stream big

stream big

THE TRIUMPHS AND
TURMOILS OF

twitch

AND THE STARS
BEHIND THE SCREEN

LIVE

nathan grayson

ATRIA BOOKS

New York   Amsterdam/Antwerp   London   Toronto   Sydney   New Delhi

ATRIA
BOOKS

An Imprint of Simon & Schuster, LLC
1230 Avenue of the Americas
New York, NY 10020

First Atria Books hardcover edition February 2025

ATRIA BOOKS and colophon are trademarks of Simon & Schuster, LLC

For information about special discounts for bulk purchases,
please contact Simon & Schuster Special Sales at 1-866-506-1949
or business@simonandschuster.com.

The Simon & Schuster Speakers Bureau can bring authors to your live event. For more
information or to book an event, contact the Simon & Schuster Speakers Bureau at
1-866-248-3049 or visit our website at www.simonspeakers.com.

Interior design by Davina Mock-Maniscalco

Manufactured in the United States of America

1 3 5 7 9 10 8 6 4 2

Library of Congress Cataloging-in-Publication Data has been applied for.

ISBN 978-1-9821-5676-3
ISBN 978-1-9821-5678-7 (ebook)

contents

----

why twitch matters

The elevator pitch for Twitch, back in its earliest days, seemed tailor-made to be met with incredulity. "You wanna watch *someone else* play video games? Instead of playing them yourself? What's the point?" But that was 2011, and this is now: Twitch has become the largest livestreaming service on the World Wide Web, with over 7 million creators broadcasting to over 100 million viewers per month. Twitch's founders, clearly, were onto something. For millennials and Gen Z, the platform took a near-universal childhood experience—sitting next to a friend on the couch and cracking jokes as they hopped, bopped, floundered, and flubbed their way through a new video game—and removed all geographic boundaries.

When Twitch first launched, the idea of a "creator" barely existed. YouTube had only been around for a handful of years, and there were few reliable pathways toward a sustainable income for those populating the internet with entertainment. Twitch played a major role in providing accessible means by which creators could generate an income, implementing ideas like paid subscriptions to individual streamers, which ultimately led to consistent work schedules and a crop of creators that didn't just fizzle out. As a result, Twitch was able to pioneer many of the features and outsized personalities that form the DNA of the modern internet that we now take for granted on YouTube, Instagram, TikTok, and whatever social media platforms might come after. Meanwhile, the unique alchemy produced by streamers and chat—a rectangular box next to every broadcast where viewers can react in real time—birthed a community like none other. The presence of chat meant that streamers and viewers were in a constant dialogue with each other, producing an endless torrent of memes and ideas that continually reinforced the foundations of a larger community. In the old days, Twitch was in on it, too, regularly soliciting streamers for feedback and hiring numerous employees from said community of streamers, viewers, and tinkerers. It even went so far as to commemorate this by adopting a slogan from a community member (whom it eventually hired): "Bleed Purple." This simple sound bite spread like wildfire because it encapsulated a sentiment common among early Twitch users: that they were part of a rambunctious, strong family, even if there were only thousands of them at that point. It did not take long for Twitch to transform from a loyal family into a juggernaut technology company and a driver of both video game sales and culture. There were other, bigger platforms out there at first, but none of them were even remotely like Twitch. And so, it grew and grew and grew.

As of 2023, over 2.5 million concurrent viewers were watching Twitch at any given moment, putting it in league with—and often well beyond—mainstream television networks like CNN and Fox during prime-time slots and major events. According to Twitch's own stats, that added up to 1.3 trillion minutes—or 22.4 billion hours—watched in a single year. Alongside stats from unofficial trackers that have been monitoring Twitch since its inception, that puts Twitch's lifetime hours-watched total at 105.3 billion. This reflects the platform's broadened appeal: Where once Twitch attracted a small subset of gamers who primarily tuned in to watch tournaments between players of the highest skill levels—aka esports—Twitch streamers now cater to every imaginable niche—arts and crafts, news and politics, travel and outdoors, music and concerts, and even just sitting around and chatting. Young people visit the site to be entertained and informed—or, depending on who they choose to watch, for their daily dose of reality TV–like drama. Streamers, in turn, keep them company for hours and hours every day, whether while out and about or from the comfort of their bedrooms.

You might hear that job description and think it sounds cushy, but the truth is rarely so glamorous. Streaming—even just the garden-variety "play video games from your room" version—is work. Top streamers broadcast nearly every day of the week, often for eight to twelve hours per day. They can't just sit there and stare blankly at a screen, either; if they're not lively, animated, and talkative, audiences will go find someone who can better hold their attention. Twitch's secret sauce, interactive chat, is also its greatest challenge: Chat is akin to an anthill where every ant hopes to be individually acknowledged. Streamers are expected to keep a running dialogue with their chats, even when they're comprised of tens or hundreds of thousands of concurrent viewers. At the highest levels, it's like performing for a stadium full of insatiable onlookers.

The streamer-chat dynamic makes for broadcasts that, much like video games themselves, are interactive. Depending on the particular community, chatters might try to get a rise out of a streamer, help them through a difficult portion of a game, or even aid a streamer when they're clearly going through a hard time in their personal life. This, too, can be a double-edged sword: Few fans are as loyal as those of Twitch streamers, but lines get blurry quickly. While many viewers pop in for just an hour or two here and there, others watch—actively or while working, doing chores, etc.—for the full eight-plus-hour gamut every day. As a result of this, they come to believe that they truly know a particular streamer, or that perhaps through repeated, fleeting interactions, they're becoming friends. This largely one-sided connection has become known as a "parasocial relationship." The potential pitfalls of this new form of fame are many. For instance, I spoke to two different streamers, Ben "CohhCarnage" Cassell and Ben "DrLupo" Lupo, about their respective approaches to an especially heartbreaking dilemma: Viewers will occasionally come into chat and feel comfortable enough to discuss the craterous lows of their mental health, up to and including suicidal ideations. But Twitch streamers are not therapists; they do not have the tools to capably and safely diffuse these situations or the emotional bandwidth to engage with such viewers regularly. Streamers and their teams have found that they must re-sist the urge to give longtime fans a shoulder to cry on, and instead develop comprehensive plans to pass them along to more capable sets of hands, lest the streamers risk the slow, painful dissolution of their communities.

It's tempting to believe that what happens online stays online, but some fans take their adoration so far that they show up in creators' home cities—and even on their doorsteps. Best-case scenario, these uncalled-for meet and greets prove alarming but ultimately harmless. A couple streamers I spoke with, however, experienced much more harrowing outcomes. In 2021, Kaitlyn "Amouranth" Siragusa had garbage outside her home set on fire by a suspected arsonist, and on two separate occasions in 2022 and 2023 dealt with a stalker she believes flew to her location all the way from Estonia. Clara "Keffals" Sorrenti, meanwhile, felt the full fury of what she's termed "parasocial hatred" from a pair of websites dedicated to unearthing targets' most intimate information: their childhoods, careers, family connections, and locations. This resulted in a so-called swatting—in which bad actors online trick a fully armed SWAT team into showing up at a creator's place of residence—and a series of forced relocations to evade potentially mortal peril.

This kind of toxic relationship can sometimes go the other way. Another creator, Dream, found himself embroiled in controversy after leveraging his own parasocial fame to get too close to fans for others' comfort—exchanging flirtatious DMs and, according to accounts that Dream disputes, sometimes taking things even further. Revelations linked to this pattern of behavior led to a community schism: For months, fans and ex-fans exchanged verbal volleys and dominated Twitter trending topics in a seemingly endless dispute over whether their formerly wholesome streamer had gone too far.

Despite appearances, most Twitch channels are group efforts. This starts with moderation—keeping chat from getting too rowdy, typically on a vol-unteer basis—but big names hire and often pay other people to help them with tasks as far ranging as video editing, stat tracking, negotiating deals, scheduling, and running in-game guilds. Top streamers are now enterprises unto themselves; Cassell, for example, is backed by a team of twenty-seven, thirteen of whom receive regular compensation for their roles. Siragusa, one of livestreaming's biggest female stars, runs her own company of eighteen and retains additional teams to advise her on financial and legal matters. Hasan "HasanAbi" Piker keeps his operation much leaner, but he's nonetheless become a political institution, coordinating with the well-oiled machines of nationally known figures like U.S. representative Alexandria Ocasio-Cortez and presidential aspirant Marianne Williamson for blockbuster broadcasts. They see in Piker what numerous companies see in Twitch streamers: the opportunity to reach an audience often unavailable even to household-name celebrities, with an intimacy and a face that audience legitimately trusts.

Yet it also must be noted that in the grand scheme of Twitch—and online platforms in general—megastar creators are anomalies. In the wake of a 2021 Twitch leak that revealed creator pay across the platform, pundits pointed out that just 25 percent of Twitch's top ten thousand highest-paid streamers made minimum wage or greater. That's far less than 1 percent of the millions of total streamers. The notion, then, that this is a burgeoning new career field, where anybody can succeed if they just try hard enough, is patently false. This mirrors other platforms like YouTube, where under 1 percent of creators generate an income. But the modern platform landscape is a little more complicated than those stats make it out to be. Many people have come to use online platforms—especially TikTok—to advertise pre-existing businesses and events. Content creation has become a means to an end, rather than the end itself, and creators a piece of a much larger puzzle. This presents additional moneymaking opportunities to both full-time content creators and those who start accounts to draw attention to, say, stores or video games. But it also means that growing and maintaining a presence on these platforms is a multifaceted full-time job, even if you're not being paid like it. On YouTube, TikTok, and Instagram, as well as Twitch, you have to be a savvy businessperson on top of being a talented content creator to turn views into revenue; moneymaking on these platforms is often tied up in sponsored deals with third-party brands, which creators have to be proactive about seeking out. Rather than a passive-income or get-rich-quick scheme, being a streamer is hard work. Breaking in requires not just a dedication to streaming for hours per day, but deals, connections, and a panther-like instinct for pouncing on opportunities when they present themselves. Take the story of Emme "Negaoryx" Montgomery, who pushed so hard to capitalize on a viral stream moment, her thirteen seconds of fame, that she ended up breaking a rib. But still, she decided to soldier on, streaming as much as possible and attending numerous events . . . until she broke another. This torrid period took such a physical and emotional toll on her that she ultimately had to step away from Twitch for a time.

These may not all be names you've heard before, but they are by almost any measure famous, with millions and millions across the globe hanging on their every word—and regarding their every game and product endorsement as gospel. It's no surprise, then, that shortly after Twitch began to sniff success, companies began salivating in its general direction. Ultimately, Amazon— a colossus among tech giants, one of the biggest companies in the world— acquired Twitch in 2014, ushering in a new era that crept in subtly but surely. Twitch, flush with newfound resources, initially passed what it could on to creators in the form of flashy new features. But the company also grew at a dizzying pace and ultimately lost its way. Indebted to a corporate benefactor cracking its knuckles with increasing impatience at the idea of extracting a profit, Twitch over time drifted from its community-first focus to a more nakedly money-grubbing model. This meant underpaying streamers—many of whom already struggled to earn a living wage while providing Twitch with the majority of its content—relative to other platforms and pressuring them to run regular barrages of broadcast-interrupting ads, decisions widely disliked by both streamers and viewers. Monetization-related features moved to the forefront as the company's commitment to its community—once expressed by in-person, feedback-gathering appearances at numerous events and close connections with individual streamers—receded into the halls of history. Twitch is not alone in this regard. In recent times, Twitter (now X) has massively degraded its product in pursuit of profit, laying off staff in droves, transforming a once-useful verification system into a subscription service meant to confer privilege to those vain enough to pay, and repeatedly breaking features large and small that users didn't even think were in need of fixing. More subtly, TikTok has pushed its shopping and e-commerce features to the forefront, transforming the app from a portal to a world of quirky discoveries to basically the same thing as any other social video platform, with every discovery starting or ending with somebody trying to sell you something.

That does not change the reality, however, that platforms are defined by the people who use them—Twitch perhaps most of all. Its culture is unique, born of hyper-passionate niches that through technology became supercharged into a pastime with a global audience. Where, say, YouTube could be likened to a nation with highways and byways crisscrossing between disparate states, Twitch is more like a city where all the major players know each other. Everybody uses the same lingo, references the same touchstones. Cameos are common, especially among the top streamers. If all the creators and viewers responsible left tomorrow, Twitch would no longer be Twitch. This is the central tension at the heart of the platform: Twitch might bleed purple, but people are livestreaming's beating heart regardless of which brand's flag they fly. And yet, as Twitch, the company, has grown in terms of viewership, prominence, and prosperity, it has strayed further and further from this north star. Communication has grown indirect and oftentimes insufficient, resulting in confusion and controversy. Streamers have come to feel like stones being squeezed for every last ounce of profit rather than pillars of a platform that values each of them individually. Viewers have ceased to view Twitch as a special little slice of the internet, as a driver of online culture. Now it's just a delivery mechanism for content.

In the process of reporting, I came to realize there was only one lens through which to tell Twitch's story: the creators themselves. Rather than by putting together a chronological account of Twitch's financial triumphs and tribulations through its various eras, Twitch is better understood through its streamers. The innovations, personalities, and struggles of nine exemplary streamers reveal why Twitch is one of the most important internet culture and business stories of the twenty-first century. The goal is to paint a holistic portrait of both Twitch as a platform and, more importantly, the people who through hard work took livestreaming from a hobby to a behemoth.

Viewers often feel like they *know* their favorite streamers, but the truth

is, even in the most revealing moments, fans are still getting a show, a performance. Following streamers in their everyday lives shines a light on what it
really means to be a content creator contending with Big Tech and the toxicity
of the internet: the ups and the downs, the fears and the insecurities, even the
unglamorous busywork that undergirds the whole operation. Technological
innovation is often not a top-down process, but one where content creators
bootstrap solutions or demand features, and these in turn took Twitch's business to the next level. To demonstrate these dynamics, I met streamers where
they were at, spending days with them in their homes and at events, and
communicating back and forth with them for months or years after. But on
Twitch, creators are only part of the equation; sometimes they're not even
the stars of the show. I also spoke to dozens of friends, family members, fans
of streamers, and Twitch employees. I endeavored to examine these people
who are also, increasingly, becoming institutions themselves with staffs of
anywhere from a few to a few dozen and empires worth tens of millions of
dollars. This collage of stories demonstrates how creators have shaped and
been shaped by Twitch, an ever-evolving platform, from its unassuming rise
to its celeb-stacked pandemic boom to what's beginning to look like a fall—
or perhaps a slow descent into corporate malaise.

But Twitch, whose live format renders it trapped in an eternal present,
never stops marching forward. By the time you read this, the streamers depicted in this book will doubtless have entered new chapters in their lives and
careers. The stories I tell here are messy and inconclusive because they're still
unfolding. However, these snapshots document pivotal moments in the lives
of streamers, capturing the days and weeks that will define the years to come
for Twitch as an entity. It's impossible to say in what state Twitch, the brand,
will be in months or years down the line, but the site's true exports—its community and culture—will continue to inform content creation, the internet
economy, and how millions of people interact online. Twitch will always be
a platform by the people, even if it one day stops being for them.

chapter one

----

community

Some people just look the part of what they do. There's no universe in which Beyoncé doesn't become a pop star. The Rock appears to have been hewn from solid granite. Nicholas Braun, aka Cousin Greg on the HBO show *Succession*, was born to play that *exact* kind of guy. As far as people who've worked at Twitch go, this is Marcus "DJWheat" Graham. Whether he's broadcasting from his office or chilling on his couch, the now-forty-five-year-old, salt-and-pepper-haired livestreaming pioneer is all wide expressions and big gestures. He moves like a cartoon character, as though he was animated to captivate. His voice booms no matter what he's discussing, the volume knob on his enthusiasm level evidently stuck at 11, never to so much as glance at 10. You can just *see*, almost immediately, why this person in particular was one of the first successful video game streamers, predating even Twitch itself. Graham can talk for hours and hours and hours, and then more hours after that. He *will*; it's just who he is. But you'll find it impossible to look away, like a snake under the spell of a master charmer.

Right now, he's talking about pinball machines, which he's turned into the centerpiece of the lower floor of his Nebraska home.

"You never have the same game twice. So the adage of 'Once you get a pinball machine, they multiply' is totally true," he says, gesturing toward favorites based on *Teenage Mutant Ninja Turtles* and *The Mandalorian*. "They're amazing, and they're actually better investments than, say, an NFT or something. They have been skyrocketing in price over the pandemic, partially because manufacturing costs have gone up and they produce less machines, but also people are like, 'I want things to do.'"

Graham's appreciation of these machines is infectious. The craftsmanship of a good pinball machine, he explains, is a thing of beauty—a clockwork assemblage of flippers, knobs, springs, switches, lights, and speakers meant to spirit you away to some fantastical realm (or a sewer where giant turtles eat pizza) amid the din of a crowded arcade or bar.

This passion, this attention to detail, is what turned him into one of the first prominent esports commentators, one of the first well-known gaming livestreamers, and eventually, one of the first Twitch employees. Where Graham goes, people gather to listen—a quality that came in handy back when he began his career. In the late nineties, when Graham first started commentating over competitive games, there was barely an American esports scene to speak of. There certainly wasn't software designed with the idea in mind or an easy means by which to broadcast online to more than a small handful of people. This eventually led him to streaming, which he also got into when the medium was in a larval form.

Graham's career was only possible because of the people he was able to draw to his early, hacked-together broadcasts. He owes everything to the community he helped build, which in turn built him. This, more than anything else, is the lesson he's taken to heart: Community is key. It's the soul of his operation, the gasoline that fuels his passion.

It's why he joined Twitch. It's also why he left.

- - - - - - -

THANKS TO HIS dad, Graham grew up with a keen interest in radio. This led to a broadcast journalism major in college, which in turn led to a realization.

"I realized that radio was fucking dumb," Graham says. "And what I mean by that is, radio has such a limited audience. And I'm discovering that as I'm realizing the internet is the future, right?"

So in 1997, after he'd graduated and begun working an IT job, Graham went to his local Best Buy and picked up a gadget that claimed it would let him start his own radio station online. Unfortunately, its audience was *significantly* more limited than radio's.

"One of the bullets on the back of the box was 'Start your own radio station' with an asterisk next to it," Graham says. "Like, you know, you need to have this stuff to run this, and of course I'm like, 'Well, fuck the asterisk.' I took it home and realized I could have five, at max ten people listen. But getting those first ten people for esports stuff was amazing."

Graham's game of choice at the time was *Quake III*, a multiplayer-focused entry in a classic sci-fi first-person shooter series without which modern genre pillars like *Halo*, *Destiny*, and *Apex Legends* wouldn't exist. But at the time, online gaming was still relatively new, and competitions with money up for grabs were a niche within a niche, especially in North America. Big matches were infrequent and inconsistent, and central sources for news about them were difficult—sometimes impossible—to come by.

Initially, Graham commentated largely for the benefit of a *Quake* team he was coaching; he'd watch their games and record notes for them about how they were playing. It was a teammate who gave him the idea to start broadcasting to the (relative) masses.

"[My teammate] was like, 'Hey, you should do this live like you're covering sports,'" says Graham. "And I was like, 'Yeah, why not?'"

With the help of an old friend (who's since gone on to work at Meta), Graham managed to set up a server on a media service called Shoutcast that allowed him to reach more people than his previous, severely limited approach. At the time, this was about as good as it got.

"We filled up that five-hundred-person Shoutcast server almost right away," says Graham. "And it was, like, the most atrocious thing ever. I had no idea what I was doing. I wasn't even really thinking about it, right? It took me a little while to go, 'Oh, now let me take my knowledge of radio and apply that to making an opening intro, [explaining] why you should care about this game, post-game interviews—you know, getting it all together actually.'"

Radio expertise proved valuable on the tech side of things as well. Though Graham's setup at the time was rudimentary, the bones of it were not so different from hardware utilized by modern streamers.

"It was hard as hell back then," he says. "Even trying to get mics to work and stuff was unbelievable. Nowadays everyone's got a [studio-quality microphone], and back then we were getting stick mics from Walmart. . . . But because of all the radio experience, I basically built a radio console that I could plug into a computer, which is what a lot of streamers still do today."

What Graham and his friends didn't recognize was that by broadcasting to nascent gaming audiences, they were also tapping into a force that would become essential to the DNA of livestreaming as we now know it: interactivity. *Quake* fans would gather in text-based internet relay chat (IRC) rooms and react to what was happening in matches, offer their own opinions, and of course, tell Graham when he was screwing up. (The latter desire, it should be noted, has powered far more pivotal instances of human ingenuity than anybody is willing to admit.)

"Someone could be like, 'Wheat, you're an idiot,' and I could respond to them immediately," says Graham. "We had a little bit more delay back then, but I was blown away by this instant interaction that we saw take place. So it wasn't just the commentary part of it. Once it got tied to IRC, suddenly it became the interactive experience that I think people really love today."

It's this alchemic reaction of broadcasters and viewers/listeners creating collectively—cheering, jeering, and building on each other's ideas in real time—that would later go on to define livestreaming as a medium. No longer was a broadcaster like Graham simply talking at audiences and occasionally taking listener calls or running contests. The two sides of the equation had become connected, tethered by a moment in time regardless of space. Graham knew he was onto something. But the road to fully realizing his vision of the future would prove longer than expected. And much, much bumpier.

- - - - - - -

IN THE EARLY 2000s, Graham took his first crack at making a career out of this whole "talking over video games" thing. He'd been commentating on larger and larger tournaments, and people with deeper pockets had begun to take notice. In 2004, Graham hit the jackpot: an American esports upstart called the Global Gaming League. Its owners, flush with investment cash, convinced Graham and his wife to uproot from Nebraska and move to Los Angeles for the purposes of taking esports and video game content to the next level.

"GGL let me experiment with livestreaming like crazy," says Graham. "They were helping me pay bandwidth bills that were absurd. I went to them and said, 'I want a livestream from [annual video game news conference] E3,' and they were like, 'Great, what do we need to do to make that happen?' I said, 'You just gotta get a $25,000 internet pipe to the booth on top of [what you'd already normally pay to be there].' They'd be like, 'Awesome!'"

Even mainstream celebrities were beginning to suspect there might be gold in gaming's still-untapped hills.

"GGL let us put together a hip-hop gaming league that had Snoop Dogg as a commissioner [and] Method Man and Eric V. playing *Madden* against each other," says Graham. "We were doing shit way, way, way ahead of its time."

However, this also marked the beginning of a pattern that would ultimately echo forward to Graham's time at Twitch: a company making good, forward-thinking decisions, followed by bad decisions, followed by decent decisions, followed by worse decisions. For Graham, it was whiplash inducing.

"They would do these great esports events," he says. "They were paying players. They were putting out good prize money. They were getting good sponsors. But then they'd do something stupid like say, 'We want to rename esports to vsports so then we can own the name.' So you can imagine what it was like, especially for me—knowing what you know about me and Twitch— working for a company that has these moments of brilliance and then the dumbest fucking ideas you could ever imagine."

Needless to say, vsports, as a name, did not catch on.

Graham got an even bigger break in 2005, when a television producer named Mike Burks approached him at an esports event he was casting.

"I think I was casting in a Hawaiian shirt," says Graham. "It was all sorts of goofy, awkward gaming nerd geekiness happening here. Occasionally you'd see a mom that came with their kid or whatever."

Burks, not from the world of gaming at all, stood out—his twenties a distant memory, very tall and rocking a hairstyle older (both in fashion and literal age) than any of the competitors at the event. Burks was impressed by Graham's ability to commentate effectively all by his lonesome without a large behind-the-scenes crew feeding data into his ear like traditional sports broadcasters typically had. Burks revealed to Graham that he was working with DirecTV on a pilot for what would become the company's esports offering: the Championship Gaming Series (CGS). Graham leaped at the opportunity to ascend beyond his small online niche and grasp at televised legitimacy.

"I wouldn't give up the experience ever," says Graham. "It was years of live television. I don't know where I could have ever gotten better experience. It was brutally hard."

But CGS was vanishingly short-lived, beginning with a pilot in 2006 and then folding in 2008 after just two regular seasons. Graham estimates that DirecTV spent tens of millions of dollars on CGS, but it failed to find the kind of audience the company was looking for. This, too, served as a lesson for Graham, albeit one of a different, more sobering sort.

"I think working for DirecTV is the first time I started seeing, 'Oh shit, this is how companies exploit gaming for advertising dollars, profit, etc.,'" he says. "On one hand, I was OK with that because they were at least pushing the envelope. But the reality of it is, two years later when they shut everything down, you feel the hangover of it all. Gaming is also the first thing [companies] are willing to jettison."

This left Graham at a loss. His grand hope for gaming had failed, and the traditional entertainment industry rejected him like white blood cells fending off an infectious disease.

"I started realizing there was no landscape for people like me [in LA]," he says. "I had conversations with William Morris [now WME] where I basically pitched them the idea of Twitch, and they were like, 'This shit is never going to be big,' and laughed me out of their offices. It was absolutely crushing."

Faced with a lack of direction and mounting financial uncertainty,

Graham and his wife moved back to Nebraska, and Graham resumed working in IT. It was, as he describes it, a "long fall" from his lofty days in live television, but it was a living. But when the content creation bug first bit him, it had burrowed deep. Despite the near-fatal damage prior years had done to his spirits, Graham resumed creating shows on a website of his own in 2009. To support his hobby, he made his PayPal info public. After just forty-eight hours, viewers had kicked in $5,000.

"At the time I was like, 'Oh my fucking god. That's huge. I don't even know what to do with this,'" says Graham, echoing a sentiment Twitch streamers—supported in large part by viewer donations and subscriptions—would later espouse.

Ensuing success led to interest from Ustream, an early livestreaming platform originally created in 2007 to aid deployed soldiers in communicating with their families, but which went on to host broadcasts from politicians, artists, and video game streamers. Ustream's founders sought out popular personalities, including Graham and a whole host of esports luminaries, to provide content. Graham believed in Ustream's tech and vision, so he went to bat for the company and persuaded others in the esports space to start streaming there. But the relationship soured quickly. While Graham and other gaming streamers brought a consistent audience to the site, Ustream's eyes often wandered elsewhere.

"We would come to them and be like, 'We're gonna do this huge *Quake* thing, and we're gonna advertise it and put it all over the place,'" says Graham. "'Will you give us [placement on your] front page?' And they'd be like, 'Well, we would, but we're gonna have Snoop Dogg do a fifteen-minute chat on his channel, and we want to keep that up [on the front page] the whole time . . . .' Yes, they'd get an explosion of users for Snoop Dogg, but that didn't make anyone want to come back. Snoop Dogg wasn't coming back and streaming."

Snoop Dogg was a household name, but his presence on Ustream was functionally a stunt, a gimmick. To build a real audience, the site needed homegrown personalities who were consistent.

"[Ustream] were like, 'Hey, we need to focus on these people who we spent so much money to bring on board,' but there was never really any stickiness," concurs Justin "Gunrun" Ignacio, an early esports streamer and commentator who came over to Ustream because of Graham. "The viewer base would just go off platform."

Moreover, money was quickly becoming an issue.

"[Ustream] gave me, like, no money," says Ignacio. "My two thousand viewers would make [me], like, a couple dollars."

It was around this time that the founders of a competing streaming platform called Justin.tv, also created in 2007, began to realize they'd need more than cutting-edge livestreaming tech to succeed. The site began as a single channel on which founder Justin Kan livestreamed his life 24/7, an alluring gimmick that attracted attention from mainstream publications and TV shows—and which, for better or worse, led to some of the first-ever instances of swatting during a livestream. After a handful of months, however, Kan and his compatriots decided to broaden their horizons. With plans for expansion came a need for more content creators with different styles of broadcast. Back then, though, there was no template, no guide on what a good stream looked like. People just threw whatever they had at a camera to see what stuck. And then sometimes, they immediately thought better of it and gave up.

Initially, Graham did not like what he saw.

"[At first] Justin.tv was kind of a joke because most of what was on there was garbage," he says. "It was, like, someone with bad video and audio going live for thirty seconds and then not being live. There were a few gems in there, but it was mostly garbage or pirated content."

But Justin.tv kept studying the space and expanding. Before long, the company started trying to poach Ustream creators with the goal of building out a vertical dedicated to gaming. This initial ambition was followed by a period of second guessing, explains then-COO of Justin.tv Kevin Lin. Lin and Kan had watched esports titans like Graham get sent packing by traditional television behemoths and came away thinking it was just too early to bet the farm on video games.

"A lot of those TV attempts basically died," says Lin. "The industry was reeling from [the fact that] DirecTV and those other TV companies had promised all this wealth and money to the esports industry, nascent as it was, and then it got canceled. . . . And so we felt it was too early to really deep dive."

Yet, it was hard to ignore the obvious potential of games to become a truly mainstream force somewhere down the line. Meanwhile, something resembling today's creator economy was beginning to take shape on other platforms—to gain a silhouette and spine, if not a recognizable face or body.

"YouTube was pretty new," says Lin. "Creators were struggling to understand how advertising works and [were] feeling like, 'Wait, I get paid 80 cents per one thousand views? That doesn't seem like it's actually going to sustain me.' But it was starting to work. You were starting to see creators that were making maybe tens of thousands of dollars per year. . . . We started doing research and found that gaming was the third largest category on YouTube at the time."

And then a watershed moment happened: Lin, Kan, and numerous other Justin.tv employees got really, really into *StarCraft II*, the 2010 sequel to one of the greatest strategy games of all time.

"[The original *StarCraft*] was pretty much the only content I would watch on Justin.tv," says Lin. "Flash-forward a bit, the *StarCraft II* beta test comes out in 2010. A bunch of our employees got access to the beta and just started playing nonstop. . . . Just noticing our own behavior: We were going home and watching *StarCraft* videos on YouTube just to get better at the game. We were playing in the office every single day. And we had that sort of proverbial light bulb moment of 'Wait a second, should we just lean into this?'"

In calls and meetings with creators, Justin.tv talked a big game. Graham also found that, on a more basic level, the company's executive team actually gave him the time of day, a far cry from the dearth of attention he felt his concerns were receiving at Ustream. But eventually, for Graham and others in his scene, what it came down to was money.

"Justin.tv started talking to people like me," Graham says, "[esports commentator Sean 'Day9' Plott], [Ignacio], and other people in the gaming space, and they're like, 'What would get them to use Justin.tv over Ustream?' . . . And I was like, 'Money. I hate to say it: It's because none of us are making money. We have been kind of unsupported as gamers over time, and all we want to be able to do is support our hobbies. The company that first helps support gaming and second helps us put money in our pockets to leverage this passion we have for gaming—or esports or *StarCraft* or whatever—that's what we want.'"

In response, Justin.tv's team said they were interested in spinning up a partner program for streamers that would offer better pay to Graham, Ignacio, and others. And so, Graham made up his mind: He'd paddle his operation—now a small network with multiple recurring shows featuring himself and other hosts—over from Ustream to Justin.tv, and he'd encourage other gaming streamers in his scene to follow suit. But almost immediately, he found himself in choppy waters.

- - - - - - -

GRAHAM, OF ALL people, knows how streamers feel when Twitch's missteps leave them in a giant, foot-shaped crater. He knows this because he was perhaps the first person to whom it ever happened. It was 2011, and Twitch wasn't even Twitch yet.

"We signed with Justin.tv," says Graham. "It was a pretty big deal for us because at that point we were running basically a production company. We had all of these lower thirds and intro videos and links everywhere. And I said to Kevin Lin, 'You know, you guys have been great, but please don't fuck us.'"

About a month and a half later, Justin.tv announced that its gaming efforts would be spun off into a new company and site called Twitch while the Justin.tv mothership would continue playing home to other types of broadcasts. A last-minute name change might not seem like the biggest deal, but if you're a creator dealing with graphics, advertising, and a fundamental rebrand to suit your new online home, it's the kind of thing that throws a jumbo-sized wrench into your plans.

"I remember that being a very heated telephone call with Kevin," says Graham. "Basically I called him and said, 'Kevin, you fucked us! We just spent all this money to redo all of our graphics and all this shit. Now we're going to have to put another $5,000 into changing all this stuff and hiring the right people to do it. And this is exactly what we asked you not to do.'"

On Graham's end, the principle of the thing mattered more than the material challenges. He'd jumped ship from Ustream in part because he felt like Justin.tv leadership had the creator community's best interests at heart. But then, suddenly, it seemed like he was dealing with the same set of problems as before stacked on top of each other, disguised in a slightly different trench coat.

Lin, to Graham's surprise, took it well. He apologized and offered to pay the costs.

"We weren't really creatives," Lin explains of Justin.tv's executive team at the time. "None of us actually streamed, and the thought of graphical assets didn't come to mind. We just didn't think about it. It was an honest mistake not informing people more ahead of time. We didn't realize, 'Oh crap, creators have all these assets?' But of course they do. We see it every single day with our own eyes. . . . [Running Twitch] was a constant, iterative learning process, and that was a key learning."

The incident, minor though it was in the grand scheme of things, is in Graham's mind emblematic of what made Twitch work in its formative days.

"If one thing was true from the very beginning, it's that Justin.tv's original founders knew what they didn't know," says Graham. "They respected the opinions of others who had a perspective, a lens, experience in the space. That went a really, really long way."

All the way, it turns out, to Lin offering Graham a job just a few months after that tense phone call.

"I think what Kevin saw was someone who understood livestreaming— who really cared about not fucking the creators," says Graham. "This is the lifeblood. This is what needs to be the most important thing."

Twitch's community-focused hiring approach neither began nor ended with Graham. In its early days, Twitch also hired Ignacio and numerous other esports luminaries like Ben "FishStix" Goldhaber, who'd previously created a website that served as a centralized resource for esports streams. This quickly snowballed into a creator-first approach not just to hiring but to everything else.

"We had this very specific rubric of 'How do we drive love, fame, and money for streamers?'" says Goldhaber, Twitch founding team member and now-former director of content marketing. "When you put it that way, it sounds kind of cold and calculating. But what that meant was that we spent all of our time talking to the people who were creating gaming content and asking, 'What do you want? What do you need to succeed?' The first couple years of product development at Twitch was really just interviewing streamers, figuring out what they wanted, and building it for them."

Twitch wasn't just calling streamers on the phone, either. It quickly gained a reputation for its presence at countless video game conventions, tournaments, and events, many of which attracted thousands or tens of thousands of people. During this time, video game events were experiencing a rapid growth spurt in tandem with a widening embrace of video games and geek culture at large. PAX, which grew from 3,300 attendees in 2004 to 70,000 in 2011, did not carry the same sort of nerdy stigma as the (allegedly) B.O.-soaked *Star Trek* conventions of yore. Video games were becoming cool. Twitch, though intended to create connections that would bypass hills, seas, and other harsh realities of our mortal plane, grew at first through boots-on-the-ground word of mouth.

"I don't think you could possibly overstate how important it was for us to be at these events and tournaments," says Goldhaber. "At a lot of these, there was a Twitch partner lounge. At others, there were at least a few reps from Twitch there. I think that made an incredible difference, just to show the community that we cared, show the streamers that we cared. It also elevated streamers. . . . The Twitch parties became legendary, right? Having these exclusive parties made them feel very special. It built a sense of community around Twitch and was an aspirational goal for prospective streamers."

The strategy was a conscious one on the part of Twitch leadership. It was intended, Lin explains, to work both ways, bringing the gaming community into the Twitch fold and ensuring that employees were hearing suggestions, questions, and concerns directly from creators.

"We encouraged people—everyone in the company, whether you were a brand-new junior employee all the way to a senior leader—to talk to creators," says Lin. "We allowed people—and paid for them—to go to one event a year. Could be [Penny Arcade Expo], could be E3, could be an esports tournament. And while there, we'd set them up with creators to have a deep dive or casual conversation. This would help people understand how to talk to creators, how to extract good questions, good ideas, good problems and then turn them into product or feature ideas."

The goal was to foster a sense of community with all Twitch creators, even if they weren't on the verge of bursting through the stratosphere and achieving superstar status.

"People would come along and set up these relationships with creators," says Ignacio, "even if they never became, like, huge, huge top streamers."

Graham remembers the moment that solidified this approach: a get-together with partnered streamers at one of the first Boston-based "East" versions of the annual Penny Arcade Expo (PAX).

"We just rented out a sushi bar and invited all these esports people that were streaming on Twitch and Justin.tv," says Graham. "What every attendee walked away with was exactly what I was searching for for so long: [that feeling of] 'I love that Twitch cares about us, what we do, what we say, what we'd like them to build,' etc. It became very clear to everyone at Twitch that we needed this to be our marketing."

Graham quickly found himself on the front lines of this effort. His job, in effect, was to persuade esports players and teams to stream on Twitch, a prospect they initially found bewildering. Why, after all, would they want to spend months with their fingers on keyboards and heads in the clouds, devising galaxy-brained strategies, only to give everything away in broadcasts rivals could watch?

"I spent a year literally explaining what Twitch was," says Graham. "I spent six months of that arguing with players and teams [about whether] streaming on Twitch would be bad for them, because their opponents would tune in and watch them and understand their strategies. I was up against so much resistance. But I was just like, 'Let me show you how successful [Plott] is being, and all he's doing is talking about games.'"

Little by little, Graham eroded the esports community's suspicion. It helped that he was, in many ways, the ideal person for the job. He was a bona fide livestreaming pioneer, and he knew in his heart—from countless hours of experience—that Twitch was onto something.

"I've never enjoyed sales, but to me this was the best version of sales, which is evangelism," he says. "I truly believed livestreaming was the future."

The idea that Twitch cared—that not just the company but the entire streaming community was a family—became central to Twitch's identity. Even Twitch's slogan, "Bleed Purple," was initially a community creation. Shannon Plante, an eventual Twitch employee who was, at the time, just a fan and moderator for streamers and the Twitch subreddit, came up with it in 2014 after attending a video game convention in the UK. On Twitter, she decided to thank Twitch for, essentially, giving a shit. She hashtagged her tweet #BleedPurple, riffing on the slogan of a local hockey team.

"I was thanking [Twitch staff members] for being involved not just for streamers or large video game studios and trying to build those relationships, but for caring about indie developers," says Plante. "I was just basically being a fan of how everything felt so tight-knit back at that time. I really wanted to inject myself in that because it gave me energy. It was just such a wonderful buzz."

Before long, Twitch staff let her know that employees had begun using the slogan internally, as well as at parties: "There was a party in 2014 where they had started to use it printed out on regular paper, pasted on the walls, because that was the budget they had for parties back then," says Plante.

Twitch hired Plante for a community-focused role in 2015, and it used the slogan to announce that she was joining the company. "That was really special for me," she says. "And then it became something I started to see on every banner and billboard that they made. They made it their official thing after that."

"Bleed Purple" became Twitch's official slogan, Plante believes, because the underlying sentiment resonated not just with Twitch employees, but everybody who used the platform.

"It was something that took off because of a strong sense of community," she says. "It wasn't just me or Twitch staff who said it. It became something that streamers, smaller and larger, began to use constantly. Everyone felt that way. It was a very contagious sense of identity and inclusion."

In some cases, Twitch wound up stopping major event streams from falling apart at the seams. Ignacio proved instrumental in this regard. Before Twitch hired him, he was a community college student living with his parents, with short black hair and an unassuming, blue jeans–clad style, which disguised a person with boundless expertise in a field that had just barely begun to exist. Streaming was just a hobby, but Ignacio had a preternatural knack for squeezing blood from stones, hacking together a livestreaming setup involving obscure Russian software to ensure his video game streams looked better than anybody else's without his modest computer going up in flames. Before long, he gained a reputation for using his whiz-kid know-how to save esports events whose livestreams were collapsing under the weight of high-end graphics and rickety internet connections. That piqued the interest of folks like Lin, which led to a job at Justin.tv. Before long, Ignacio, whose irrepressible enthusiasm made him talk so fast that it seemed his mouth couldn't keep up with his brain, was helping Twitch solve tech problems at its San Francisco home base and in the field.

For Ignacio, working at Twitch was a dream come true, but as Twitch came to both embed itself in the gaming community and rely on esports for viewership, he got a front-row seat to the most precarious elements of the platform's business.

"I feel like I have all this personal PTSD from handling these tumultuous moments in the field of 'Oh wow, this is something that's never happened in existence. I need to solve it immediately for this event to not be a crippling failure,'" he says.

Some events, like the debut of livestreaming on Xbox 360 from Germany, were pure pressure. Others, like the 2012 Battle.net World Championship in China, were surreal.

"I just remember being in the server room trying to solve this issue, and then [former NBA basketball player] Yao Ming comes in, and everyone's like, 'Yao Ming really wants to see production right now!'" says Ignacio. "I was like, 'Oh cool, I'm just trying to do my work' while being a crazy twenty-one-year-old wearing a bunch of *StarCraft* swag and trying to fix crazy things."

Even though Twitch had made strides in low-latency video tech, livestreaming remained—as in Graham's mid-2000s Global Gaming League days—expensive. At first, Twitch had to pay another company called Akamai to handle especially large viewership spikes and avoid overloading its own servers.

"Whenever there was a major event, we'd call Akamai and tell them, 'Hey, we're thinking we're gonna get, like, thirty thousand viewers for this, so let's pay you some money and get this set up.' But if it broke, like, eighty thousand [viewers], we'd have to pay a much higher cost for it," says Ignacio. "We'd have to forecast esports events so we wouldn't die from the cost of [overflow]. I had one of the keys for that. So did [CEO] Emmett Shear. I liked using the nuclear missile analogy when it came to that, like 'OK well, there goes however much money that was.' We had a giant red thermometer of 'Here's how much money was being lost, and we need to make this money up somehow.'"

Lin, perhaps because he had no other option, came to view even these moments through an optimistic lens.

"We had so many failure points, whether it was at ingest or on our systems," he says. "It was constant, constant breaking. But it was also a great signal of how much people wanted us to exist. They would suffer through all these pain points that were out of anyone's control in many cases."

Graham always maintained hope that Twitch would eventually stop bleeding green.

"[Twitch's founders] were thinking about 'What does our infrastructure need to look like in three to five years in order for us to be a sustainable business?'" he says. "They were spending money like a startup, but in my opinion they were hyper-focused on the two things that were going to determine their success: creators and infrastructure."

- - - - - - -

IN THE BEGINNING, Twitch didn't have many ironclad rules, at least compared to today's time-honored terms of service that outline who stays and who goes when it comes to granular forms of racism, sexism, harassment, and numerous other varieties of inappropriate conduct. Of the few rules in place back in 2011, one towered above all the rest: Video games only. No non-gaming streams allowed. Those, upon detection, would be banished to Justin.tv, forced to roam the wastes with 24/7 livestreams, truck driving streams, farm streams, and whatever else people could think of to broadcast that wasn't gaming.

"Anytime we found anyone, any content, even if it was a talking head show," says Lin, "we would message them and say, 'Hey, you can't do this here. You have to go to Justin.tv. Twitch is really about video games.'"

As far as standard-setting edicts go, it was a pretty simple one—at least, on the surface.

"We felt like it was pretty obvious: The majority of the screen real estate should be a video game," says Lin. "You can place yourself in the corner or whatever. That was totally fine for a while, but of course our community loves to push the envelope. So eventually, people would just put a tiny little corner of video game, to test the line."

Once early streamers started getting in trouble for that, they flipped the dynamic on its head, giving games center stage but broadcasting even more audacious main events down in the corner of the screen.

"You have the camera where all the [actual] content would happen in the lower third," says Ignacio. "So they're 'playing' *World of Warcraft*, but . . . they're having a crazy party or doing a dating game or something over Skype."

This taught Lin, Graham, Goldhaber, Ignacio, and numerous others a lesson that seems obvious in hindsight, but that flew in the face of conventional wisdom at the time: Livestreaming is powered by personalities. Everything else—even God-tier video game skill—plays second fiddle. It was the beginning of a seismic shift that would ultimately send shock waves to every corner of the internet. Now there's a personality for everything, whether it's politics or detecting scam artists. Younger people, in fact, primarily get their news from creators rather than traditional sources. Twitch learned early the power of a friendly face.

"While a lot of the impression at the time was that people wanted to watch who are skilled [gamers], it really is about personality," says Lin. "Esports was just starting to be understood by the industry and consumers, and so we had this concept that it was all about skilled play, when the reality is, people were watching for the streamer, the personality. . . . You don't have to be that good. It helps if you can do both."

But even though Justin.tv would seem a more natural fit for streams that emphasized personality above all else, Twitch's focus on gaming provided glue for an otherwise formless medium. Games—often lengthy, or in the case of competitive hits like *StarCraft* and *League of Legends*, potentially endless— gave streamers something to react to, to talk about, every day. Consistency allowed viewers to form habits and build schedules around their favorite creators. They could expect streamers to show up with a daily dose of comfort food, as opposed to the dissonant blend of gimmicks and stunts that had come to characterize other livestreaming services. Technology provided the dance beat, but gaming taught everybody the steps.

"No one knew what their script was going to be if they were just going to sit in front of the camera and talk all day," says Graham. "You did have guys like [Justin.tv streamer] Marijuana Man where literally he smoked marijuana and then would talk and listen to music, and that's why some people showed up. But it really came down to: Were you building community around your content? And the gamers were building a community."

Community led to a consistent audience, and it did not take long for prospective streamers to realize that Twitch was where the viewers were. Twitch cemented this community dynamic by working in collaboration with Plott—one of the most popular streamers on the platform at the time—to create a button that allowed viewers to subscribe to their favorite streamers for $4.99 per month, granting perks like exclusive chat emotes. Subscriptions became badges of honor to viewers, a sign of commitment, bolstering group cohesion and boosting streamers' (and Twitch's) revenue. Twitch's user base, meanwhile, grew and grew, from 3.2 million in 2011, to 20 million in 2012, to 55 million in 2014. It did not take long for Justin.tv's founders to realize which arm of their operation was buttering their bread: In 2014, Justin.tv and Twitch's parent company rebranded to Twitch Interactive, and it shut down the Justin.tv website to focus on Twitch.

Still, it was, to some extent, that first Garden of Eden–like moment that came to define Twitch's culture: A single rule decreed from on high, almost immediately defied. Twitch streamers would spend the following years trying to skirt the outer edges of rules and norms, while Twitch would try to define what rules and norms even were. Some of this outside-the-box thinking led to pioneering innovations: While early stars like Plott were by-products of the esports world, others like Ben "CohhCarnage" Cassell and Saqib "Lirik" Zahid ascended to new levels of stardom by playing a variety of different games— rather than esports standards like *StarCraft* and *League*—and anchoring broadcasts with affable personalities. Those streamers, more so than Twitch, also set the bar for what was an advisable amount of time to spend streaming. They set it high.

"[Zahid], back in the day, was one of the first streamers who was ever just like, 'I'm streaming eight to ten hours a day,'" says Goldhaber. "That's part of why he blew up. That became the meta of how you grow an audience on Twitch."

Upping time spent streaming conferred a multitude of benefits. Twitch spent much of its lifetime structured as a series of categories organized by number of viewers, and the more hours a streamer spent in a category, the more chances they had to scrape viewers from the underbellies of bigger names who are logging off for the day. Moreover, there was the spectacle of it all: Lengthy streams represented a sort of endurance feat, whether they came in the form of a single marathon broadcast that lasted for twenty-four-plus hours or multiple broadcasts that lasted ten-plus hours, perhaps every day, indefinitely. Viewers came to revere that level of dedication, as they did with YouTubers who'd post multiple videos per week, or even per day. Eventually, they started to rely on it. At that point, for streamers, there was no turning back.

Nowadays, burnout is a major topic of discussion among top streamers, and it's natural to wonder if early Twitch employees thought to pump the brakes and encourage, well, breaks. At the time, however, most weren't thinking of what the Twitch landscape might look like in a decade.

"At the time it was so novel, the idea of playing video games for money or for a living," says Goldhaber. "It's easy to take for granted, but the concept of [a] creator—someone who makes their entire full-time living on the internet—barely existed at the time. So I can't recall a lot of conversations where [burnout] was a big concern. I think it was mostly elation that people were making a full-time career doing what they loved, and we were facilitating that."

Twitch's own work culture was also not the healthiest, which might have contributed to that particular blind spot. As with many startups, passion could turn into toxic work habits.

"I had no concept of work-life balance," says Ignacio of his early days at Twitch. "Grind culture was the meme of the era."

But while Twitch might not have contemplated the long-term impacts of streamer labor at the time, those norms, once solidified, certainly informed the company's future thinking; it's not uncommon for modern-day Twitch contracts to demand upward of 150 or 200 hours per month of live time from big-name creators.

Other creator-born innovations were more straightforwardly beneficial to both the creators and the company. In 2014, a channel called Twitch Plays Pokemon moved beyond the idea of a streamer entirely, allowing thousands of viewers to simultaneously input commands into chat to collectively—and chaotically—pilot a player character through the 1998 Game Boy hit *Pokemon Red*. The concept went viral, with millions ultimately tuning in and creating memes based on the broadcast's most absurd triumphs and failures. Twitch staff came to view it as a watershed moment, one that—thanks to the resulting news coverage—showed mainstream media that Twitch had bottled millions of Pikachus' worth of lightning. Its community was doing the unthinkable, in large part because nobody had ever thought of anything like this before. Twitch users were dreaming up entirely new forms of entertainment.

"I think [Twitch Plays Pokemon] completely changed the way people looked at Twitch," says Graham. "They finally went, 'Oh shit this whole interactive format and medium is the future. It will define this industry for a long time to come.'"

Other early streamers, like Steven "Destiny" Bonnell, innovated by pairing gaming prowess with offensive language and shock humor, echoing back to edgy pockets of early YouTube and forward to the perpetual drama engines that power large portions of Twitch today. Bonnell has since been indefinitely banned from Twitch for "hateful conduct," according to Twitch, but other streamers of the era prone to harboring questionable beliefs or casually employing inadvisable language—Chance "Sodapoppin" Morris, Jaryd "Summit1g" Lazar, and Zack "Asmongold" (who has not disclosed his last name) among them—are now about as popular as they've ever been.

Following in this grand tradition, every era of Twitch has had its crop of edgelords, some of whom took things too far, others of whom are still around today. In 2016, Tyler "Tyler1" Steinkamp began a reign of bellowing, profanity-laden toxicity that got him banned from his game of choice, *League of Legends*, for two years. In 2017, Paul "Ice Poseidon" Denino became famous for repeatedly courting real-life controversy until somebody swatted him on an airplane, at which point Twitch banned him. In 2023, Adin Ross—who'd already committed countless other infractions—finally got the boot after moving to another platform entirely and allowing antisemitism in his chat. Félix "xQc" Lengyel, once Twitch's biggest North American star and still a top streamer, has been suspended for everything from porn to airing copyrighted content to cheating in a Twitch-hosted tournament. The list goes on, as it does on other platforms, each of which have adopted their own content moderation policies over the years—some, like YouTube, gradually clamping down, while others, like Twitter (now X), have come to allow all manner of toxicity, even as advertisers have fled. Despite Twitch's wholesome modern-day marketing, it was founded on edgelords.

"It was the Wild West," says Graham of livestreaming's earliest days. "People think there's edgelords now—there are—but everyone was an edgelord back in the beginning."

Graham, to some degree, counts himself as part of that lineage. As an example, he points to a 2007 pre-Twitch stream in which he hosted an event called "Strip *Halo*," which pitted adult actresses Mia and Ava Rose against viewers of Graham's show in games of the popular sci-fi first-person shooter, and if viewers won, the Rose sisters had to remove articles of clothing. This was near the peak of the era in which video games were considered a male pastime, at least as far as marketers and gatekeeping subsets of the fandom were concerned. Graham feels like he contributed to a status quo of objectifying women, one that informed the Twitch community's future hostility toward female streamers.

"Some of us were like, 'We can all be Howard Sterns on the internet,'" says Graham. "I'm not overly proud of all that."

Early Twitch was characterized by a male-dominated culture among streamers and their communities, as well as in the halls of Twitch's offices.

"We did attract a certain kind of bro-y gamer guy," says Goldhaber. "The majority of the partnerships team was a bro-y gamer guy [type]. A lot of bro-y gamer guys."

Partnerships, the team on which Graham spent his first several years at Twitch, were instrumental in Twitch's early success. At the time, Twitch hand-selected which streamers achieved partner status, granting them additional moneymaking features on the site, a direct line of communication into Twitch, and the ability to attend exclusive parties. This gave Twitch's partnership team outsized influence and led to accusations of favoritism, especially where moderation—what happened when streamers broke the rules—was concerned.

"There was such a lack of structure," says Graham. "On one hand, that was great for creators, because as partnerships [team members], we want to look out for other partners. . . . But [partners] really only got banned for the most egregious shit."

"In the early days, everyone did everything," says Goldhaber. "We all kind of tapped in for moderation. I don't think we had a lot of consistency."

While Twitch standardized its moderation practices more over the years and eventually put together a dedicated trust and safety team, Graham believes that too few people doing too much work led to a reactionary moderation approach rather than a proactive one.

"A lot of [moderation] was 'Just let it keep going until we really need to change it.' It was forced reaction. 'This happened, now we need to do something about it.' . . . Did the [rules] evolve gracefully over time? No. Did support evolve gracefully over time? No."

These growing pains left scars. Racism and sexism—never explicitly allowed on Twitch, but addressed slowly by staff (or not at all) in the platform's early days—were able to snarl their roots around the bases of many communities. Long-standing issues sprouted from this tainted soil: regular harassment of female streamers both on Twitch and off, by streamers and viewers, as well as the practice of spamming chat with an emote of a Black streamer named Mychal "Trihex" Jefferson anytime a Black person appeared on-screen, sometimes as a dog whistle for slurs. That's just the tip of the iceberg of old-school Twitch toxicity, and though the company has worked hard to curtail those issues with significantly better enforcement of its own rules and built-in moderation tools streamers can deploy at will, the platform will never be able to fully erase the stain on its culture.

"If you've seen [Netflix mystery movie] *Glass Onion*, one of the main characters is a Twitch streamer, and he's an awful fucking human being," says Cristina Amaya, a former customer service rep at Twitch who went on to become a director at esports event company DreamHack. "That's the joke, right? All these awful people are representative. That's what people think of our platform."

This insufficient approach to self-moderation and self-regulation also revealed the downsides of Twitch's cross-pollination within its own community. Twitch employees regularly mixed and mingled with streamers, who they regarded as peers despite a power imbalance in which employees could grant streamers status both socially and—when it came to site features—at the press of a button.

"Not to downplay it or say it's acceptable, but first of all, everyone's in their early to mid-twenties drinking a lot at conventions," says Goldhaber. "Twitch employees and streamers were all partying together, and they were all young. . . . So yeah, [streamers and employees getting together] definitely happened. That kind of thing was not all that surprising."

"There was a bit of a bro-y culture," Goldhaber reiterates. "There was *a lot* of drinking culture."

In a few cases, these dynamics led to unsavory outcomes, though they would not come to light until much later. In 2020, a streamer who went by the handle Vio accused Hassan Bokhari, then accounts director of strategic partnerships at Twitch, of abuse of power and sexual assault that took place both before and after the two began dating in 2015. She said Bokhari would use his status as a Twitch employee—one with special access to Twitch partners—to lavish her with perks like a username change, a special holiday package meant for Twitch partners (she was not one at the time), and eventually partnership. When the two met up in person at a 2015 video game convention, Vio said Bokhari immediately began pressuring her with unwanted sexual advances. This turned into a pattern across multiple in-person encounters, until she, in her own words, "gave in."

"I was preyed on, manipulated, gaslighted, violated, and sexually assaulted," Vio wrote in a 2020 post about her experiences with Bokhari.

According to a report by *Kotaku*, this led Twitch to hire an external investigator and ultimately dismiss Bokhari from his role.

A wave of similar stories came out around the same time as part of a #MeToo movement in the Twitch and content creation space. These focused not just on Twitch employees but other empowered individuals: managers and agents, some of whom had already begun to draw flak for negotiating predatory contracts and secretly skimming money off the top of deals between creators and brands. Omeed Dariani, then CEO of Online Performers Group, one of the biggest management firms in livestreaming, faced accusations not unlike those leveled at Bokhari, with a streamer saying he engaged in predatory behavior at a 2014 video game convention. After word of his alleged actions got out in 2020, numerous streamers dropped the firm, and it ultimately shut down.

Even if justice was eventually served in some cases, the impact of the male-dominated, drinking-heavy culture that sprung up around Twitch shaped the environment. In 2020 alone, over one hundred people, mostly women, came forward to accuse industry figures and streamers of abuse and exploitation. At the time, Twitch issued a statement saying it had banned several streamers and would "continue to assess accusations against people affiliated with Twitch and explore ways Twitch can collaborate with other industry leaders on this important issue."

Both prior to and following this reckoning, Twitch employees who were not white men found themselves in protracted uphill battles within the company.

"[Early] Twitch was gaming nerdy white dudes," says Amaya, who worked at Twitch from 2017 to 2018. "They never brought in people that did makeup or [other non-gaming types of content creation]. And even when those people were at Twitch, when I was there, they never really got a voice in the room."

"It was always a fight," says a former Twitch employee, who chose to remain anonymous out of concern for future job prospects, who worked on diversity and charity programs at Twitch. "It was never, 'Hey, let's just do this.' . . . Everybody was fighting over the limited opportunities to get in front and be seen as somebody leading a project because it was the only way to get promoted. That means people who excel at things that are important to the company that are administrative—which tend to more often be women or marginalized identities—don't get promoted as often."

One example of this, according to the former Twitch employee, was Twitch leadership's response to the idea of a Black History Month celebration on the platform—now a successful annual tradition that spotlights Black creators every February.

"[Leadership] fought me like hell over the first Black History Month," the former Twitch employee says. "They didn't want to tweet it. They said it wouldn't do well. A guy on the team at the time was like, 'I don't think this tweet will even get five hundred retweets.' That Black History Month tweet from [Twitch's] first Black History Month was their best-performing tweet for almost a whole year."

A 2020 report from GamesIndustry.biz painted an even more severe picture of Twitch's diversity-related lapses over the years. In the piece, former Twitch employees from all prior eras of the company's history spoke of multiple instances of sexual abuse, incidents where female streamers were scrutinized and punished for non-rule-breaking attire, and dismissals of concerns from employees of marginalized backgrounds, such as racist language both in the workplace and in Twitch chat. At the time, Twitch issued a statement saying that it "takes allegations of this nature extremely seriously," but also, "many of these allegations are years old, and we've taken numerous steps to better protect and support our employees and community, and will continue to invest time and resources in this area."

Lin, who was part of Twitch's C-suite from its inception until 2020, acknowledges that Twitch leaders made mistakes when they were young and "flying by the seat of our pants," but they also tried to course correct later on.

"Consciously we tried to change this," Lin says. "A topic we spoke with a bunch of our friends in the industry about was 'How do we increase diversity? How do we proactively do this?' The hard part there is, we were running a business, and we had investors. When we talked to investors, it was constantly 'Well, why aren't you hiring experienced people?' And the reality of what came before us was, most of the experienced people were male and white."

Studies even back in 2011, however, showed that the lack of women and minorities in tech wasn't merely a pipeline problem. People from non-white, non-male backgrounds reported disproportionately worse experiences in the workplace, which led to turnover. In other words, we've known for quite some time that companies play an active role in growing (or thinning) that part of the workforce. Still, Lin insists he and other Twitch leaders did their best, improving hiring practices, creating a streamer ambassador program with a focus on diversity, and implementing weekly meetings where anybody in the company could ask questions.

"We actually cared about this stuff," says Lin. "No one will believe it, but we did. Could we have done better? One hundred percent. But a lot of this feedback [from the GI.biz article] is, like, any company is like this. Oh, an exec doesn't listen to you? Yeah, guess what? There's two thousand people in the company. Sorry, it's impossible to talk to two thousand people every single month. It's not possible. Maybe technology can solve this one day."

The former Twitch employee who chose to remain anonymous views that potential solution as part of the problem: Twitch leaders like Lin and former CEO Emmett Shear, she says, had a tendency to view Twitch through a lens of technological neutrality—to believe that they'd somehow created a platform that was unaffected by the prejudices of those who made it.

"Nobody wanted to admit that users are racist," says the former Twitch employee. "Every time I would talk about how the top users on Twitch's platform for a long time were mostly white and men, people would just say, 'That's just what people feel is the best content on our platform.' I'm like, 'So you think Twitch is completely neutral on this?' And they're like, 'Absolutely.'"

Graham believes he grew as a person over the course of his time at Twitch. He came to recognize the double standard that impacted colleagues like the aforementioned former Twitch employee who opted remain anonymous, whom he ended up mentoring. "We could literally say the same thing in a room," says Graham, "and if I spoke it people would say, 'Oh that's [Graham] for you,' but if [she] spoke the same thing it would be 'That's insubordinate and [she] is hard to work with.' . . . I think she was constantly labeled incorrectly because she cared about community and was passionate."

However, despite early ripples that would turn into future tidal waves, Graham retains a forgiving view of the first few years, before Twitch—and its problems—grew several times in size.

"I think where Twitch was falling short, or where we had problems, was just having a lot of work and not enough people to do it," Graham says of Twitch's startup days. "The growing pains were the hardest part. It wasn't that the ideas were bad. It wasn't that the vision and the mission weren't right. It was always that we needed more people to do more things so we could accomplish more."

- - - - - - -

MORE PEOPLE WOULD come in 2014 and the years following. Many more.

When Twitch got big enough, the major tech giants came sniffing around. Amazon emerged as the early favorite, its main competition in this clash of tech titans being Google, already the owner of YouTube. Upon hearing rumors that an acquisition was nigh, Graham feared a future in which Google would strip Twitch for its (by this point global) livestreaming infrastructure and roll the rest into YouTube. Effectively, this would have meant no more Twitch—and by extension, no more Twitch community.

"I didn't want Twitch to get sucked into YouTube," he says.

Twitch leadership, it turns out, felt the same way.

"Our biggest hesitation around Google was, we were certain to just become another cog in the YouTube machine," says Lin. "By comparative scales to YouTube, we were still quite small. Would we ever really get the attention and resources we needed? Or would we just get absorbed entirely . . . when we still had all these big ideas, products, initiatives?"

Google also pitched Twitch on its broader strategy around games, but Lin "wouldn't say that was very convincing" at the time. Amazon, on the other hand, seemed more sold on Twitch's vision of the future.

In 2014, Amazon acquired Twitch, spurring long-term change that would shake the company to its core.

"We had this dream of ten years down the road, what Twitch's place in the games industry could be, and that eventually became a project internally called 'developer success,' which was about building these audience-interactive games," says Lin. "The easy example we'd use was *Hunger Games*. Imagine you're playing *Hunger Games*—like games and audiences buy stuff while the game is live—or, at minimum, you could easily pull your viewers [from a stream] into a game."

Lin and others at Twitch wanted to keep exploring those ideas, but they'd hit a wall: cost. Twitch did not publicly talk numbers on this front until 2022, by which point it was a very different company than it had been in 2014, but the outline of the problem has been present since day one: As Twitch gains more viewers, it grows more expensive to run.

"Bandwidth is expensive," says former Twitch software engineer Theo Browne. "The more data you have and the further the distance it has to travel, the more expensive it gets."

"We were profitable up until 2012, but as Twitch started to really take off, the cost just outpaced our ability to continue to improve monetization," says Lin. "Twitch is an expensive site to run, and [then-CEO of Amazon Web Services] Andy Jassy gave us a lot of freedom to continue to build. As long as we kept growing, he was cool with it."

With the Amazon acquisition came some pretty immediate benefits, chief among them integration with the mega-corporation's popular Prime program. Amazon decided to use Twitch to sweeten the Prime pot: If a user signed up for Prime, they'd receive a free monthly subscription to a Twitch streamer of their choosing—meaning Amazon was effectively paying for millions of Twitch subscriptions per month. This put cash in streamers' pockets and allowed Twitch to keep building.

"We sunk a lot more money into Twitch's continued growth and development," says Lin. "Amazon had a lot of patience there, I think, because things like [Twitch] Prime were working."

This also meant resources for rapid expansion, the kind that would have been inconceivable before Twitch became a beneficiary of Amazon's mighty money spigot.

"We ended up ballooning from when we got bought," says Lin. "[At the time] we were at two hundred and forty people across the globe. Just one year after we grew to a little over four hundred, because we had all these resources and were encouraged to do so. Our [Amazon] integration team was like, 'Yeah, you should go faster. Just grow!'"

But that's also when the troubles began.

"It became somewhat unnatural," says Lin. "We'd been historically very careful about hiring. We talked about it all the time. Myself, Emmett, [and others] would ask, 'Do we really want to grow this much? They're telling us to, but it feels unnatural. What's right? Do we stay at this size?'"

After a little over a year, Graham and others on the more community-oriented side of the company began to feel the impacts of Twitch's accelerated growth.

"The biggest downhill we saw after the Amazon acquisition is when we started hiring people that did not believe in the things that made Twitch successful in the first place," says Graham. "I think Twitch hired a lot of people who had good Silicon Valley résumés, that could make a PR splash—but at the end of the day [who] were total fucking boomers who could not grasp what Twitch was, how it worked."

During this time, Graham transitioned between different director-level roles that focused on everything from features to Twitch-produced live shows and events. As he almost always had, he continued to stream as well, something that was becoming rarer and rarer among Twitch employees. With that in mind, he took it upon himself to advocate for what had come before—or at least a more robust understanding of it. But a new layer of management made that difficult.

"The new guard created this sense of—and it was supported by individuals like Emmett, I'm not sure why, maybe he was too passive—everything that needed to be done needed to be new," says Graham. "One of the reasons I think people felt I was a disruption within Twitch is because I would force the function of history. I'd be like, 'You know, we used to do this,' or 'We tried this, and it failed. Why are we trying it again?' [They'd say], 'Oh, well it worked over at Twitter or Pandora.' But we weren't Twitter or Pandora. We're not Facebook. We are Twitch."

Ignacio also moved around within Twitch during this time period, switching from working under Lin to working under Graham. He realized he enjoyed being involved in more creatively oriented projects within the company, but he, too, could feel the company's foundations shifting beneath his feet.

"People were brought on who'd never used the platform," says Ignacio. "They focused on social media, too. They launched a system similar to Twitter likes and a friend system because they were trying to compete with Facebook for a while. . . . We all agreed it was a weird move, and even if you liked it, we didn't do it right. And we gave up too fast."

From 2015 onward, Twitch slowly expanded beyond the realm of video games, catering to a wider audience than in its pre-Amazon days and growing commensurately. Between 2014 and 2015 alone, Twitch went from 16 billion minutes watched per month to 20 billion, with a peak viewer count of 1 million concurrent viewers in 2014 and over 2 million in 2015. Some of Twitch's non-gaming efforts bore fruit that sustains the platform to this day: "Just Chatting" streams—in which creators interact with their audiences sans a game—are some of the most popular on the platform, and many creators now focus on artistic pursuits, outdoor activities, or trawling the internet and gawking at other people's content instead of ranking ever upward in games. But these broadened horizons also turned Twitch into a graveyard of half-baked projects: a karaoke game for streamers called *Twitch Sings* that, despite proving costly, never caught on and was eventually shut down; a merchandise program that split revenue with streamers; a store that also gave streamers a small cut of resulting sales; and countless site features and Twitch-produced shows. Meanwhile, teams—numerous and diffuse as a result of Twitch's continued expansion well past the one-thousand-employee mark—competed as often as they cooperated, resulting in a plethora of projects that never cleared the runway. Twitch wanted to expand, but it failed to pick a direction and stick to it. And all the while, it struggled to synergize with Amazon, whose game development efforts hit snag after snag.

"Amazon Game Studios finally hit it big with [2022 role-playing game] *Lost Ark*, but the first, like, seven years of Amazon Game Studios was a complete disaster," says Goldhaber. "[For Amazon] the buying of Twitch was supposed to be like, 'We have a game studio, and then we market it on Twitch.'"

Twitch continued to grow in popularity, though arguably more because of what was happening around it than inside it. In 2018, *Fortnite*—a battle royale shooter in which each match sees a hundred players compete to be the last one standing—took the platform by storm, with the game's fusion of candy-colored cuteness and high-stakes blood sportsmanship catapulting creators like Tyler "Ninja" Blevins to previously unseen heights and hooking mainstream stars like Drake in the process. Before long, streamers were appearing in television advertisements and at the Super Bowl. It was as though the world suddenly awoke to a fact Graham and many others had known for quite some time: Everybody plays video games. Just as the *Fortnite* craze began to simmer down, 2020 brought another colossal influx of new Twitch users as the result of a pandemic-stricken populace starved for human connection. Every year brought with it a new all-time viewership high. Twitch had officially arrived.

But sheer numbers—by this point, Twitch had millions of streamers and over 100 million monthly active users—presented challenges that even Twitch's most community-oriented employees couldn't surmount. The company was forced to automate the partner program, resulting in a system that served many (over fifty thousand partners, compared to the hundreds of Twitch's early days) but satisfied few. It became impossible to provide the lion's share of big streamers with personalized attention, and many came to feel that Twitch failed to beef up its communication chops elsewhere to compensate. Streamers grew increasingly irate over suspensions they felt were under-explained, rules that seemed inconsistently applied, Twitch's unwillingness to pay licensing fees to allow streamers to broadcast music and other copyrighted material (despite other platforms like Facebook and TikTok having done so to varying degrees), and slow responses to issues like a 2021 epidemic of "hate raids," in which trolls overwhelmed streamers' chats with fake accounts that spammed hateful messages. All the while, there was a looming sense that instead of providing streamers with the tools they wanted—features that would aid with pernicious issues like small streamers' inability to be discovered by viewers—Twitch began to prioritize turning a profit. This, to a degree, was an accurate read: After years of expansion, Amazon had come to collect. It wanted Twitch to prove it could be a profitable enterprise.

Twitch didn't feel like Twitch anymore, and Graham began to feel hopeless.

"The number of dumb ideas I had to shoot down in my time at Twitch, I wish I had a nickel," he sighs, outlining an instance in which a decision from on high functionally ruined Twitch's official channel on its own website by encouraging viewers to spam chat indefinitely. "These particular employees couldn't truly show empathy for a creator. I was trying to explain to them why it would ruin a chat if I can't have a conversation with the people in it. If Twitch can't do it [on its own channel], how can it be an example for anyone else?"

When it came to decisions large and small, Graham was dismayed with his new compatriots' lack of experience in the trenches of streaming, their inability to see how all the pieces of the site fit together.

"How does [a decision] affect a moderator?" he says. "How does it affect a creator? How does it affect an audience member? How does it affect the trifecta of how these things work together? The more and more Twitch goes away from that, the worse things seem to get. We started with Amazon purchasing Twitch. This is the long-term consequence."

Longtime streamers like Ben "CohhCarnage" Cassell, who came up alongside Graham in Twitch's early days, could feel the change. And hear it, because Graham has never been one to stay silent.

"Some of what [Graham] said on his stream were the kind of things where when you hear them, you know exactly what he's talking about," says

Cassell. "When he can say something like 'I stood up in a meeting full of people and asked if anyone was thinking of the people creating on this plat- form,' when you hear something like that and get a vision in your head of literally a room full of people, and one person is standing up and asking if *anyone* is thinking of this? That's a good example of where things are now [at Twitch]. . . . I think we all kind of hope that feeling of community, of shared passion, lasts as long as it can. For Twitch, we are past that time. We are not in that realm anymore."

Other former Twitch employees with whom Graham worked have slightly different takes. While the Twitch employee who chose to remain anonymous also ultimately found herself dismayed at the extent to which Twitch took its community for granted (and discouraged her from advocating for it), she feels like Amazon helped professionalize a company where not everybody swapped out their halcyon-day beer goggles for rose-tinted glasses.

"A lot of early employees, Twitch made them, and it caused a lot of people to be ego-driven," says the former Twitch employee. "[They would] speak out of turn, but also people who were friends with creators would advocate for them to get things, and it made it really messy. I think that a lot of what [Graham], for example, looked at from the olden days [as better]—and I've talked about this with creators who say, 'Oh, Twitch was better,' too—is people saying they liked it better when they had more influence and control."

Goldhaber concurs that, even if he doesn't love the exact form it took, Twitch needed to move past its rowdy early days.

"You have to grow up a little bit at some point," he says. "As the company scaled, we're talking about going from twenty employees when I joined to one thousand employees five years later. You need some growth in terms of management, in terms of leadership. And I do think some was needed."

But as Twitch grew larger and larger, continental drift set in where em- ployees' objectives were concerned. Many wanted to see Twitch succeed, but according to Graham and Lin, others were mostly there to climb the corporate ladder.

"By nature of these big companies, these large groups of people, people aren't aligned," says Lin. "I think we were younger and much more naive, and we believed that all the other Amazon people that were coming at us to say, 'Hey, let's do something together,' were sincere in their interest in working with Twitch and not so much driven by their own selfish objectives. Ninety percent of the time, that is what was going on, and so we became somewhat jaded. We became a little less interested in exploring anything too much deeper because a lot of these conversations led to dead ends. And wasted time, debates, and arguments."

"There were people I worked with for three years, and it was not uncommon for me to hear [them say], 'I still don't understand why anyone would watch something like this,'" says Graham. "I don't know how to respond to something like that, because that's not much different than [them] coming into someone's house, taking a big shit on the living room floor, and then leaving and thinking they've done nothing wrong. I felt so hurt when something I worked so hard on was treated like it was a fad—like it was just a stop on a long road or whatever corporate ladder somebody was trying to climb in Silicon Valley."

- - - - - - -

IN HIS FINAL days at Twitch before departing in 2022, Graham attempted to sell Twitch on the idea of a program meant to foster greater empathy between Twitch employees and creators.

"Honestly, when you start at Twitch, you should be able to fill out a form of what your interests are and be matched up with a creator or set of creators, or have a list of creators," he says. "And your fucking job for two weeks should just be to watch Twitch, to chat, to subscribe to someone, to look at their Twitter. If you do that, you're immediately gonna have some sort of connection, you're going to immediately be able to build some sort of empathy, and then you have to reinforce that over time."

He is unsure if anybody picked up that ball and ran with it, but he assumes it now lies on the floor of a darkened gymnasium, gathering dust.

Graham describes his departure from Twitch as the result of "death by a thousand cuts," but ultimately it came down to a guilt-laden sense of having failed the community. Controversies over copyright issues on the platform, he says, played a big role, because he feels like he could've done more in Twitch's early days to head them off at the pass. But the hate raid epidemic—and the headline-making #TwitchDoBetter hashtag it spawned that begged Twitch for some kind of response—was the last straw.

"That was an incredibly deep cut, not only because of what it represented—a group of marginalized individuals getting raided and harassed—[but] what really pissed me off was that we didn't have a conversation with RekItRaven, the creator behind [the hashtag], for two fucking weeks," Graham says. "As someone who spent five years pre-Amazon building Twitch, all based off of creators, [that was unacceptable]. There were times in 2012 and 2013 where a creator would be like, 'Oh, I cut myself in the kitchen,' and I'd be like, 'Are you OK? Do you need anything? Can I help you find an urgent care?' We would pick up the phone and we would fucking call them because they were people, and we cared about what they were doing."

Kaitlyn "Amouranth" Siragusa, one of the most popular female streamers on Twitch, has found that a lack of consistent communication has strained her relationship with the platform over the years.

"Twitch is a weird platform because no one can really ever get direct communication from the people on the inside," says Siragusa, whose risqué content has gotten her suspended from Twitch on several occasions. "I don't really have a clear thought of whether I'm good with them or if I'm on thin ice."

But the Twitch of now is not the Twitch of the good old days. While the anonymous former Twitch employee—who worked alongside Graham and advocated for many of the same causes—understands where he's coming from, she believes Twitch has stranded itself in an awkward middle ground: It brands itself as a community leader, but in reality, the community has been leading itself for a long time.

"It puts Twitch in a really weird position because their marketing is 'We're a community, we're a family,'" she says. "But in those moments, it's very much not. It's a corporation."

The solution, she believes, would be for Twitch to drop the facade entirely.

"I think Twitch would benefit from stopping trying to sound like they're a community leader and instead positioning themselves as the best tool and the best place for communities to organize and meet and grow," she says. "For people from the old days, like [Graham], that's really hard because when your role, or your whole identity or success or popularity, has been wrapped up in being a voice of the community, it definitely feels like things are being taken away from you."

Graham is fully aware of the limits of direct one-to-one communication, especially on a site that now services hundreds of millions of people per month. But he, much like the users behind the viral hashtag, still believes Twitch can do better.

"We handled #TwitchDoBetter like a corporation. And great, but we should've handled it like a corporation that actually cares about the people that are using its product," he says. "I came to a point in 2021 where I realized that there is a complete lockdown on communication from Twitch. . . . So here I was realizing that the glory days will never return. And that's fine; companies exist. But that's not an excuse for giving up on the values the company was built on."

Graham, Lin, Ignacio, Goldhaber, and Amaya are no longer working at Twitch. Hundreds of others have also departed the company in recent years. In 2021 alone, over three hundred employees left. Since Graham's departure, the company has changed even more. In 2022, Twitch removed a contract option that allowed for a 70/30 revenue split on subscriptions in streamers' favor. This had previously only been offered to a small percentage of creators, but for years it functioned as an aspirational goal and a sign that Twitch valued the faces of its platform. The decision was met with outrage, especially when paired with increased pressure to run ads that disrupted broadcasts and turned away new viewers.

Even creators who understood from a business perspective why Twitch made these moves, like politics juggernaut Hasan "HasanAbi" Piker, struggled to bear the weight of Twitch's heavy-handedness.

"When the announcement came that the 70/30 split was no longer [available], or when I learn that I'm going to have to run more ads no matter what," says Piker, "those are things that remind me of my place, ultimately."

In early 2023, Emmett Shear—CEO of Twitch since the beginning—stepped down following the birth of his first child. New CEO Dan Clancy's first major public announcement, just a week later, was a sobering one: As part of a round of nine thousand job cuts at Amazon, four hundred Twitch employees (out of a little over two thousand) would be laid off. Some were recent hires. Others had been with the company for over half its existence.

Devin Nash, who rose out of the esports community, represented top streamers publicly and behind the scenes, and eventually came to run an agency dedicated to connecting brands with creators, was at various points about as connected to Twitch's inner workings as one could be without being an executive there. He believes that Twitch's drift off course and into a sea of corporate BS was unfortunate but inevitable.

"The story of Twitch—I was so dramatic about it in the past—is just the classic mergers and acquisitions story," says Nash. "Executives that love the company, that have the vision, that really want to build something special and understand the culture really well, they cash out. They have incredible opportunities, they're ready to move on to the next thing. No moral, ethical judgment. That's just how business works. They move on, the big corporate giant brings in people that understand [the company] a little bit less, and at the same time, they're getting so much budget to hire people at the management level that understand less, too. Before you know it, you've come to a place four or five years later where no one really understands why the whole thing worked."

"The culture of Bleed Purple," he adds, "there just wasn't anybody left at the company to tell that tale."

Plante, who first coined "Bleed Purple," left Twitch in 2017. She's still part of the community—now the director of business operations for longtime streamer Chris "Sacriel" Ball, who is also her husband—but she regrets the slogan.

"It has been weaponized in my mind," Plante says. "It's become something that late Twitch, third-gen Twitch—whatever you want to call it—has definitely used against the community. Not for the community or with the community. That's why I feel like it really doesn't fit anymore."

"Twitch is not a dead platform. The concurrent viewership is still absolutely astronomical," she adds. "It's the sense of community culture that maybe is in a coma, and someone's about to pull the plug."

Lin cannot help but ponder what would've happened if he and other Twitch executives had kept the company independent. No Amazon, no Google. Just Twitch.

"If we stayed independent, would we have been able to grow quite as fast? Maybe not," he says. "We would have had to invent additional [means of] monetization. We would've had to raise a lot more [investment] money. But I believe we would've been much more disciplined on costs and monetization building. The platform might look a little bit different than it looks today, [but also] from a policy perspective and a fun perspective."

"I'd still be there," he adds. "I never wanted to leave. I love the work. I love the people. I think we could have stayed smaller as a team. . . . Would we have survived? I don't know. I really don't. We'll never know."

- - - - - - -

GRAHAM SITS ON his luxuriously lengthy couch, but he looks tapped. By this point, he's nearing the end of a long, emotionally taxing journey through his professional history. The day has played host to no small number of unexpected cameos. Not his former coworkers—those conversations, to give you a peek behind the curtain of the journalism factory, would end up taking place later over the phone—but a flock of wild turkeys outside Graham's house as well as Graham's wife and teenage son.

The latter, who grunts a hello and then recedes into his bedroom, briefly becomes the focal point of conversation. From behind his closed door, he's audibly talking to others while playing a video game. Graham explains that his pride and joy—despite inheriting his father's formidable height—is not following in his footsteps. Instead of streaming to an audience of hundreds or thousands, Graham's son is broadcasting to just a small handful of personal friends over Discord, a popular communications app.

"A lot of kids today are streamers; they just don't do it publicly," says Graham. "They hang out in a group of eight, and it's like, 'It's this person's turn this week to stream some game' that they all sit there and [joke about] in real time, right? It's basically the same as streaming, except you're saying, 'We're doing this because we like the social aspect of it, not because we feel the need to make money or want to make a video that we're going to upload.'"

It is, in a sense, closer to the platonic ideal of livestreaming than what Twitch has made it into: the feeling of sitting on a couch with friends while one person plays a video game and everybody else hoots and hollers and talks shit. Just like the old days, but through new technology. For a generation raised in the constant blaring noise of social media, there's a clear desire to curate more personal spaces—free from the prying eyes and ears of companies and the general public. These communities, vastly smaller than the ones Graham has dedicated his life to serving, seem at first glance more capable of building themselves, of sustaining themselves, sans the need for outside interference or advocacy. In a time when global squares like Twitter collapse and algorithms wall off platforms like Instagram to the degree that people exist in their own little pockets, it's not difficult to imagine a future in which atomized communities become the norm. Perhaps, in that future, there will not be a need for someone like Graham to perform what ultimately proved an impossible task—at least, at the scale Twitch forced him to operate.

But no matter what shape gaming communities end up taking, Graham believes that in the face of corporate interests and incentive structures, they'll always need an advocate. He's getting back to it, he explains with the wide eyes of somebody half his age, at a company called Fortis, where he hopes to create a process by which community can directly influence the creation of video games. After years of putting out fires, he feels relieved to just help make something again. Maybe it'll pan out, maybe it won't, but he's glad to be back in his community-first wheelhouse.

"I want to keep fighting that fight as much as I can," he says.

chapter two

----

virality

B reaking points are strange. Sometimes they take months or years of reflection, meditation, therapy. But other breaking points happen instantly, with the viciousness of a thunderclap. Emme "Negaoryx" Montgomery learned this the hard way.

On the wings of a viral moment in 2019, Montgomery's star had finally begun to rise. To pursue her dreams of Twitch fame—or even just a middle-of-the-road Twitch career—she'd given up a college education and a career in the entertainment industry. She'd endured countless long days and sleepless nights to get her numbers up.

All of that—years of unglamorous toil—built to a single, thirteen-second stream moment. In it, Montgomery, light brown hair swooped to the side and clad in a plain white tank top, playing the popular PlayStation action-horror game *The Last of Us*, gets taken by surprise when an arrow impales an inno-cent rabbit, splattering virtual snow with disarmingly realistic bunny blood. Already in a heightened state of emotion from a previous story scene in the game, Montgomery immediately covers her face with her hands and yelps in authentic sorrow. That's it. That's the entire clip.

Much like her dearly departed lagomorphic friend, Montgomery never could have predicted what happened next. Nobody could've. The internet builds its ever-evolving zeitgeist like a free-form jazz player: It selects pieces in an almost gleefully haphazard fashion, and somehow they fall into place without bringing the whole house down. In 2019, it was suddenly Montgomery's turn to be at the center of it all. Her thirteen-second livestream moment had everything: tragedy, comedy, and spontaneity that simply couldn't be scripted. Millions of people shared hundreds of versions of the "*Last of Us* dying rabbit meme girl" clip. Literally overnight, she went from having a regular Twitch viewership of a couple hundred to thousands, all waiting expectantly to meet the woman behind the meme.

Montgomery could not let this moment go to waste. She knew what was at stake. On Twitch, chances to "make it" are few, far between, and most importantly, fleeting. There are around 7 million streamers on the platform. After analyzing data from a 2021 leak that revealed payment information for everybody on Twitch, observers found that fewer than ten thousand—less than 0.1 percent—of streamers make minimum wage or better, let alone get rich. And things were likely better by then, compared to the timing of Montgomery's big moment in 2019. But it's always been a mighty exclusive club, and one that features a revolving door; back in 2018, Tyler "Ninja" Blevins, then Twitch's most popular streamer, took a two-day break from streaming. He lost forty thousand paying subscribers, totaling out to over $100,000. Much like livestreaming as a medium, even success on Twitch is ephemeral. For every Ben "CohhCarnage" Cassell—every pillar of consistency who has managed to stick it out for over a decade—there are countless big names and no names who've burnt out and fallen off almost overnight. This weighed on Montgomery, just as it weighs on every person who hopes to turn the pipe dream of playing video games for a living into a career.

"I just said 'yes' to everything because I thought I was never gonna get opportunities again," Montgomery explained.

So, in the first half of 2019, she streamed and participated in events as much as humanly possible. During one event, a live charity drive for Red Nose Day, a campaign to end child poverty, she rubbed elbows with megastars like fellow streamers Imane "Pokimane" Anys and Rachell "Valkyrae" Hofstetter as well as movie star (who moonlights as a YouTuber) Jack Black. But she also picked up a cough she just couldn't shake. Fortunately, she wasn't sick. Her voice was just struggling after endless amounts of talking on-stream and off. But then, midway through the event, one of her coughs hit different.

"I coughed and felt something in my side," Montgomery said. "I tried to inhale and wanted to scream. It was like somebody shoving the world's sharpest sword directly inside me anytime I tried to breathe. I was like, 'I'm on camera. We're smiling and at a charity event, and I'm fucking dying. What is happening to me?'"

Montgomery had coughed so hard that she broke a rib. But she couldn't stop. By this point it was the beginning of summer, and she had too many events on the calendar. Famous streamers were just about to host a reality TV–style broadcast called *Streamer Camp*, and she'd been invited to compete. It was an enormous opportunity to grow her audience and network with some of the biggest names in the business. How could she say no? On top of that, E3, an LA-based convention that functions as the nexus of all video game announcements, was set to take place immediately after in June, and Montgomery had landed a hosting gig. She couldn't pass that up, either. So she decided to soldier on, broken rib and all. She'd just smile her way through the pain, she figured. She'd already done it once, after all. How hard could it be to keep doing it . . . indefinitely?

Then, while Montgomery was sitting on a couch and catching up with some friends, that nasty cough decided to rattle her rib cage again. Cough, cough, pop. Just like that, she'd broken another rib. The pain was so intense that her friends had to carry her to bed. The next day, a doctor told her there was really only one thing she could do to expedite her recovery: rest for a couple weeks. He asked her if she could take that much time off work. She said she could but she wasn't going to.

"He literally laughed in my face and said, 'Good luck,'" Montgomery recalled.

The day after, she was off to a premiere of the movie *X-Men: Dark Phoenix* for a stream sponsored by Fox. Mere hours after that event wrapped, she took a Lyft to the house in LA where *Streamer Camp* was being filmed and spent a week hardly sleeping and competing in livestreamed challenges alongside other streamers. She ended up leaving before everyone else, not because she had two broken ribs, which had not, you will be surprised to learn, miraculously healed, but because it was time to rush over to the LA Convention Center for the days-long, appointment-packed frenzy that is E3. Even once that ended, there was no finish line in sight. Next, Montgomery flew out to a charity summit in Memphis, Tennessee, and then to an event hosted by one of gaming's biggest publishers, EA, in Germany, followed shortly by TwitchCon—an official Twitch convention—in Europe.

"All of my viewers were like, 'What the fuck are you doing? Take care of yourself,'" Montgomery said. "I probably sounded like a crazy person to everyone, because I was like, 'I can't stop.'"

In the end, the physical toll was great. Montgomery said her body— already prone to pain from a spinal injury—remained "messed up" long after. But the mental toll was greater. There's a price when you push yourself past your breaking point. You can only put so many cracks in your resolve before its foundation starts to crumble. Going into her nonstop summer, Montgomery was already in rough shape. Just before the *Last of Us* bunny kicked off a new chapter in her Twitch career, her stepfather had lost his battle with cancer.

- - - - - - -

MONTGOMERY MIGHT HAVE ended up working in entertainment if her biological parents had raised her. That was her dad's world, after all. But Montgomery wouldn't be a Twitch streamer if not for her stepdad.

Montgomery's parents, Jackie and Joseph, split before she could even form memories. Growing up, she spent time with both, and thanks to her biological father's career in entertainment, it didn't take long for the Hollywood bug to bite.

"Ever since she was little, she wanted to act," said Jackie. "She was part of the drama program throughout elementary, middle, and high school."

"She did a lot of plays in high school, and she was always the star," said Joseph. "She was always very good."

But Montgomery, a self-proclaimed introvert despite her gift of gab, realized early on that the life of a movie star wasn't for her.

"My dad was friends with a lot of actors, and I remember we went out to lunch with one of them once, and it was like every person in the room was staring at her," Montgomery said. "People were interrupting to come over for autographs and photos. And I thought, 'She's not even being flashy or anything.' She was just trying to eat lunch. I remember looking at that and being like, 'If there's even a chance that could happen to me one day, I don't want to do this career.'"

Games found their way into Montgomery's life via a more circuitous route. When she was only six, Joseph purchased *The Sims*, a game Montgomery still adores to this day. Joseph's career, though, was all-consuming, so it was hard for him to find time for many other simulated lives. It was his husband, Dan, her stepfather, who inducted Montgomery into the hallowed halls of gamerdom. He gifted her a Sega Genesis and Game Boy Advance SP as hand-me-downs, and before long, gaming became a family affair—even though the family was spread across two coasts. Joseph would indulge his passion for interior design alongside Montgomery when he had time ("Typical gay guy that likes making rooms pretty, is what it came down to," he said with a wistful chuckle), Jackie would physically print out guides and read tips to her daughters, and Dan would lead them—mainly Montgomery—further down the rabbit hole.

Dan's game of choice was *World of Warcraft*, the massively multiplayer online role-playing game that presaged video games' surge to mainstream popularity by garnering an audience of over 10 million players and a *South Park* episode way back in the mid-2000s. Soon, it was Montgomery's game of choice as well. When she was visiting her dad on the East Coast, she'd take over Dan's computer well into the night until he, an artist, needed it for work early in the morning.

"He was so grouchy in the morning," Montgomery said of Dan. "He had an eyebrow piercing and, like, twenty tattoos. He's, like, six-five, spiky white hair, and he comes downstairs looking like he's gonna murder you with a cup of coffee. So I'd tag out."

This routine helped the two bond, and eventually, Montgomery got her own *World of Warcraft* account. Even when Montgomery was visiting her mom on the West Coast, she and Dan used the game to stay in touch.

"I'm sure I was just an annoying little kid, but anytime I would be online when he was online, I'd be like, 'Hiiiiiii,' sending him [direct messages] like 'I'm saying hi to you in the game!'" said Montgomery. "That was a way that it felt like we still were interacting with each other when I was across the country."

This dynamic took on a new significance after Montgomery became an adult. When Dan got diagnosed with cancer, Montgomery was broke and working at a voice-over talent agency that barely gave her any vacation time. She was only able to visit him in the hospital once.

"It was just awful," she said, her features suddenly sinking to sullen depths as though she was back in the room where it happened. "It was the hardest thing emotionally that I've ever had to do. And when I came back, I was like, 'I can't afford to go back and forth all the time. I can't afford to be there.' Then I heard about Twitch from a coworker when I was at the voice-over talent agency, and I was like, 'I bet if I did that, somebody could maybe bring [my stepdad] a laptop.'"

By this point, Dan could no longer play games, but Montgomery figured he might be able to live vicariously through her. There was just one flaw in her plan: She had no idea how to use Twitch. Her first stream in the summer of 2016 was a disaster. She didn't know it was possible to moderate chat, so random people came in and said "awful" things to her. This experience instilled in her a sense of urgency: She needed to clean up her online act ASAP, or else she'd only succeed in adding to her stepdad's teetering tray of burdens. But in doing a series of what she considered "test" streams, she managed to draw a small audience. Before long, people were asking her when she'd stream next, what her regular schedule was, and where else they could find her online.

"I only became a streamer because people were asking me to," said Montgomery. "It was really weird!"

She kept at it, and before long, she realized she'd backed into finding her calling. Streaming was everything she wanted: a forum in which she could radiate the charisma that had taken her so far when she was pursuing acting aspirations, but without the messy complications of traditional stardom.

From the relative comfort of her apartment at the time—a converted garage where she didn't even have room to lay down a yoga mat—she could perform for dozens, and eventually hundreds, of people. All the while, nobody could make unwanted advances or crowd her space. They were all just names on a screen, and she could make them disappear at will.

Montgomery ended up leaving the voice-over talent agency—a job that stressed her out so much that she'd regularly go into the bathroom and cry amid fifty-hour workweeks—to go back to college. This, however, still left her spread so thin as to be translucent. Between classes, commuting, freelancing to pay the bills, and streaming, she had no time to rest.

"I was not sleeping," she said. "I would literally nap in my car between classes in the school parking lot, because I just had no time for anything."

Her stream was starting to take off, but it had a ceiling. More than anything, Twitch demands time and consistency. If you can't put in eight-plus hours per day, your audience will go find somebody who can; Twitch makes that as easy as a couple of clicks. They have a plethora of options elsewhere, as well; a single streamer is effectively competing with TV, news, YouTube, and the tractor beam–like pull of scrolling on your phone. In this day and age, for better or worse, it's all content. Unfortunately for Montgomery, even when broadcasts were going swimmingly, she'd have to bail for her college classes. It was as frustrating as it was exhausting. Then her dad stepped in with some very un-parental advice: He told her to drop out of school. Again.

"I said, 'You know something, Emme? Fuck college. If this is really what you want to do, do it. Go out there, throw your whole heart and soul into it,'" said Joseph who, himself, had dropped out of high school. "You can't follow a path that's not right for you. You've got to make your own path in the world. And I knew how she's very charismatic. Working in the entertainment industry, you can tell the difference. If someone's got that special little something about them, you can tell."

But Joseph also believes Montgomery brings a little something extra to the table—something that makes her uniquely well equipped not just to entertain but to function as social glue for a community.

"She's comforted people that have been depressed and felt like they didn't belong. She's built this sweet, positive community," he said. "When I was growing up, I was the gay kid who didn't want to be gay. My personality was to take the misfits and make them feel good about what they could contribute to society. Not trying to take credit, but I think in a weird way, Emme got that from me. I always collected every type of person I could around me, and I think that's one thing Emme does so beautifully. All these people feel like they have a kindred spirit in her."

So in spring 2017, with her dad's blessing, Montgomery put College: Act Two on hold to focus on streaming full-time. Against all odds, it paid off. Her stream grew slowly but surely, right up until the viral moment that put her on the map in 2019. But Dan never got to celebrate her success with her.

"Toward the end, his memory started to go really badly," Montgomery said. "When I'd call for updates, my dad would say that [Dan] thought we were still in elementary school. He didn't know what year it was. . . . It sucks because by the time [my stream] really picked up steam, he just wasn't there enough to understand what I was doing."

"That really hit her profoundly," said Joseph. "He was an amazing human being."

"That was a hard time for all of us," Jackie concurred. "It's so sad that he never lived to see her success. He would have been so proud of her."

The end came just before Montgomery's viral *Last of Us* moment. And so, when she set aside her physical and mental well-being in pursuit of her one, fleeting shot at success, she also set aside her grief. At least, she tried to.

STRUCTURALLY SPEAKING, TWITCH is like a bowl of pudding left on the counter for too long. On top, there's a layer that keeps everything below from seeing the light of day. Over time, this layer has calcified. These days, it's basically a crust. Breaking through requires an iron stomach and a herculean will. Also: a whole, whole, whole lot of luck.

The crust is Twitch's top tier of streamers, the less than 0.1 percent who at least make minimum wage through a combination of Twitch-supplied advertisements and viewer subscriptions and donations. Some of them make millions. But once you get outside the top 100 highest paid streamers—over 90 percent of whom are male—payout numbers begin to drop precipitously. This is because Twitch is organized via a series of directories specific to individual games and activities. The easiest way to make it to the top of these directories is to have a boatload of viewers. So if, for example, you've got five thousand concurrent viewers and are in the top 10 to 20 streams in the *Fortnite* directory, you're probably good. Odds are, anybody clicking on that directory in search of a new streamer will see you without having to scroll down too far, and of those prospective viewers, a decent number will end up tuning into your stream. This is very different from other, more algorithmically driven platforms like YouTube, Instagram, and TikTok, where algorithms ladle up heaping amounts of new content based on what other people they deem to be like you have watched. The end result is a crisscrossing latticework of pipelines that's deeply flawed in a different way than Twitch—just look at all the people who have been radicalized by You-Tube—but which at least nominally prioritizes discovery of new content in some cases. In recent years, Twitch has added algorithmic recommendation features, but they don't undergird the whole operation like on other platforms. Twitch's algorithm is far less sophisticated and pervasive. This means that viewers, or more accurately movements of viewers, determine popular content rather than the programmers and powers that be behind the tech.

You might be able to see the problem here: Success begets additional success, but if you're starting from rock bottom, there's no reliable way to climb unless you go off Twitch and grow your audience using other platforms. According to statistics compiled by online publication *Dot Esports*, the top 1,000 Twitch channels accounted for over half of all viewership as of 2020. It's not just that most Twitch streamers don't turn a sustainable profit; the overwhelming majority of streamers broadcast to nobody and, on a good day, maybe pick up a single-digit number of viewers. Twitch's fantasy that *you too can become a star* if you grind your own bones to make their bread is just that: a fantasy. Odds are astronomically against creators.

This makes for an ecosystem in which, somewhat paradoxically, it's necessary for creators to promote themselves on other platforms in order to break through on Twitch. Any streamer who's serious about their career has a YouTube channel where they upload stream highlight clips every day. Everybody communicates with fans on Twitter and Discord. In recent years, TikTok, whose algorithm is scarily good at pinpointing what users like and surfacing new creators in the same vein, has become a quiet Twitch kingmaker as well.

"The streamer death spiral is what I call it," said Devin Nash, industry insider and chief marketing officer at influencer marketing agency Novo, in reference to what happens when streamers don't diversify across a variety of platforms. "Twitch has no external form of discovery. So if all you do is stream on Twitch and you don't start expanding your media profile, you don't get new viewers. . . . It's so easy to click the 'start broadcasting' button [on Twitch]. The inertia's so low on it. The amount of effort it takes to then go make YouTube videos and study each platform for what optimal content is—that's really difficult."

If you look at big names like Cassell, Kaitlyn "Amouranth" Siragusa, and Hasan "HasanAbi" Piker, they have teams handling much of this labor for them. They are, in that sense, well-oiled machines. But nobody starts out that way, and getting over the initial Twitch hump—which is also a YouTube hump, TikTok hump, Instagram hump, and Twitter hump—proves impossible for most. And even when streamers are firing on all cylinders across every platform known to man, they still face extremely long odds. Every additional platform is a slow, likely unrewarding grind unto itself, and you cannot plan to go viral. You can hope, certainly, that a clip, tweet, or TikTok will catch fire and get a shout-out from both PewDiePie and your local NBC affiliate, but it's never guaranteed.

And so, in that sense, Montgomery's bone-splintering sprint was justified: If she didn't make good on her viral opportunity, another might not come around for a long, long time. Whether intentionally or not, Twitch created a system that puts streamers in this desperate mindset. The reward for years of hard work is harder work.

But even before Montgomery's ribs decided to resign in protest, there were dire consequences to the nonstop work she felt pressured to do.

"The *Last of Us* thing going viral was a weird combination of the highest professional high and the lowest personal low because my stepdad passed," Montgomery said. "I was like, 'I don't want to be on camera. I don't want to talk to people. I'm so depressed.' It was awful. I streamed through it and clearly was not doing well."

To cope with both the emotional burden and the sheer amount of time she was spending sitting at her desk and chatting with her newly enlarged audience, Montgomery said she began to dissociate.

"The way I would describe it is, I would hear a sentence that came out of my mouth after it had been said, and I'd be hearing it like it was new information," Montgomery explained. "Even though it was me, it didn't feel like it. It felt like being a passenger with somebody else in the driver's seat. . . . I ended up figuring out with a lot of therapy that it was because I was spending so much time and energy trying to power through when mentally I was like, 'I should not be here right now.' Eventually my brain was like, 'OK, mentally, you won't be here.' One of my viewers was like, 'You tell the same stories over and over on stream.' And I was like, 'Oh, I had no idea.' My brain was just on autopilot."

Montgomery's Twitch chat moderators tried to lend a helping hand, but it got chewed up by the blender that was her work schedule.

"One of the things we were trying to do as a moderator team was get her over there, to see if we could, for example, have her father pay for the flight or hotel," said Nicolas Lee, a research engineer who regularly volunteers to help keep Montgomery's chat free of harassment and other rule-breaking behavior. "We wanted to give her some family time. Ultimately that never manifested because she was always so busy, and [her dad] was always so busy as well."

Montgomery's viewers were aware she was having a hard time, but she kept enough to herself that they only saw a small, dark shadow peeking out from behind the scenes.

"Negs is a pretty private person," said a longtime viewer named Thomas Hay. "She did share about her stepdad in Discord and on [social media], but for the most part she kept that off stream and asked us to as well. . . . I was worried the whole time, but I trusted her judgment with what she could and could not do."

"I was not aware of or don't remember her stepfather passing, but I definitely remember the two ribs cracking," said Alex Caldwell, another viewer who's followed Montgomery for years. "But I didn't realize it was because she was putting in so much effort to capitalize on that moment."

Caldwell was especially blindsided to eventually learn the full extent of Montgomery's troubles, as he'd once helped her out of an agonizing jam before. All throughout Montgomery's first year of streaming back in 2016, she was plagued by pain from a severe spinal injury she'd suffered while working at Disneyland when she was younger. Streaming from a ragged chair for hours and hours each day reaggravated it. Noticing this, Caldwell, completely out of the blue, donated $1,400 to Montgomery so she could buy a better chair. It was the first time he'd ever given her money, and Montgomery says he hasn't done it again since.

"While I didn't know her as a person then, she and her community had helped me through some difficult times, and I wanted to thank her for everything," Caldwell explained, noting that he wouldn't have done it for any other streamer. "There's no price I can put on the help and steadiness they gave me in a time when everything in my life was upside down, even if they don't realize it helped."

"I just sobbed on stream," Montgomery said of the moment when Caldwell gifted her the chair. "I couldn't believe that someone—especially someone fairly young who wasn't, like, in his thirties with a 401k—would be so generous and so selfless. That chair is a lifesaver. It relieves more pain for me than actual pain relievers do."

But in 2019, Caldwell, too, was stuck on the outside looking in.

"I was saddened and concerned for her," he said, "but since there was nothing I could do at that time for her personally, I just kept supporting her in chat and Discord."

Montgomery kept powering through her injuries and grief until July 2019, a full six months after the *Last of Us* dying bunny clip engraved its name in the internet meme walk of fame. Finally, perhaps mercifully, she hit a wall.

"I was so burnt out that I was really scared for my future with streaming," she said.

She decided to go on a brief streaming hiatus to rest her body and mind. But you can't take a hiatus from being a viral meme.

- - - - - - -

NO MEME EXISTS in a vacuum. The moment the internet latches on to something its collective consciousness finds funny or resonant, it adds that visual, sound, or format to a pantheon. Within months, days, or even minutes, a new meme is combined and recombined with every single imaginable prior meme that isn't *completely* played out—and also many that are.

Things get weirder when the meme is a person.

Initially, gawkers slid into Montgomery's DMs to learn more about the mythical bunny girl and wish her well.

"I got so many comments with people being like, 'It's just so refreshing to see someone connect with the characters and not try to hide how emotionally affected you are,'" Montgomery said. "I remember feeling that day like, 'Oh shit, I get why people do this as a long-term career and want to grow.'"

Others, however, followed the time-honored online custom of reaching out purely to get mad at somebody they didn't know. This, said a very specific kind of commenter, was just more evidence that women are prone to pesky, pointless emotions—unlike sensible, rational men, who would rather yell at a woman they'll never meet than go to therapy.

"People were like, 'Why are you crying over this rabbit?'" said Montgomery. "So I clipped the thirty seconds leading up to it to show people I wasn't just crying about the rabbit. I was crying because I was worried about [*Last of Us* main character] Joel. So many people replied to that saying, 'Oh shit, what? I didn't know that!'"

But that was far from the end of it. Months passed. The clip took on a life of its own. Several lives, actually. After an initial flurry of attention on Twitch, YouTube, and Twitter, terminally online types began replacing the background of the clip—the part where the video game was—so that it seemed like Montgomery was reacting to games that were nothing like the gritty, gut-wrenching

Last of Us. They began subbing in moments from games that were popular with younger audiences on YouTube: *Minecraft, Undertale, Five Nights at Freddy's.* Unsurprisingly, this resulted in a new round of angry messages, this time from viewers who had no idea they were watching edited footage.

"I started getting hate and even death threats from people DM-ing me and being like, 'You stupid fucking cunt. It's just *Minecraft,*'" Montgomery said.

Things proceeded to take an even more upsetting turn when another content creator made an avatar—that is, a playable character—of Montgomery in a virtual reality game called *VRChat.* They even made it a selling point of their stream, titling it, "The *Last of Us* Bunny Girl Plays *VRChat.*" Concerned that this streamer might start spewing hate speech or otherwise defaming her character, Montgomery consulted with a lawyer. He told her they could probably force the streamer to stop with a copyright claim, but that it had a high chance of backfiring. Hell hath no fury like an online community scorned, as many victims of targeted harassment campaigns have learned. Ultimately, Montgomery decided it wasn't worth the risk.

"I have friends who, for example, made a comment about PewDiePie, and his fans harassed them for months on end," she said. "I get hatred when whatever thing I did goes viral, but people don't stick around on a daily basis. That's what would have happened if I had pursued legal action. . . . In hindsight, I did the best I could given what my mental health state was at the time."

Lee, a moderator of Montgomery's Twitch chat, was present for the whole saga. He views it as symptomatic of a wider online malaise.

"Even now there are people who come into chat and still say, 'Hi bunny streamer' and stuff like that, without acknowledging her with a name or as a person," said Lee. "To some of these people still coming in, she's just the meme. I think that it gets to this whole loss of empathy and humanity that you see prevalent on the internet, but that's a whole discussion in itself."

In this way, Montgomery's online life has ended up somewhat resembling that of an actor's, despite her long-standing concerns. People have found ways to approach her unbidden, to dehumanize her without regard for the fact that her life carried on after the thirteen fateful seconds they witnessed on-screen. But while she has mixed feelings about how everything has played out, she doesn't hate the outcome. In early 2021, she went viral again for a reason that brought things full circle: During a stream, she publicly told off a sexist chatter so effectively that nearly 7 million people watched and shared the resulting clip. She did so simply by asking the viewer to square his pointless rudeness—apropos of literally nothing, he asked Montgomery what color her thong was—with his own perception of himself as a good person. "I'm sorry if that's hard for you to hear because you think you're the hero of your own story, but you're a footnote in everyone else's," she said at the time as part of a completely improvised multi-minute rant.

Once again, the unpredictable spontaneity of livestreaming made this clip resonate, only this time, Montgomery was in the driver's seat.

"I've had a lot of people say, 'If it had been me, I would have thought of a comeback two hours after,' or 'I would have tried to say that, but I wouldn't have known how to say it,'" Montgomery said in the same surgically measured tone that defined her takedown of the chat troll, the same one that makes her so endlessly compelling that people have no problem listening to her talk all day long. "A lot of people have been like, 'You said it in a way that I couldn't and made it seem like you already knew what you were going to say.'"

In the end, was it all worth it? The physical and emotional pain, the overwork, the harassment? That's a deeply thorny question. But reactions like those—or the sheer volume of positive messages she's received with the *Last of Us* clip now on its fourth (or fifth or sixth) life on TikTok—have recolored her perception of an intensely difficult period of her life.

"All I've ever wanted to do with any kind of work is just make a positive impact in some way," said Montgomery. "I had a period for a while with streaming where I didn't think I was putting as much good out into the world as I was getting. But now, the number of times people have been like, 'My roommate would always show me clip compilations of [the *Last of Us* meme] whenever I was having a bad day, because it never fails to make me laugh.' If anyone says any content I've made has made them laugh or smile, I think that's the coolest thing in the world. I could never achieve anything else with streaming for the rest of my life, and that would still be awesome."

- - - - - - -

MONTGOMERY SAYS ALL of this from the comfort of a cozy couch in a spacious home. Her partner, Mark, sits next to her as their family of pets—two normal-sized cats, one cat as big as a human torso, and a dog named Oryx, from whom Montgomery derived her streaming handle. Things have changed significantly since Montgomery's days of broadcasting from a cramped not-garage.

Without a doubt, the grueling work she did in 2019 helped propel her to new monetary heights. According to the 2021 list of all payouts on Twitch, she's made over $200,000 from streaming since 2019, and that doesn't include money from deals she cut with brands sans Twitch's direct involvement, nor does it factor in money she's made pursuing an additional career in video game voice acting. The latter is also a direct result of her viral moment. If she hadn't become the *Last of Us* bunny girl, she wouldn't have gotten the opportunity to be an on-camera host at E3, where she ended up hitting it off with the developers of popular restaurant simulation series *Cook, Serve, Delicious*, who in turn offered her a breakout voice acting gig in 2020's *Cook, Serve, Delicious 3*.

Lee looks at all of this and sees a series of "externally imposed random events." On one hand, Montgomery never could have predicted how things were going to play out, and it's impossible to pinpoint the single, crucial "butterfly flap," as Lee puts it, that made her instead of breaking her. But on the other hand, she almost certainly upped her odds of success by being so dogged in her approach. Did she need to push as hard as she did, though? Did she really benefit from giving it her all and then some, or was Twitch the only real winner?

"There were all these instances where things could have gone other directions, things could have petered out," Lee said. "In many cases, they do. How many people create how many hours of streams? And so many of those could be really funny, really poignant, really big moments, but with lack of audience, lack of platform, they evaporate. There has to be a balance between capitalizing on unique opportunities and pushing a bit beyond your means. But you can't push so far on everything that you end up dropping it all."

Montgomery continues in therapy to work through the burnout and emotional strain she suffered, but those around her believe she's managed to emerge with the core of her person intact.

"As a streamer, she is more willing to say, 'No,'" said longtime viewer Thomas Hay. "But for the most part, if you look at an old stream from 2017 and a stream from 2021, Negs is the same person. Negs is still Negs."

"[Montgomery's job] is definitely hard," said Mark. "I think I've seen that more than anybody, especially in the past two years. It's rewarding to see her succeed, but it's also hard to watch someone grind their bones down. And like, I'm so ecstatic that she's up there and she's just crushing these goals, but she's still that person in pajama pants on the couch eating chips, right? . . . It's scary, weird, and interesting, but not life-altering. She's always gonna be her."

Watching Montgomery record a voice over session for an unannounced game from the voice acting booth in her downstairs room proves a surreal spectacle. "HELLO DARLING," she bellows so loudly that it's audible through the booth's soundproof glass. She puts her hand on her hip and channels a character who's posh enough to border on pretentious. In her mannerisms she comes across as distant and greater than—the polar opposite of the welcoming presence she presents on stream and in real life. Her dad was right: She's a talented actor.

But she also comes across as light and loose—like an immense weight has recently been removed from her shoulders, and now, suddenly, she's capable of leaping a hundred feet in the air. This is because in the wake of additional, non-stream-related medical complications that arose in 2021, she had to take a couple weeks off. This time, though, the break followed a period during which she'd already only been streaming once or twice a week while pursuing gigs in a plethora of other fields: voice acting, hosting, and tabletop role-playing.

"So then I take two weeks off and come back to one thousand fewer subscribers and two hundred and fifty to three hundred fewer average viewers," Montgomery said. "I was like, 'I've been grinding for five years, and all it took was a couple weeks to make it go down this much.' But in a weird way, it was freeing. Those two weeks were the best I felt mentally in five years. I finally just got a break where I wasn't on camera."

This also helped her realize she's diversified her career to the point that she doesn't *need* to throw her heart, soul, and spine into the thankless meat-grinder anymore. Now she can lean on brand-sponsored streams that pay a flat, predictable rate as well as the aforementioned jobs in voice acting, hosting, and tabletop.

With platforms like TikTok allowing regular people—not just internet celebrities—to more reliably go viral, Montgomery's story can serve as a cautionary tale. It's easy to fall into the trap of believing that nothing matters more than capitalizing on a viral moment, that if you just push hard enough, you'll break through and find yourself on easy street. From there, you might imagine, you'll spend the rest of your days loving your work and being loved back by it. But the truth is that even dream jobs are still jobs, and content creation—while certainly a privilege compared to the drudgery or manual labor of many more traditional jobs—is hard work. If you allow it to, the eternal, inglorious grind will consume you, mind and body. Nothing is worth that price.

Free of precarity, Montgomery has branched out with two YouTube channels that explore her passions: makeup, stolen Disney animatronics, and the game that started it all, *The Sims.*

"Even though I'm probably working about the same hours, it doesn't feel like it anymore because I'm not grinding on Twitch and equating my worth to viewership and subscriptions," Montgomery said. "Doing this has made me fall in love with creating content again."

chapter three

----

recognition

The sun has set on one of the biggest days of Tanya "Cypheroftyr" DePass's life. Under the faint, golden glow of light from a nearby bar, the forty-eight-year-old Twitch streamer and activist sits at a table inside a pandemic-born outdoor enclosure on a Manhattan street. Her plate is empty. She's finished her drink. She's surrounded by a small handful of friends. It's a triumphant end to a very long twenty-four hours.

But it's not really an ending. Instead, it's the start of something exciting but also uncertain. DePass, a native of Chicago, Illinois, is in Manhattan for a movie premiere. The movie is about her. Soon this short film focused on her career—titled *Game Changer* and directed by WNBA star and filmmaker Tina Charles—will air on BET, a major cable television network. But at this moment, only DePass, her friends, and audiences at the Tribeca Film Festival have seen it. Just a few hours later, she's still taking it in.

DePass gazes out into the street, away from those who've gathered around her spotlight. The air hums with the sound of voices from nearby tables, but in this moment she is alone, set apart.

"I'm worried it's going to change everything," she says of the documentary. "I don't know how famous people handle it."

Prior to this day, DePass has played video games and tabletop role-playing games like *Dungeons & Dragons* while over ten thousand people have simultaneously watched. Hundreds of thousands of people have viewed clips she's posted online. She's spoken in front of breathing, chattering flesh-and-blood audiences at numerous conventions. But this is something different, something new. She's gone beyond the world of games, beyond the community she's painstakingly built for herself and others like her.

"I don't want people to treat me differently, but I know that they will," she says, shifting uncomfortably in her seat. "Oh god, what if I get recognized at the airport? I will freak out."

- - - - - - -

DEPASS FOUND VIDEO games early in life. Raised by a single mother in circumstances that necessitated food stamps, she couldn't afford games of her own, so she picked them up through arcades and a single, well-placed source somehow familiar to pretty much everybody who's ever been a child: "that one kid in the neighborhood who had everything new." Her mom regarded games as childish, but that didn't stop DePass from buying her own console, a Super Nintendo, once she started earning money as a teen.

Games didn't become a career for DePass until long after. Her early professional life led her down myriad crisscrossing roads. At various points she was a clerk at a grocery chain called Jewel Osco, a secretary in the field of law, and an office manager. Eventually she found her way to higher education, where she spent much of her adult life aiding international and exchange students.

DePass, who is Black and queer, maintained a connection to video games throughout adulthood, both playing and writing about them. But she never fully felt like she belonged. This came to a head in October 2014, when major video game companies hand-waved away a lack of representation in popular series like *Assassin's Creed* and *Far Cry* by saying, essentially, that playable female characters took too much additional work to animate. At the time, DePass decided to go to the same place as many of us when we're in our feelings, for better or worse: Twitter. There, she tweeted a simple phrase: #INeedDiverseGames.

"I saw [companies saying] it was too hard to animate women," DePass said, "and yet another round of games coming up for fall and holiday 2014 where we once again got the rugged, brown-haired, blue-eyed white buff cis-dude protagonist whose whole goal was probably saving some chick. Or he was broken and sad because his wife, his daughter—whoever—had been killed. The usual MO. I was just mad about video games, so I tweeted that out and went to work. It was trending by the time I got to work."

DePass's tweet, far from disastrous, proved to be a rallying cry for thousands of gamers and games industry professionals similarly fed up with playing as innumerable variations on the same white guy in the majority of big-budget video games. For her troubles, DePass received so much online abuse that her friends called her to say they were worried, but self-described as "obstinate and ornery," DePass just kept on tweeting. Before long, tweets led to a Tumblr, and then a more professional blog, additional written work, podcast appearances, and a host of other responsibilities.

Around the same time, DePass took up streaming on Twitch as a hobby when she wasn't bogged down with her day job. For her, it functioned as an outlet, a chance to play games she loved like *Dragon Age* in front of a small, enthusiastic crowd. Then she got laid off.

"I was like, 'All right, this is my sign,'" she said. "'I'm gonna see how this goes until unemployment runs out. If I can make a job out of it, great. If not, oh well, I tried.'"

To her surprise, it worked out. In 2016, DePass founded a not-for-profit foundation called I Need Diverse Games. From there, she pushed for increased representation in games both publicly—at and in collaboration with conferences and conventions—and privately by doing consulting work with numerous studios and companies.

One of those companies is Twitch, with whom DePass has a complicated relationship. Actually, "complicated" probably doesn't do it justice.

- - - - - - -

IT'S THE DAY of the premiere of *Game Changer*, and DePass is in her hotel room, getting ready. Nerves haven't quite gotten to her yet, but they're circling overhead like vultures, waiting for her to drop her guard. She sits in a chair and fidgets with her shirt—a black button-down—before announcing that she's going to go off camera and change it. Her Twitch audience, who she's invited to be privy to this moment, encourages her to take her time. Not long after returning, she leaves to change her shirt again.

"I'm freaking out a lot," she says later that day from the Tribeca Film Festival's outdoor theater on a pier in Manhattan. It's a fittingly immense environment; steel beams loom overhead, supported by towering pillars, while a gargantuan screen occupies all but the very edges of moviegoers' peripheral vision. Despite a light breeze and the summer sun, it's almost like being inside. Still, glimpses of the nearby Hudson River and numerous buildings peek through. You can't keep the city out.

DePass is no longer streaming. This moment is for her. Why, though, this one and not the small, more intimate moment she chose to share with viewers earlier? In part, she explains, she decided to stream earlier in the day so that international friends in other time zones could come along for the ride, if only briefly. But also, she didn't want to give people a window into glitz and glamor without first reminding them of the sweat and tears that brought her to this big stage.

"I try to keep grounded," she says. "I don't ever want to be like, 'Oh, look at me. I'm super important.' I don't ever want to get to the point where people don't think I'm a real person."

- - - - - - -

FOR MANY TWITCH streamers, the border between personal and professional is porous. There is an advantage to creating the illusion that they're separated from viewers only by the thin pane of an LCD screen—that if viewers just keep reaching out and trying to make contact with their monetary donations and paid subscriptions, they might push through to the other side and befriend their favorite streamer. But the illusion must be convincing. Some streamers spend just as much of their time on camera—thousands of hours per year— discussing their personal lives as they do playing video games. Viewers, in turn, donate and chat so much that they become known quantities, names streamers shout out on a regular basis. It's like getting juicy gossip from one of your best buddies. Sure, they're talking to hundreds or thousands of people at once, but it feels like they're really talking to *you*.

DePass detests this illusion. She wants to remain authentically grounded—not to put on a pantomime of groundedness to get viewers in her corner. For her, overfamiliarity is as much of a no-go as fame. She bristles when fans act like her BFFs—after all they ever really see are small, hand-selected slivers of her personality. On stream, she is first and foremost an entertainer, sometimes an educator, and in multiple senses of the term, a role-player. But she's not a friend. What she presents—what any Twitch streamer presents—is unavoidably a persona. You cannot get to know a persona. Even the most layered persona is still a cardboard cutout of a well-rounded human being.

DePass maintains this tricky balance with a rule: Viewers in chat must refer to her by her handle, Cypheroftyr—not her real name. That way, they can't get too chummy. They can't role-play as her friend. Many viewers, especially after being warned, abide by this rule. But some don't.

"In those cases where you've tried and you've expended emotional energy to make it better but they still don't get it, that sucks," said DePass. "We've had to kick people from our Discord because of it, where they just didn't get the boundary. They didn't understand. And no matter what you did, they didn't get it. At some point you have to go, 'OK, here's my wall. It's going back up. See you never.'"

DePass walks a difficult line. She seeks, above all else, to facilitate community on Twitch. As a queer Black woman who is also decades older than the lion's share of Twitch users, she considers herself a "minority within a minority" on the platform. She wants to create a space for others who might not have one on Twitch and in video games, to function as social glue even while she keeps her distance.

"I am far too aware of the power of visibility and am someone who's Black, who's older, who's doing things outside of Twitch but is still on the platform," she said. "At a certain point it's not just about you. If I wanted to stream for me, I would stream to an unlisted YouTube link. But there's a community that we built together, and I don't want to lose that. I don't want to alienate people from a place that they like congregating in.''

Despite the nuance of DePass's position, many fans get it. They even see this as part of her appeal on a platform where some big names pretend they don't wield tremendous influence in order to maintain that same pernicious illusion—that they're just regular, approachable people rather than powerful public figures.

"That's what drew me in, actually," said a Ukrainian artist and regular viewer of DePass's channel who goes by the handle Lethendralis. "I find this professional and polite attitude to be refreshing and something others should imitate. I've seen how damaging it can be when prominent creators cultivate a trusting, family-like relationship with their fans, only to then use it for personal gain or validation—usually both. As someone in their thirties, I find this trend very troubling, seeing younger people putting their trust [in] and being swayed by opinions of people they don't really know and who are showing them a carefully constructed image of themselves."

C. S. Conrad, who goes by "Adeana" when she broadcasts on Twitch, is a French writer, editor, and sensitivity consultant who follows DePass's example when it comes to her own streams on Twitch. She, too, keeps her real name away from her Twitch channel and tries to maintain a healthy distance from her audience.

"Watching Cypher, I learned a lot about how to care, be warm, and [empathize] while not setting precedents for boundary-breaking with chat," said Conrad. "Cypher also has a huge role as an educator, if you are just willing to stay, be quiet unless you have anything to bring to the conversation, and listen. I also appreciate Cypher's space: the safety of her space and how she curates it. That is what sets her apart for me. . . . For someone like me with a lot of social anxiety, it's been incredibly helpful to be in Cypher's chat and to be told when I step out of bounds. You sincerely apologize, you try hard not to do it again, and you move on. That's all you have to do."

At the end of the day, no matter how much socializing and game playing goes into it, streaming is work. That reality informs the other side of DePass's personal/professional divide: Turns out, friendship doesn't always mix with a job that, from the outside looking in, seems to center around being everybody's friend. DePass learned this the hard way toward the end of 2020, when a promotional deal with hardware manufacturer Nvidia meant she got to stream the year's hottest game, *Cyberpunk 2077*, prior to its release. This was a big opportunity, a chance to draw in numerous new viewers who were champing at the bit for even crumbs of gameplay footage and pull in a paycheck on the side.

But by this point, the massively anticipated sci-fi role-playing game already had a reputation. Via pre-release promotional materials, the gaming community had gotten a glimpse of its custom character creation tool, which allowed players to decide their character's physical attributes. One element in particular rubbed swaths of would-be fans the wrong way: Characters' gender identities were determined entirely by their voices, not appearance or any number of other player-chosen attributes. What computer-controlled non-player characters heard, they would react to in a way that reinforced the traditional notion of a gender binary. In a setting that specifically focused on human beings transcending the limits of the flesh, game developers could seemingly only imagine male and female. This led to criticism, specifically that the game was transphobic, or at the very least willfully ignorant of trans experiences. At the time, two of the people who moderated DePass's Twitch chat and kept it free of harassment were trans. DePass had considered them friends for years and decided to let them know ahead of time that she'd be participating in the *Cyberpunk 2077* promotion. They did not take it well.

"One person decided I was a transphobe for even touching the game," said DePass. "Another person decided not only was I a transphobe, but they said I was planning action against trans folks, which was a lie. Those were two long-term friendships, but everything they knew about me didn't matter. In that moment, they decided that I must be hateful because I did my job."

Vanessa "PlesantlyTwstd" B, a fellow streamer who also helps moderate DePass's chat, was at a loss at the time.

"No one cared that the contract in question was with one of her biggest partners," she said. "No one cared that, you know, she was probably going to be one of maybe three total Black people who were going to be able to showcase the game. . . . And keep in mind that she's doing this on top of trying to run a charity. So these are things that you're asking her to actively deny income on. You're asking her to kind of put her livelihood in jeopardy for it."

Ultimately, this disagreement led to a schism in DePass's community despite her goal of facilitating greater diversity in games. But this is, to an extent, what happens when communities are the product of platforms engineered first and foremost not to bring people together but to turn a profit. As long as opportunities for growth, sustainability, and representation remain scarce, push will necessarily come to shove, even where cooler heads might otherwise have prevailed.

Members of DePass's community were shaken by the incident.

"I felt baffled, hurt, and confused at the time, [because] I had no real understanding of why the people who left did so as violently as they did," said a DePass community regular named Kaylin Evergreen, who is trans. "I feel the question of 'Is *Cyberpunk 2077* transphobic?' is so fraught and up to individual opinions, and thus while my own feelings on the game are conflicted, I felt they were wrong to [react to] a simple streaming of the game in such a way."

DePass's ex-moderators declined to comment.

- - - - - - -

DEPASS ALSO REJECTS the signature blend of overfamiliarity and fame that comes with Twitch success for another reason: She's seen what can happen when it spirals out of control. In 2019, DePass was forced to ward off the increasingly threatening advances of a viewer who exploited loopholes in Twitch to functionally stalk her and her community.

It began at the tail end of 2018, when DePass was discussing the harassment some streamers face for applying Twitch's LGBTQIA tag—which was intended to help like-minded streamers and viewers find each other with a couple quick clicks—to their broadcasts. DePass contended that the tag also allowed would-be harassers to easily scope out potential targets and that, as a result, Twitch had a problem on its hands. Two viewers belligerently disagreed, at which point she decided to ban them from her chat, because that's not the sort of discussion she was trying to facilitate.

That should have been the end of it, but it wasn't. One viewer directly messaged DePass, as well as her moderators and viewers, demanding to know why he'd been banned. In the weeks that followed, multiple users with handles that referenced the name of that viewer showed up in her chat and—after they, too, got banned from chat—sent direct messages to DePass's viewers. Weeks turned into months. Tactics escalated. Trolls grew more organized, taking aim at channels DePass sent viewers to visit, harassing streamers and viewers with targeted messages, and accusing those who blocked them of toxicity and racism. It made DePass anxious to stream, because she never knew where this incensed viewer and his gang of infinitely re-spawning clones might pop up. Slowly but surely, she locked down her Twitch channel and presence on other platforms, like Discord, leading to a community that felt decidedly less open than the one she had hoped to facilitate.

All of this arose from an expectation of access. Some viewers believe streamers owe them a chunk of their lives or, failing that, *a very, very good* explanation as to why that access has been taken away. Which, if viewers do it for long enough, is really just another way of obtaining a chunk of a streamer's life. DePass's harasser explained as much.

"I attempted to DM her and her [moderator] to seek clarity on why I was banned. It was met with silence and name calling," he said in a direct message in 2019, explaining the rationale behind the ensuing months-long crusade carried out by him and his friends. "After that my friend who had also been banned came to me and told me she had gotten him banned from a stream he was a regular [in]. I felt this action was extremely unjust."

In reality, though, streamers don't owe viewers who break their channels' rules anything, just as you shouldn't be expected to send a lengthy logical proof to somebody you've blocked on Instagram. But streamers, as public figures with audiences whose sizes are available for all to see, ride the line between human and institution. Or at least, it *feels* like they do, which in turn makes it easier to forget they're people.

"The more 'famous' someone becomes, the easier it is for trolls and racists and whatever to hurl things at you, right?" explained Eugenio "DMJazzy-Hands" Vargas, DePass's close collaborator on tabletop role-playing shows like

Rivals of Waterdeep and *Into the Mother Lands.* "Because then not only does that racist person not see you as a whole human being, but also the audience writ large sort of has this degree of separation from you as well. It's a slippery slope snowball situation where the less people see you as a person, the easier it is for them to be shitty to you, and who wants that?"

Back in 2019, DePass's harasser bore this idea out by conspiratorially speculating that he and his cronies had gotten banned from DePass's and other streamers' Twitch channels due to DePass's nefarious financial influences, rather than the obvious fact that they'd spent months kicking the proverbial hornet's nest.

"Maybe her mob is all finance based," he said despite a total lack of evidence. "Explains her power trips, too."

At the time, DePass pleaded with Twitch to do something, but even after she spoke to some members of Twitch's staff in person, it remained possible for viewers to get around channel bans in this manner. The harasser and his friends kept at it off and on for more than a year.

"Twitch didn't do a lot in regard to that person, even after I had a chance to meet with some of them at their office," DePass said. "It's hard because I do know people who work at Twitch, and I know that they hate this, and I know they're doing what they can. But they're not on the teams that can actively affect change. On the other hand, as a company that exists basically off everyone's content and ad revenue and everything else, how do you reconcile not protecting your streamers?"

In 2021, this specific loophole came back to haunt Twitch in a big way. Late that summer, malicious users began using bot software to coordinate hundreds of dummy accounts such that they would all arrive in streamers' chats at once to spew slurs and other hateful language. These "hate raids" would overwhelm the chats, replacing a pleasant conversation or a waterfall of memes with miles-long lists of vile insults. DePass, along with many other Black and queer streamers, was a regular target of these attacks, which persisted for months, until Twitch, initially caught off-guard, was able to create new features that made it more difficult for harassers to create fake accounts and join Twitch chats. During this time, streamers who couldn't go a single broadcast without getting hate-raided grew so exasperated that they organized a strike called #ADayOffTwitch, which temporarily reduced Twitch's overall viewership by hundreds of thousands of people.

While DePass does not believe her harasser from 2019 was involved in 2021's hate raid epidemic, his tactics echoed forward: Hate raids also followed individual streamers between Twitch channels and communities on associated platforms like Discord. If you were a streamer of a marginalized background with a friend who was getting hate-raided, odds were, the trolls would be banging down your gates next. Most importantly, hate raids would not have been possible without the ability to quickly and easily create a limitless number of Twitch accounts, which could then be used to circumvent bans. As Twitch struggled to contain the problem—and savvy users within the streaming community stepped up with hate raid–halting tools of their own—attacks grew more targeted and vicious. Where insults wouldn't do, trolls begin disseminating personal information like real names and addresses.

These unwanted info dumps come with an implied threat: "We know where you live." It is not an idle one, either. Among online denizens for whom boredom has evolved into full-blown sociopathy, there exists a practice known as "swatting," in which especially cavalier trolls call SWAT teams on targets of their ire. While swatting is often intended as a prank, it can have dire consequences, as experienced by the likes of trans politics streamer Clara "Keffals" Sorrenti, wildly popular NSFW streamer Kaitlyn "Amouranth" Siragusa, and leftist news kingpin Hasan "HasanAbi" Piker, all of whom have found themselves in the literal crosshairs of police. None of them were harmed, but the impacts of such experiences ripple outward, not necessarily ending lives but absolutely upending them. During a June 2021 broadcast, Twitch's most popular streamer, Félix "xQc" Lengyel, said police squads had been showing up at his home "almost every day," to the point that he and his then-partner were forced to move. "I was genuinely scared that I was going to die," Lengyel said at the time.

In a 2021 interview, Siragusa also noted that swatting presents multiple dangers. Siragusa is an animal lover, and dogs—of which she has two—are a common police target. She explained that though she has, as a result of all the swatting calls, been forced to cultivate a "decently good" relationship with local law enforcement, she's still not confident enough to arm herself in the face of other threats, like a suspected arsonist who set her garbage on fire in August 2021. After all, if police repeatedly show up and see a gun every time, it ups the odds a cop might eventually pull the trigger.

"In Texas, the impulse is to get a firearm," Siragusa said. "But if one finds themselves getting swatted often, it switches from a defensive asset to a liability. If you hear something go bump in the night, the impulse to arm oneself isn't something a popular streamer can do without adding reciprocal risk of endangering oneself more if the disturbance is due to swatting."

For somebody in DePass's position, it's hard not to be concerned: After all, swatting is often the culmination of a series of stalking behaviors: incessantly sending harassing messages, digging up personal information, posting addresses, and in the cases of Sorrenti and Siragusa, physically showing up at those addresses. On Twitch, there are countless examples of how quickly these tactics snowball, how dangerously blurry the line between the internet and real life truly is.

DePass is especially wary of this side of Twitch fame because she's had her own brushes with it. The most severe occurred during the Seattle-based 2019 installment of PAX West, one of the most popular annual video game conventions in the world.

"It got to the point where people were putting out a hit list on Twitter and Reddit of women and marginalized people at the convention," DePass said. "I had to have a security escort for half the convention. . . . What if somebody finds their way onto the same elevator as me? What if I wake up and someone is outside my hotel room door? What if someone figures out my flight plan or is arranging to be at a panel I'm on? That is not ever how I want to live my life."

But she already is, to an extent. DePass said that as a precaution, she keeps "whatever the longest legally allowed knife is" on her where possible, along with some mace. Whether online or off, for her it all goes back to boundaries. Once people start blurring lines, it's hard to get them to stop. Inches given become miles taken, and the line between the internet and real life turns to little more than a smear on the ground.

"The dude that stalked me on Twitch, his whole reason for being mad was I told him he couldn't sit there and be queerphobic and harass me, and then he spent two years stalking me after we banned him from chat, because he felt he had every right to be there," she said. "When people fixate in an unhealthy way or when they have decided that you don't deserve your accolades and accomplishments—when people fixate to the degree that they're making these creepy YouTube videos or are showing up in your streams or doing whatever—they are past reasoning with. At that point, it makes me afraid. I'm not invulnerable. I'm also not going to show this fear to people, because that's what they want. But it's always in the back of my mind."

- - - - - - -

IT'S SUMMER 2022, and DePass sits in a tan plastic chair so uncomfortable that it must have blackmailed somebody to get a gig at the Tribeca Film Festival. Everybody in the audience does. But she's the only one in the socially distanced crowd intently watching herself on the gargantuan screen.

As part of the *Game Changer* documentary, the screen displays a clip from *Into the Mother Lands*, a Twitch tabletop role-play show starring DePass and an all–people of color cast, which takes place in a game and setting DePass spearheaded the creation of. In the clip, Vargas, the season's dungeon master (an interactive storyteller, basically), sets up the stakes of the episode: "Welcome back to the season finale of *Into the Mother Lands*," he says to viewers in a voice that mixes pleasant playfulness and honeyed grandiosity. "[Introducing] our leader, our creative director, the person who made this all possible, the person whose channel we take over every Sunday night, the one who brought us aboard, the one who came up with the idea for all of this and the reason we're here: Hi Tanya, how are you doing?"

"You're gonna make me cry, you bastard," DePass replies in the clip, her voice cracking.

This proves prophetic. Back in Tribeca's makeshift theater, tears stream down DePass's cheeks as she watches the scene unfold, even though it played out live just a handful of months ago. She hugs Vargas, who is sitting in the seat directly next to her.

DEPASS HAS MORE than earned a victory lap. But there's always more work to be done. While many streamers discuss communities in self-aggrandizing terms, pointing to the emote-spamming masses as totemic monuments to their personal brands, DePass recognizes them for what they really are: projects. This goes double when you're creating a space for those who might not have anywhere else to go. You can never stop inviting people in. Left to its own devices, a door not actively held open has a way of slamming shut.

Everybody around DePass—whether friend, fan, or both—agrees that this is her greatest strength: She never stops trying to find ways to make room for more people.

"More than almost anyone I know in the space, she really does walk the walk in addition to talking the talk," said Vargas. "She puts together the shows, she makes a space for the people that she knows and the people that she doesn't to work and put their stuff out there. She pays them for it, and she doesn't pay them peanuts. If she can't do it right, then she's not gonna do it at all."

"She reaches out to us all the time and says, 'Hey, I'm doing a thing. I mentioned your name,'" said Brian Gray, a moderator for DePass's channel who's known her longer than Twitch has existed. "That's what anybody will tell you about her: She is always doing for others as well as herself. A lot of the cool stuff I've gotten to do, it's because of her either letting me know about an opportunity or specifically suggesting me for an opportunity. I think even though she may be tired of being called famous or being in the limelight, that work of hers will never stop. She'll never stop elevating others with talent that she recognizes."

This is especially crucial in the tabletop role-playing scene, which has exploded in popularity on Twitch in recent years thanks to "actual play" shows like *Critical Role*. But despite the ability of games like *Dungeons & Dragons* to transport players to imaginary realms on the furthest outskirts of human comprehension, the scene around these games and live shows has remained painfully white.

"The tabletop scene classically, or at least as it's been presented, has been dominated by white men for a very long time," said *Critical Role* star and video game voice actor Matt Mercer, noting that women and people of color are, in reality, an indelible part of D&D's history, but societal perception fails to reflect that. "For me, it's been important to be open to listening to different perspectives and acknowledge unconscious biases that have been baked into me. People like Tanya are openly having these conversations in a very real way, not a way that's sugarcoating things."

Mercer, whose show according to 2021 Twitch payout data made nearly $10,000,000—more than any other channel, albeit with pay split among a whole company—dating back to 2019, is the kind of influential figure DePass regularly consults. Mercer considers her a friend, but that doesn't mean he doesn't learn from her when push comes to shove.

"Correct and move forward," Mercer said, summing up a broader philosophy he picked up from DePass and other non–white/male figures in the tabletop scene. "Even if something isn't necessarily your fault or a fault of culture or whatever it may be, do not get defensive. Do not let that instinct to be defensive get in the way. Just correct and move forward."

Two of DePass's shows, *Rivals of Waterdeep* and *Into the Mother Lands*, have carved out sustainable niches for themselves, with the former running for over ten seasons and the latter pulling in $360,000 on Kickstarter for a version of the game everyone can play. Both feature all-POC casts. Neither, however, holds a candle to the predominately white *Critical Role*, whose Twitch channel has over 1 million followers, in terms of sheer audience size.

This status quo is why DePass feels the need not just to bestow opportunities on friends and confidants but also up-and-comers who just need a small push onto bigger stages.

"She continually expands that roster, that community, that stable," said Vargas. "When we were looking for more folks to work on *Mother Lands*, we were getting suggestions from all over the place, and not all of us on that team knew everyone we brought on board. But we asked folks who needed maybe a bit of notoriety and a bit of recognition—a bit of a chance—because they were doing good work, and now it's time to level them up."

"She's a bastion of the community," said Vanessa B, fellow streamer and close friend of DePass. "She is the showcase and the kind of pinnacle of what strength looks like. She is adamant and focused on her goals. There's not a lot of people who know how to have unwavering strength like that. On the flip side, I hate that for her because I think it robs her of a lot of opportunities to just relax. She is always on the clock, and that sucks."

Vargas pointed out that in some ways, *Mother Lands* is a response to this conundrum. It takes place in an afro-futurist setting where people of color exist sans the baggage of racism and slavery.

"Both *Mother Lands* and *Rivals* are excellent representation projects, but they're also just great shows," Vargas said. "Tanya and I joke all the time about 'My god, if we have to get invited onto one more diversity panel at a convention. Just let us talk about other things!'. . . . It's such a testament to Tanya's talent and work ethic that she is such a powerhouse in all of these other ways and still is such a champion of representation and diversity. She is all those things while just also having the ability to create good shit."

- - - - - - -

TWITCH STREAMERS, YOUTUBERS, and TikTokers, and even creators who only dabble in social media to promote their projects—musicians, artists, and game developers—all regularly throw around the word "community." It's become one of the internet's most overused yet least well-defined terms. Generally, when creators use it, they're referring to the audience they've built around themselves, but when you're sitting beneath that umbrella, it can take on all sorts of additional connotations. For some creators, community is a means to an end, whether that's raising money for charity or elevating their own public profiles. For others, community is the point, and what comes before is little more than song and dance in the name of attracting like-minded individuals. Many fall somewhere in between.

DePass certainly does, though she's more on the latter end of the spectrum than the former. It bears remembering that she started out as a writer and a blogger rather than the face of anything; I Need Diverse Games was never supposed to be about her. But during her time building a community, platforms like Twitch, YouTube, and TikTok reknit the fabric of the internet. Slowly but surely, appearing on camera—emphasizing your most charismatic

qualities for hours each day—became the de facto way to build and maintain a community online. People like DePass found themselves straddling
an uncomfortable line: They didn't sign up to be sorta (or in some cases
very) famous. That comes with its own set of challenges that appeal to a very
specific subset of people. But now everybody with a career that involves the
internet at least occasionally has to put on their influencer hat and lace up
their influencer shoes. They've got to smile for the camera. They've got to
manage communities. They've got to endure the sporadic rage, harassment,
and invasions of privacy that come with those things. "The job," even if you're
just somebody posting art online or, in DePass's case, playing and making
games, now includes several other, unasked-for jobs.

It's not an ideal internet for everyone, but for the time being, it's the one
we've got. Creators like DePass do their best to build something better within
that framework, to stomach the parts of the job they don't feel cut out for in
service of those in their communities. Fame is one thing; recognition is another. Creators like DePass do not seek fame, but they deserve recognition.

- - - - - - -

DEPASS AND VARGAS have spent *Game Changer*'s premiere on a roller coaster
of emotions. They've cried, taken pictures, whispered like schoolkids, and
gripped each other's hand tightly for support.

But more than anything else, they've laughed. In some cases, this is because the larger-than-life documentary DePass has delivered a killer line—the
entire crowd cracked up when, in the process of critiquing games for including
hardly any Black hair options, she says, "I don't know why in the apocalypse,
everyone thinks dreadlocks is just gonna happen. They need maintenance!"—
but mostly because the movie is finally here. No more anticipation, no more
worrying. Nothing has gone disastrously wrong. It's good. DePass and Vargas
exhale delirious relief.

Game Changer ends. The credits roll. The audience claps. DePass, visibly rigid even as she laughed, cried, and sighed through the documentary,
finally leans back in her chair.

"Oh fuck," she whispers incredulously. "We did it."

chapter four

----

technology

Iťs a warm afternoon in Los Angeles, California. The sun bathes a hillside dotted with homes that range from nice to luxurious. Palm trees bob in the breeze as blades of light pierce through their branches. There's an idyllic quiet to the scene, save for the odd passing of a car as it climbs to ever more secluded heights. Otherwise, hardly anyone is around.

Youna "Code Miko" Kang answers the door of a multi-story home, which is surrounded by a large plastic fence meant to obscure the first floor's interior from prying eyes (in case someone is dedicated enough to go through the trouble of getting there in the first place). Clad in a black hoodie and flip flops, she nudges aside a growing pile of delivery boxes to extend a greeting. Over the course of the next few hours, more boxes will arrive.

Immediately upon walking into the house, it's hard to miss what lies just past the entryway: a bar littered with vitamin bottles and decorated with plastic replicas of animal skeletons. There are also numerous trash cans adjacent to the front door, enough to fill a dumpster. And more boxes. In the elevator up to Kang's room, there are more boxes still: the discarded packaging of an entire DJ setup. This is what it looks like when four streamers of wildly differing specialties share a home, though Kang explains that her housemates—Irish Twitch star Rebecca "JustAMinx" (who has not divulged her last name) and dynamic chess duo Andrea and Alexandra Botez—are only sporadically around.

Kang's room is a realm unto itself, a jungle of monitors and cords hanging from walls and ceilings. This is because, of everyone's in the house, hers is the most unique broadcast of all: Much of the time, Kang does not go live as herself. Instead, she puts on a high-tech motion-capture suit that animates her virtual on-screen avatar, Code Miko, in real time. If Kang waves, so does Miko. If Kang speaks, so does Miko. If Kang so much as twitches an eyelid, so does Miko.

Kang is what's known as a VTuber, short for "Virtual YouTuber." VTubers stream and make videos as alter egos who often resemble video game or anime characters. Many of them craft elaborate fictionalized backstories meant to further immerse viewers. Miko, for example, is a video game character who proved too glitchy for a starring role in a big-budget blockbuster, a comically modern spin on the classic tale of a struggling Hollywood actress. This gamer-friendly premise—plus uncannily high-fidelity animation and Kang's natural knack for humor—caused Miko to blow up. For a time, it looked like she would become Twitch's next big thing. She was a breath of fresh air to both viewers and other streamers. They couldn't get enough of her. The sky—or some pixelated approximation of it—was the limit.

But in 2022, Kang hit a crossroads. Multiple crossroads, actually. In real life, she lives with regular Twitch streamers, but online everyone sees her as a VTuber. In truth, she's not entirely either. She's some secret third thing, and it's unclear where she belongs. Since her peak in 2021, her Twitch viewership has declined steadily. Moreover, she's in the midst of a crisis of purpose: Originally a developer and animator, Kang isn't sure her heart is in performance anymore. So she's shifting her focus—or trying to, at least.

"Throughout the last few years, I've just been fighting at streaming and my internal battles," she says, sitting in her office chair with her legs folded against her chest. "I would feel miserable. I would feel bad about streaming, and then just force myself to get on and force myself to be funny or entertaining. And

I never could. So I decided to take a break and focus on things that make me happy, like building and tinkering."

As for what comes after, she pauses before adding: "We'll figure it out."

- - - - - - -

CODE MIKO WAS—LIKE most good ideas—born of desperation, albeit desperation of a self-imposed sort. Kang had just been laid off from her job at an LA-based animation studio in 2020, close to the beginning of the pandemic. Instead of seeking out a new full-time job, she decided to purchase a $20,000 streaming setup, "around $12 to $13,000" of which went toward the motion capture suit alone. Inspired by a youth spent playing games like *The Sims* and watching movies like *The Matrix*, Kang had been kicking around the idea of Miko since 2014. The chance to finally pursue her grand vision was just too tantalizing to resist.

"I got into real-time tech, and I was like, 'It's possible. Holy shit, it's actually possible,'" Kang says.

Her career as a digital puppetmaster got off to a rocky start. Especially in the West, VTubing had yet to become an established livestreaming genre like it was in Japan; at the time, Kang barely even knew what a VTuber was. And though Miko technically fit the definition of a VTuber, she didn't really look the part, largely divorced as she is from the 2D anime aesthetic that signals a connection to the Japanese culture from which VTubers originally emerged. Miko was fully 3D and—while still stylized in appearance—moved like a real human being. She didn't completely fit in anywhere, and for a moment it seemed like she might be *too* ahead of her time.

For the first few months of Miko's existence, she was far from a surefire success, with Kang pocketing just $300 a month from Twitch. On the hook for a $2,000-per-month LA apartment, Kang feared she'd have to pack it in and return to the corporate world. But then she hatched a plan that would go on to lay a veritable mountain of golden eggs: She'd let her audience pay to screw with Miko.

"Basically I made my stream into an arcade game where viewers can come in and toss 25 cents and make things happen," says Kang. "Exploding Miko, people want to do that over and over and over. They never get sick of it. Or muting me, or spawning dead bodies, or spawning half-naked guys running around [in the background]—things like that. People just loved creating chaos in my streams, and that's how I was able to get out of debt."

Interactivity was the name of the game, and Kang made it more direct than just about any other streamer before her. Miko blurred the line between improvisational performer and video game. Chat was no longer a teeming anthill of impotent observers, the core appeal of Twitch that had long been overdue for some innovation. Viewers could poke and prod at her in ways large and small, and Kang would have to roll with the punches, even if that meant going, "Oh no!" for the tenth time in a single day as she once again exploded.

This feature set paired well with the personality Kang had crafted for Miko: She was kind of an asshole—intentionally, mind you—more obliviously unfiltered than actively malicious. She'd regularly blurt out rude or strange comments to viewers and, once her stream began to pick up steam, guests. Kang savvily recognized that to make it on the cliquey livestreaming platform, you had to ingratiate yourself with the locals. So, as quickly as she was able, she transformed herself into Twitch's premiere talk show host. Her character-driven shtick paid dividends: Instead of treating internet stars like Imane "Pokimane" Anys, Charles "Moistcr1tikal" White, and Jason "Dunkey" Gastrow with reverence, Kang, as Miko, acted like she either had no clue who they were or did not care. Turns out, this is because Kang actually did not know much about most of her guests. She decided, for the sake of both comedy and her own composure, to keep it that way.

"I had no notes because it was funnier that I didn't know who they were," says Kang. "Then I could make fun of whatever they did. And if I looked them up, I got really absorbed into who they were and it would make me so nervous."

Purposeful distance allowed Kang to barrage guests with awkward questions. Miko's boisterous, sometimes crude interjections—bodily functions were a regular topic—would fluster big streamers in ways viewers had never witnessed when they were nestled safely in the confines of their own channels. And then of course, sometimes viewers would make Miko explode, which had a way of catching guests off-guard. As long as Kang had a willing dance partner, this dynamic led to comedic fireworks. And she usually did, because a Miko interview was good content for streamers on the other side of the desk, too. On a platform like Twitch, staying on top means always searching for fresh droplets of novelty. For a brief time, Miko provided the juice.

Her unique sense of humor also allowed streamers with less giggle-inducing shticks to flex their comedic muscles. In February 2021, for example, Kaitlyn "Amouranth" Siragusa, a hugely popular streamer best known for risqué antics that pushed the boundaries of Twitch's rules, got grilled by Miko. The two quickly found themselves delighted by their comedic compatibility, especially where more absurd matters were concerned.

"I was actually thinking about doing a stream once where I go off camera and literally bring in a man—a forty-year-old bearded man with a beer belly eating Doritos—and see my chat's reaction," said Miko at one point during the stream.

"Even better," replied Siragusa, "wait until you're on somebody else's show and you're trying to acquire a new audience, and you just have that [man] chilling in the background. And you're like, 'I'm actually gonna change into [my real-life form] right now. Hold on!' And then he comes on. So you fool new communities. . . . That'd be really funny. It'd probably go viral."

Then the two shared a lengthy laugh. (Sadly, Kang never actually pulled off this bit.) Kang and Siragusa streamed together again later in the year, with many viewers discovering through Kang's broadcasts something that had always been true, albeit underestimated, of Siragusa: She was funny. This aided in catapulting her career to new heights.

With sudden interest in Kang's streams came equally sudden scrutiny. The chaotic nature of her streams meant it was easy for her—or her audience—to accidentally break Twitch's rules. In short order, she found herself temporarily suspended three times, once for a Miko outfit that Twitch deemed "too revealing," once for a "D pic" gag where viewers could donate a dollar and the letter D would appear on Miko's phone (Twitch thought she was asking for literal dick pics, apparently), and once because she made the mistake of displaying somebody else's email address on stream while discussing with Siragusa the harassment female streamers face, an apparent (though minor) violation of Twitch's rules around personal information. The latter infraction got Kang suspended for thirty days, often a prelude to a permanent ban.

"It really, really, really hurt me," she says. "At the time I was growing. Finally I was growing. And I didn't understand. A thirty-day ban when I'm finally growing out of my little hole that I've been in for such a long time. Twitch just bans my account, cuts it all off. I was so heartbroken."

Kang took issue with Twitch's treatment of her because she felt like she'd just made a few mistakes. Nothing she did was intentionally in defiance of the big purple rule book. Plus, Miko was an animated character. Constraining her felt like a waste of her creative potential.

"What's the point of having animation if you're not gonna be wacky with it?" says Kang. "That's why I love Adult Swim so much. They go freakin' nuts. They do crazy shit that real people can't do."

So she could avoid crossing it, Kang even wound up asking Twitch where the line was in a characteristically Miko way. First she asked her partner manager at Twitch if she could depict projectile vomit. That would be fine, she was told. Then she asked if she could depict projectile diarrhea. That, her partner manager replied, was not fine.

"So I go, 'OK well, what if you had a face where a butt is, and it's vomiting?'" says Kang. "'Is that OK?'"

Kang was able to appeal her thirty-day suspension and get Twitch to reduce it to two weeks. Even so, two weeks is a lot of time on Twitch, where paid subscribers start making for the door after just a few days of inactivity. When Kang returned, she shared with her audience how hurt she was. During a February 2021 stream, she teared up and told viewers that from then on she'd try to avoid jokes that "cross the line."

Over time she's come to view suspensions—and especially her first few, which made headlines—in a different light.

"In some ways, getting banned is a good thing for your career," Kang says, referring to temporary suspensions, which Twitch users call "bans" even though they're often not permanent. "Each time I got banned, my career cata-pulted even more. People were talking about it. People were tweeting about it. People were sharing that I got banned. Everything, my social [channels] all just grew a lot more from that ban."

But Kang's big return broadcast following her two-week suspension, a comedy game show she'd developed during the time she wasn't able to stream, did mark a different sort of turning point. By that time, it had started to become apparent that Miko didn't quite have a *thing* of her own. Through interviews and game shows, she'd been able to bring out new sides of other people's personalities, but who was she outside the gleam of somebody else's spotlight? Plus, on Twitch, where viewers expect full-time streamers to be live for eight or more hours per day, interviews weren't sustainable. There were only so many popular streamers, and wrangling one—let alone several—on a regular enough basis to support a daily show proved impossible.

But Kang couldn't turn Miko into just another Twitch streamer.

"I get told by many content creators: It's supposed to be [about] person-ality," says Kang. "You're supposed to be selling you, you, you. I get that. But for someone like me, I just have trouble with it. I don't know how to sit and play a game and be happy with it every single day—or be proud of myself for that. All I can think about when I'm playing a game is, I could be making this right now. It just stresses me out."

- - - - - - -

IN 2020 AND 2021, Kang was far from the only VTuber whose career was taking off.

The current iteration of the trend traces its roots back to a Japanese creator named Kizuna AI in 2016, whose simple, anime-like appearance and bubbly personality inspired an entire industry of imitators. By late 2018, two Japanese agencies, Hololive and Nijisanji, had rolled out dozens of characters inspired by both anime and Japanese idols, the latter of which refers to manufactured performers—often young women and girls—who are akin to pop stars, but with an even greater emphasis on carefully crafted personas and close relation-ships with fans. Idols join groups, which regularly induct new members and "graduate" older members who eventually age out. It's a gargantuan industry in Japan, with over three thousand groups active. According to the BBC, the idol business is worth $1 billion per year.

Elements of idol culture naturally jibed with livestreaming, where creators dial their personalities up to 11, functionally turning themselves into characters, and parasocial relationships abound. But so, too, did some of idol culture's murkier elements: Individual VTubers became intellectual property owned by agencies, irrespective of the performers behind them. Anything that broke the illusion of a character was obscured, including work schedules and pay. Creators were also barred from speaking on countless non-authorized subjects and were generally forbidden from talking to the press or non-VTuber creators. Harassment of performers, also a common issue in the idol world, quickly became a hot-button topic among fans of VTubers as well, especially after a series of incidents ended in Hololive "graduating" impacted VTubers instead of defending them.

While companies like Hololive would go on to debut English-speaking VTubers in 2020, the medium gained a foothold in the West in large part due to a proliferation of indie VTubers during the pandemic. New, easily accessible motion tracking software made it possible for anybody to download a program and use their webcams to transform into a VTuber, just as cheaper broadcasting equipment and Twitch's own innovations opened the floodgates during the early days of livestreaming.

"The technology became far more off the shelf," says Justin "Gunrun" Ignacio, a former Twitch employee who went on to found VShojo, a United States–based VTuber agency that lets performers maintain ownership of their characters. "At the tail end of 2020, people were able to create their own apps that would mimic what these organizations or people that kept it really secret were able to do and put it out there."

With everybody stuck inside, interest in Twitch was at an all-time high. A new generation of creators swarmed the platform, and many opted to be VTubers.

"I think initially it felt like a way to break into streaming, which is already super hyper-competitive, especially on Twitch," says Tyler Colp, a journalist who's reported on VTubers for *Vice* and *PC Gamer*. "If you're a cat girl or a shark girl or something, maybe you stand out more than other streamers."

Some of these indie VTubers moved less like anime characters and more like cardboard cutouts of anime characters, but that was enough to cast the beginnings of a spell. The creators playing them—crafting their backstories, interacting with fans, collaborating with other VTubers—did the rest.

For female streamers especially, VTubing also represented an escape from the worst ravages of online harassment. The internet's wiliest coyotes can't dox you if they don't know who you are. They can't catcall you or insult your appearance if they have no idea what you look like. Sure, they'll find other ways to be weird—and they absolutely do—but a VTuber avatar is a solid first line of defense.

"There's a lot of women that are VTubers," says Colp. "It's not easy being a woman on Twitch, obviously. I think part of the reason why [VTubing] became fairly big is that there's definitely streamers that just felt more comfortable having an avatar and having that layer—that distance from your actual face and everything."

"[VTubing] totally goes against a lot of the other negative things that come from social media," says Twitch's former champion of community Marcus "DJWheat" Graham, "the [need to physically] conform to a certain standard and all this shit. It's great."

These days, even custom avatars—as opposed to widely available generics—are relatively easy to obtain.

"You can find people on Fiverr and immediately sign up and get a VTuber made," says Ignacio. "Or there's apps that let you make yourself like in [a video game], too. People are finding success by using mobile apps now to create their own VTubers and set a video on a green screen and upload it to TikTok."

To further reinforce the illusion and protect creators, Ignacio's agency, VShojo, goes so far as to remove personal information from the internet for VTubers under its umbrella.

"At Twitch, it always really hurt hearing those stories about creators having those issues, getting doxxed, getting swatted," he says. "Going into VShojo, I wanted to dedicate support to preventing that from happening. So yeah, we invest heavily in protecting all of our talents and removing their personal information from the internet—hiring the right security to be able to handle that."

At first a niche, VTubing rapidly grew into a cornerstone patch in the billowing quilt that is livestreaming. As of 2022, two of the top ten most-watched female streamers on the entire platform, Ironmouse and Shylily, were both VTubers, the former after hosting a thirty-one-day marathon broadcast in which she broke the record for most subscriptions ever for a female streamer. Ironmouse, a pink-haired anime girl with a distinctly childlike voice, also demonstrated VTubing's more subtle appeals: In real life, she's just a normal person with a chronic illness called common variable immune deficiency, which leaves her highly susceptible to infection, as well as a lung condition. She is, effectively, housebound in a location not generally known for its livestreaming community. But online, none of that matters. When she goes live, she's a glamorous demon who sings and dances—and who, according to her backstory, might literally be Satan.

The fictional element is a big part of VTubing's appeal for fans, too. Real people are complicated, and that goes for streamers as well. VTubers offer an opportunity to pretend a real person is just a character—and to, in some cases, project desires and fantasies onto them.

"I think there's definitely a lot of male viewers that think they're a better alternative [to real female streamers]," says Colp. "You can imagine a lot for their character that isn't the person that's actually streaming. The gap between the person and the avatar leaves room for that imagination . . . It feels like they're able to control or have input into what [some VTubers] are doing and get that attention back in a way."

Ignacio sees VTuber storylines as an opportunity for *everybody* involved—not just creators—to play a character. He thinks that's a major part of why VTubers have become so enormously popular.

"It's also [often compared to] WWE kayfabe where we're suspending disbelief to a certain degree to enjoy media in a way we wouldn't traditionally be able to do on normal Twitch streams," he says. "It's something cool about idol culture that I got to witness in Japan in person, where it's like, 'This is the character we're all playing in this moment. Me as fan, this is what I'm expected to do here, and I'm getting such validation from my friends who are also here [for] a cool, unique experience.'"

For better and worse, VTubing means that both parties can—if they so choose—ignore the messy realities of the human experience. They can lose themselves in a character.

"It's sort of an agreement that we have," says Colp. "A lot of [VTubers] follow after Hololive and Nijisanji. They want to have that layer of secrecy."

- - - - - - -

KANG, UNLIKE OTHER VTubers, has never been much of a fan of the fourth wall. Sure, Miko has a backstory, but the entire concept—glitchy character without a game to call her own—is fourth-wall breaking, and that's before you even get into the part where she made her name off interviewing real people. Kang feels like, at this point, she's no longer even really playing a character.

"When I first started Code Miko, I was like, 'I can't do this for a very long time,'" she says. "For me it's become more of an extension of myself. I can't play another person."

It's this fact that's a source of great strength for Miko, the streamer, and of endless insecurity for Kang, the human being. There's nobody else quite like her on Twitch. Her brand of oddball humor is one of a kind, and she exudes it naturally. Even as we're talking, one of her cats begins kneading the back of the other, and her commentary is a roller coaster.

"What is this? What's going on? I mean, he's not humping," she says. Then, after a brief pause, she looks the cat directly in the eyes and, in a low rumble, commands, "DO NOT STOP."

After a period of laughter, she explains that this is just who she is, on camera or off: "People are so surprised to see my serious side," she says, "even my roommates."

Despite that—and despite a demonstrable ability to go jab for jab with some of the funniest people on Twitch—Kang doesn't feel like comedy is her calling.

"I still don't think I have what it takes to be a funny performer," she says. "I just do it, and sometimes it lands and sometimes it fails."

It's a feeling that has welled up over time. Experience has doubtless sharpened her wit, but it's also dulled her reflexes. Now she has connections and a community to worry about. She can't just joke about who or whatever she wants. So she frets and second-guesses. Worst of all, she reads the comments.

"Especially when I get in my head—which has been a lot recently, all the time—I'm like, 'Am I being too cringy?'" Kang says. "I think that happens when you read too much [about yourself] on the internet . . . You accidentally scroll down and read something mean, and then it just burns in your brain, and you think everybody thinks like that. And then the next time you perform, you just keep thinking, 'Are they right? Am I super cringy? Am I not funny? Am I just a tryhard?' All this self-doubt."

Kang finds joy in performing when she's able to let go of all that and just exist in the moment. She also finds inspiration in other comedians like fellow Twitch streamer Dennis "PaymoneyWubby" Richardson and television host Conan O'Brien—so much so that she's even taken improv lessons in an attempt to improve her craft. But she also knows, in her heart of hearts, that she doesn't want to be doing this day in and day out. Not all the time, anyway.

"What I want to do is livestreaming media, but it's not good to do it every single day," she says. "I think it would be better if it was a show format where I take a break, I work on something, I come back, and I do it for a month . . . I'm just gonna make something cool and then go back into my cave."

- - - - - - -

IF YOU TUNE into Code Miko's Twitch channel on the right day, you won't see Miko at all. Instead, you'll be greeted by Kang herself, in the flesh, with only a thin veil of pretext. During these broadcasts, she calls herself The Technician, but for all intents and purposes, she is herself. In some ways, she's her truest self, as she generally spends these broadcasts tinkering or building new features for Miko.

"When I do Technician streams, that's when you know I'm building back end. That's when I'm like, 'OK, I can't do any Code Miko right now. I've got to work on my tech,'" Kang says. "I think with Code Miko, there's an expectation for there to be something [special]."

Over the years, Miko has noticeably evolved. Where at first she wouldn't have looked out of place in a C-tier PlayStation 3 game, now her facial features verge on photorealistic, and her hair—a physical feature which often looks plastic-y even in modern games—flows and tangles with a subtlety that verges on uncanny.

Only it's not just Miko anymore for whom Kang is building. It's a whole company, called MikoVerse. Any time Kang talks about it, she immediately lights up.

"I built Code Miko, and the first thing that I got was so many people wanting to be Code Miko themselves," she says. "I really wanted to create a solution for other people so that they can also be a VTuber in a 3D environment. And so I created MikoVerse, which essentially takes what I created for Code Miko but democratizes it and creates it for the masses—and also makes it multiplayer so people can collaborate with each other."

In Kang's ideal envisioning of MikoVerse, VTubers will inhabit houses in their own neighborhoods and will be able to interact with each other and viewers in full 3D. This might mean hanging out and yucking it up, or it might mean playing games in which, for example, hundreds of viewers, as cute little frogs, try to complete an obstacle course while Miko mercilessly skewers them with a sword.

"It really is a new type of medium," she says. "[Right now] you have an audience, and they're always looking at [what you're doing] as a video feed or, whether it's YouTube or Twitch, a 2D type of video frame. We want to get to the next level, where it's 3D, and you can interact with your streamer or content creator."

She wants any kind of character appearance to make sense in her massively multi-Tuber online game. "It's unlimited about what you can be," she says. "You can be an advanced avatar [like Miko] if you want, or you can be a *Minecraft* character."

At the upper end of that spectrum, especially, that presents an imposing technical challenge: Avatars like Miko—using costly rigs and body suits to replicate every eye roll and flick of the wrist down to the most minute motions—are way more data intensive than a typical video game avatar.

That makes transferring information about what they're doing over the internet and creating a shared world massively difficult. But Kang says her nine-person (and growing) company is up to the task.

"In order for us to have that kind of range, we need to be incredibly innovative in the networking space—how data gets transferred to many users with PCs," she says. "My team has been working tirelessly to make that happen."

Kang has also been working tirelessly. Perhaps too tirelessly. For a while, she tried to stream as consistently as possible and pour herself into developing MikoVerse, as well as Miko herself. She kept at it until she "burned out real bad."

"I would get consistent on Twitch, and then I'd be like, 'I can't do this,'" she says. "I was constantly getting sick. . . . This is where I came to the conclusion that I can't be a consistent every single day streamer. Even consistently streaming Thursday, Friday, Saturday, Sunday was hard for me."

"No matter how much I lied to myself that I could keep up with everything, I just couldn't," she adds.

So, in 2022, she started taking a week off from streaming every month. And she began spending more time doing traditional streamer stuff, like reacting to YouTube videos (including a video of teens reacting to Code Miko), to fill in gaps when she couldn't debut a Miko upgrade or test out a MikoVerse feature on her audience. As she expected, viewership has dropped off.

"The sad part is, my audience doesn't know, really," she says. "They just think I'm lazy because I haven't been putting out as much content as I used to on Twitch. I've got my strong base who love and support me, but I've had many viewers leave because they're like, 'Oh, she just doesn't care about us anymore.'"

Kang cannot, however, allow Miko to languish completely. Despite not being technically alive or a real person, she's MikoVerse's best customer.

"I would get part-time help from MikoVerse staff to help me with Code Miko and sustain it, because as the first customer of MikoVerse, it's important for Code Miko not to fail," she says. "You know how Pixar makes little shorts, and every short that Pixar makes is actually a test of their newest software? That's kind of how I see Miko."

Kang might have mixed feelings about her own performance as Miko, but she's unconditionally proud of her company. She beams as she boasts that every employee is salaried and has benefits, as well as a 401(k). Compared to many streamers—whose teams are largely made up of volunteers—it's certainly a step up. She notes, however, that some of her employees are engineers who "took a pay cut" relative to their previous jobs because "they believe in the vision." As a result, she feels like everyone is counting on her.

"We're gonna raise [funding] soon so that we don't run out of money," she says. "It's monumentally stressful. It's a lot of pressure. I cannot let them down."

- - - - - - -

THE STAGE OF the Streamy Awards pulsates with every imaginable shade of pink and purple. On the monitor, however, there is but a single word: "VTuber." YouTuber Miss Darcei tears at an envelope while remarking that her nails are too long for the job. Fellow YouTube star Ian Boggs looms over her, clamoring to know who the winner is.

"Code Miko!" the two shout in unison.

Kang, clad in a black dress, nervously scampers up blue-hued stairs to claim her prize. "Oh my god," she says. "Thank you so much. . . . Thank you to my mom for letting me become a 3D VTuber. Thank you to my partner Louis for tolerating me. And thank you to my community, who made this all possible. Thank you!"

It's December, the tail end of a frequently dispiriting year for Kang. But she made it through, and now she's walking out the exit door with a trophy from one of the internet's biggest award shows—the first *ever* awarded for Best VTuber.

She can't rest, however. She cannot afford to take the remaining weeks of the year off and bask in her accomplishments. I text her to ask how things are going.

"We are in massive crunch," she replies, "to try to survive as a company right now."

- - - - - - -

AS OF APRIL 2023, it's still unclear whether or not MikoVerse will succeed in securing necessary funding.

"Our company is kinda at a fork in the road, so everything has been very sensitive," she texts, replying to my inquiries for the first time in months. "Just trying to survive atm, unfortunately."

It is not for a lack of effort on Kang and Co.'s part, but others in the VTuber space wonder if there's sufficient desire for what she's trying to build. Certainly, VTubers want to level up their tech, but the big questions are how and how much. They already can—and regularly do—collaborate with each other by placing their avatars against the same backdrop using relatively simple methods made possible by basic livestreaming software and a couple free VTuber-specific programs. Do they need to inhabit a shared, 3D virtual world on top of that? Or rather, will they want to regularly? Or will it prove to be a gimmick that gets old fast? And to what extent will a 3D space appeal to creators and fans drawn to VTubing by its connections to purposefully less realistic, hyper-stylized anime designs?

Ignacio believes the future of VTubing could lie in a variety of different directions.

"To me, anime is a style, not a lower-fidelity version of what people can do with 3D video," he says. "I never was a fan of saying [one is better than the other]. . . . As we get closer to photorealism, we approach the uncanny valley as well. You lose the anime aesthetic once you get to a certain detail level."

He points instead to the ways fidelity has already increased in the world of VTubing, often accentuating individual characters' identities rather than putting the spotlight on the environment *around* them: "There are the pins you're wearing on your outfit," he says, "which indicate who your close friends in the space [are] and the kind of anime you watch, or the kinds of things that are powerful to you."

Shindigs, a VTuber who has gained a reputation for wacky experiments that turn broadcasts into everything from an interactive high school anime to a Sherlock Holmes mystery where Twitch chat functions as Sherlock's intrusive thoughts, thinks VTubers "predominately" prefer 2D at the moment.

"With 2D, there's a lot more support and assets," says Shindigs, who has dabbled in both 2D and 3D for his own VTuber model. "Sometimes it can be cheaper than getting a really high-fidelity 3D model. There are free options for 3D, which work, but I think if you really want a super high-fidelity 3D thing, you still have to invest."

Shindigs has also dedicated his platform to spotlighting other unique VTubers, giving him a unique perspective into which ways the winds of technology are blowing. He believes that 3D is where many VTubers want to go, even if it's not necessarily where they'll end up.

"I think everyone has an aspiration to go 3D," he says. "There's just the general sense that everyone wants a 3D model because they either want to do *VRChat* or do concerts where there's full-body tracking. Going with full-body tracking is almost leveling up your avatar in a way. Now you can move in a 3D world. Now you can move your hands. But I don't think fifty years from now, everyone is gonna be 3D. Just because the number is bigger doesn't mean it's a better version of live 2D. They live together. One does not live on top of the other."

At the peak of the medium, some have aspirations to go even further than 3D. Filian, a popular independent VTuber with millions of followers across Twitch and YouTube, has hinted at plans to bring her avatar into the real world.

"I want to do an IRL [augmented reality] stream, where I get augmented reality into real life. That is something I'm kinda working on," she says during a stream, after friends joke about the idea of videos in which a VTuber avatar puts viewers through a gauntlet of real-life challenges. "I've got, like, two guys on it right now. The only thing I know about is, it's gonna cost me. . . . Not $50,000, but it's gonna be expensive. I can afford it, but it'll set me back."

Whether digital or physical, bleeding-edge tech will always remain expensive. It's the nature of the beast. Shindigs thinks that for the majority of VTubers, affordable programs that help cross the cost chasm will be key.

"The next evolution for 3D," he says, "is probably cheaper and more accessible full-body tracking implementations before we see someone do something really crazy, because it's pretty cost restrictive right now."

A VTuber who goes by the handle Fofamit—and who works on 3D

VTuber tech like Kang—concurs. She believes the winner(s) of the VTuber arms race will be the first to provide software that's both convenient and free, the former to account for the fact that some elements of VTubing still aren't available right now and the latter because the indie VTuber scene was built on free apps. The tension here is a familiar one to anybody who follows tech: A once-grassroots scene is expanding and becoming lucrative, raising questions about cutting-edge ambitions versus what will actually serve the creators who built the scene in the first place. Just as Twitch, flush with Amazon cash, eventually lost sight of what streamers wanted, is somebody like Kang—who wants to build an entire digital kingdom from the ground up, even though that's not necessarily what creators are asking for—missing the forest for the trees? Are her ambitions getting the best of her?

"There's tons of companies that want to do it," Fofamit says. "There's a few of them out there that seem like they know what they're doing, and they're going in the right direction. There's a lot of them that don't understand the space and only seem to see the dollar bills. But in order to succeed, I think someone needs to release something for free. . . . They have to compete with free apps that are made with dedication and love and nothing else."

The company Fofamit works for, Obskur, aims to do exactly that, with 3D scenes and customizable Miko-style interactivity. But Obskur's goal is first and foremost to create broadcasting software that marries the functionality of several preexisting livestreaming apps—to create the single-most convenient package for streamers of all types—rather than to create an ambitious metaverse-style world that, like other metaverses, may or may not service an existent need.

"My goal is maybe not that your grandma could use it," she says, "but your mom could use it, in terms of approachability."

NinjaGato, a VTuber who's spent extensive time with early versions of MikoVerse—doing everything from building a home to conducting interviews alongside their viewers—describes the process of importing a preexisting VTuber model into MikoVerse as "very simple." As long as it exists as a virtual reality modeling (VRM) file—commonly used among VTubers—the process is about as straightforward as it gets.

"You load a file from your machine or a publicly hosted web link," Ninja-Gato says.

Fofamit does believe VTubers at least want the option to inhabit a world together, as evidenced by the fact that it's not uncommon to find them in *VRChat*, a popular virtual reality game that allows players to create their own avatars and explore user-generated worlds. But Fofamit believes that dethroning a known quantity like *VRChat* could prove difficult, and she's not convinced VTubers will want to dive into that sort of deep end all the time.

"I've spoken to a lot of larger creators I know, and everyone likes the idea of having full-body tracking," she says. "But at the end of the day, when you're playing a video game, you're sitting down.... They just use full-body tracking once in a while because it's a pain to get into."

Kang wants MikoVerse to simplify sophisticated motion tracking and make it quick and simple with a webcam instead of wearable hardware, another on a long list of proposed features. For now, though, the focus in the first public tests with non-Miko VTubers is on interactivity. True to classic Miko form, a MikoVerse test video posted by a creator who goes by the handle Sugarcube saw viewers in Twitch chat donate money to punch her with a boxing glove before dropping a piano on her milliseconds later. Another test by a VTuber named Obkatiekat went similarly, except viewers hit her with a car.

In this regard, everything has come full circle, back to when Miko first blew up because viewers loved to, well, blow her up. On a platform like Twitch, ambitious technologies have their place, especially among VTubers, whose setups seem to get more elaborate by the day. But ultimately, none of it matters without the core spark that big-banged the entire Twitch universe to life in the first place: interactivity. Viewers remain thrilled by the idea that they might be able to reach through the screen and impact their favorite creator—doubly so if it involves vehicular manslaughter, apparently. While it's impossible to predict the future, one has to imagine that the next great leap forward will enhance that connection even more. If Kang can deliver on her vision of a shared world in which VTubers and fans get up to zany mischief together, then both the real and digital worlds are her oyster.

But as we've learned from online trends too numerous to count, accessibility and convenience trump bleeding-edge tech. There's a reason NFTs went bust and the grander dream of the metaverse seems doomed to follow, despite Facebook's billions. It is extremely telling that TikTok, an app where all users have to do is swipe up, ascended while Facebook stumbled. If you have to explain at length why somebody should want something in the twenty-first century—if they cannot intuitively discern the reason why for themselves—then odds are, they probably just don't want it.

- - - - - - -

AT THE TAIL end of April 2024, Kang launches a Kickstarter for MikoVerse. It is, in many ways, a last-ditch effort.

"Our company was hanging by a thread," she says during a stream to commemorate the beginning of the crowdfunding drive, in which individuals can contribute small (or large) amounts of money to the project in exchange for digital and physical rewards.

The days leading up to this moment were filled with trepidation. Every member of MikoVerse's small team "poured their heart and soul" into ensuring that GIFs and videos—one of which features a dedicated theme song with MikoVerse-themed lyrics—popped off the page. Kang and Co. wanted the world to know exactly what they'd spent the past two years doing their best to bring to life. They hoped to buy themselves a new beginning, or at least go out with their heads held high.

Months of intense work left Kang with little time for anything else.

"I still haven't been able to see my sister's baby yet," she says, noting that the baby is now over three months old. "I've been working so hard on this, I haven't had time to see my sister's newborn."

Kang settled on asking fans, family, and whoever else might be interested for a total of $15,000 out the gate, with "stretch goals"—ambitious additions offered at various monetary tiers—up to $150,000, which she believed the project "might" hit during the Kickstarter campaign's month-long duration.

On the day of the campaign's launch, MikoVerse's Kickstarter pulls in $15,000 in ten minutes. It breaks $100,000 after just two hours. Several hours later, it's at $150,000. On stream, Kang is a speechless, snot-and-tear-strewn mess. She feels like she's in a dream.

"I can't believe this," she says to thousands of viewers. "Wake up! You're late for your Kickstarter! Wake up!"

As far as Kang is concerned, the crowdfunding drive answers the big question surrounding MikoVerse—Does anybody actually want this?—with an emphatic yes. On the first day alone, nearly one thousand people speak with their wallets, a whopping twenty of whom pledge $1,000 and two of whom offer up $10,000. Those who are enthusiastic about MikoVerse's sales pitch are *very* enthusiastic. Kang decided to bet on them, and it paid off.

"Just seeing a few people in the Discord server, that was enough for me to keep going," she says. "You guys didn't give up on me. You continued to support me through my wacky ideas."

It remains to be seen if wider audiences will feel the same way. The Kickstarter is certainly a start, but many modern video games cost millions of dollars to produce and require hundreds of thousands or millions of sales to break even. There's still more to be done. Much more. MikoVerse has been granted a second lease on life; now it's time to use it. Kang admits that the company is not sustainable yet, though she believes it will be once the team hammers a few core pillars into place, monetization chief among them. That's a tall order, the kind of thing bigger companies have dedicated teams larger than MikoVerse's entire workforce struggling to puzzle out. But now Kang can potentially bring others into the fold.

"The fact that we have so many backers, it's real factual data for [game publishers who might want to work with us]," she says. "It gives us another chance."

More importantly, Kang has bought herself the most precious resource of all: time.

"Keep in mind, guys: This is just the beginning now," she says of Miko-Verse, which remains in a relatively early state even after two years of development. "This is still just the beginning."

While she plans to finally meet her sister's baby, she's "absolutely not" going to take a vacation. She's got time now, but not *that much* time.

"It's like I got handed a 1UP," she says. "You've got to spend that super wisely."

But now, even if only for a brief moment, Kang can stop tunnel visioning. She can imagine a future again. She thinks that once MikoVerse is a sustainable and likely larger company, she'll step down from her position as CEO. Miko, effectively, will stop leading MikoVerse. But she'll never stop being Miko.

"I wanna be able to go and do more content creation," she says. "At the core, I do love creating and founding projects and stuff. But I think we can all agree that at some point if the company grows large enough, you do less creative and more business. If it gets to that point, I want to step back and do more creative. Go back to my roots."

chapter five

----

consistency

To walk into Ben "CohhCarnage" Cassell's home is to enter a realm of domestic chaos. Dogs bark, then—seconds later—pivot to regarding you as they would a lifelong friend returning from an interminable journey. A small herd's worth of cats gingerly sniff you before turning the kitchen countertop into a war zone for your attention. At the urging of Cassell's wife, Laina, Cassell's three young sons look up from a table of toys to greet you. Then they scamper off in different directions—blond blurs bursting with barely contained energy—making sounds not of this world. The cacophony ebbs and flows but never abates.

Cassell and Laina navigate the ever-shifting scene with composure that suggests they wouldn't have it any other way. The home they're building is a testament to this. Expansive yet isolated, it occupies a pasture of property in a remote portion of North Carolina. It's the site of numerous construction projects large and small: twenty-year-old windows being replaced, trees being cleared out to make room for Laina's horses, stone being removed from large portions of the home's exterior to fix a decade's worth of water damage born of poor decision-making on the part of the house's previous owner.

Cassell calls it a "fixer upper."

"We're getting there," he says—hair shaggy and free-flowing, unconstrained by the signature black, red, and white beanie viewers are used to seeing him wear on stream—as he shows off his house's high-ceilinged, halfway complete living room. All the while, animals and children flit in and out of both eyeshot and earshot.

Then Cassell opens a door to the house's basement. Stairs lead down to a narrow hallway. The walls are white, unobtrusive canvases for a cornucopia of collectibles: life-sized replicas of swords from *Final Fantasy VII* and *World of Warcraft*, guns from *Fallout* and *Cyberpunk 2077*, a shield signed by an entire game development studio.

This miniature museum, however, is just window dressing compared to the main event: Cassell's streaming room, the nerve center of his operation. A gargantuan green screen takes up the back wall, with two separate desks in front of it supporting a jigsaw puzzle–like array of interconnected computer monitors. Should Cassell prefer a cozier broadcast on any given day, there's also a couch in the center of the room surrounded by microphones and a tablet so he can read Twitch chat. Adjacent to these are a giant TV and, of course, more memorabilia—much of it emblazoned with Cassell's own logo. On one of the desks is a pile of identical beanies.

What's most striking about this room, however, is not the sights, but the sounds. It's perfectly silent—almost eerily so. Upstairs may as well be a different world.

- - - - - - -

CASSELL, THIRTY-EIGHT, BEGAN streaming in 2013. At the time, Twitch was in its infancy, having just split off from pioneering streaming service Justin.tv —which was eventually folded into Twitch due to the latter's popularity—in 2011. The idea of a "Twitch streamer" had yet to enter the collective consciousness, or even really catch on in gaming circles. Despite all the trends, stars, and watershed moments that have come and gone since, Cassell has remained one of Twitch's anchors. While others from his era have dropped off or burnt out, he's doggedly clung to a rung near the top of the Twitch ladder, ranking among Twitch's one hundred most-viewed streamers, according to streaming analytics site SullyGnome, and its twenty-five highest-paid, according to data from a highly publicized Twitch leak in 2021.

This has been no easy feat: In Twitch's early days, a sufficiently dedicated creator could go live with a procession of different games, relying on the strength of their personality and hardcore gamers' intrinsic interest to sustain their channels. Over time, though, Twitch audiences—attracted by watershed moments like the *Fortnite* boom of 2018, which catapulted Twitch into the mainstream and birthed stars like Tyler "Ninja" Blevins, and the pandemic in 2020, which boosted Twitch's viewership numbers to record highs while everybody was stuck inside—have come to prefer streamers who relentlessly chase the latest trends, focus on individual games like *Fortnite*, *League of Legends*, and *Grand Theft Auto V*, or eschew games altogether in favor of Twitch's top category, "Just Chatting," in which streamers talk to their audiences and react to content from other platforms. Where Cassell grew his audience on Twitch, many new breed streamers must spread their efforts across Twitch, YouTube, Instagram, TikTok, and Twitter to stand a chance of finding an audience in a saturated market.

Purely video game–focused variety streamers, as Cassell's kind are known, have grown rare in the face of numerous shifts, and conventional wisdom is that there's a hard ceiling on their potential for success. Even peers who started streaming at the same time as Cassell pull just hundreds of viewers at a time—not tens of thousands like he does.

But Cassell has nonetheless managed to maintain a niche at the top through sheer consistency. Every day, almost without fail, he logs on to play the latest blockbuster game, an intriguing indie from the most obscure depths of ubiquitous PC game store Steam, or something in between. Every day, tens of thousands of his 1.5 million followers watch him simultaneously.

In an era of gimmicks, drama between streamers (which translates to voyeuristic views from those who want The Tea), and streamers who are afraid to quit playing games they no longer enjoy for fear of losing their viewers, this makes Cassell distinctly old school. He shuts everything else out and focuses on playing games. He believes he's able to stay the course—rather than panicking and pivoting when numbers slip and slide—because a varied life prior to his decade on Twitch lent him perspective.

"Most streamers are a lot younger than me," Cassell said. "A lot of these guys have become big streamers in their late teens, early twenties. Their life has been streaming. I didn't start until I was thirty. I've worked so many jobs, and some of them have been terrible. I like to think I have a good foundation for understanding just how fucking amazing of a job this is."

"[Other streamers] are constantly feeling like they have to move forward or they become irrelevant," he added. "You're making five times as much as you would in a normal job, but you're talking to me about how you feel like you're a failure."

That's not to say Cassell was never in the shoes of younger, edgier streamers. When he first began streaming in 2013, he fell into the same trap that continues to ensnare many to this day: broadcasting for as many hours as humanly possible in fear of his viewership falling off a cliff.

"I had that same mindset that a lot of these younger guys do," he said. "It's just 'The more I stream, the more successful I'll get, the more money I'll make.' It's a sick cycle that never stops. They will light themselves on fire like a sun and see how long they can burn until literally they run out of fuel."

It was relatively straightforward for a younger Cassell to devote himself to Twitch, though, because at the time it was just him and his then girlfriend, now wife, Laina—they'd yet to become parents—and his previous life as an IT worker had led him to an unfortunate revelation: He didn't want to dedicate his life to being an IT worker. At the time, his primary passions were video games and DJ-ing. But while he enjoyed the performance element of DJ-ing, he wasn't much for staying out at after-parties and networking. Twitch, he soon came to find, combined everything he loved without forcing him to bump sweaty shoulders with strangers until 4 a.m.

"This takes the public-facing element I've loved from DJ-ing," he said. "This takes the community management aspect I've loved from leading guilds. This takes the passion for gaming I've had. This takes the IT know-how of running everything and doing it how I want. Every background I'd had in my life had led to that moment."

Cassell only created a Twitch channel to show a friend in his massive multiplayer online role-playing guild—basically, a big group of players that socializes and tackles challenges together—a new game called *Defiance* so his friend could decide if he wanted to buy it or not. Originally, Cassell intended his Twitch traipse to be a one-off, a friendly gesture toward a fellow gamer. But then dozens of his guildmates piled into chat, boosting his viewership and, therefore, his visibility on Twitch. Unbeknownst to Cassell, he'd done everything right. After a handful of days and a fortuitous encounter with a big streamer at the time, he found himself with four hundred simultaneous viewers.

"This was my first week of streaming," Cassell said. "I was like, 'Yeah, this Twitch thing is easy!'"

At the time, Twitch was a vastly smaller platform than it ultimately became—with around three hundred thousand active streamers at 2013's outset compared to 8 million in 2022—and opportunities for sudden success were more plentiful. But even then, Cassell's experience was far from the norm. It did not take long for him to learn that the hard way.

"I experienced a microcosm of most streamers' entire careers in those first three months," he said. "I had this huge spike of initial success. At the time I didn't know why. But the next two and a half months were a constant decline."

Cassell streamed for twelve to sixteen hours per day to try to right his rapidly sinking ship. He let other responsibilities and his relationship languish. He played his absolute favorite games, but numbers continued to dwindle.

"It was kind of bonkers for him to be working that much," said Laina. "He was obsessive about it, to the point that he was stressing out, losing weight, not eating well, and really just overworking himself."

"At that point I was like, 'Fuck this,'" said Cassell. "'It's not paying the bills. My channel is obviously failing.'"

As a last-ditch effort, Cassell took a two-week step back and reevaluated. He returned with a significantly more scientific approach.

"I started making tools to track other streamers," he said. "I started making data dumps where I would take the top games on Twitch and parse the [total number of new viewers] they had. I took all the stuff I learned in my IT job and threw it at streaming."

He also made some adjustments that were uncommon on Twitch at the time, treating streaming like a job with consistent nine-to-five hours and adopting a swear-free family-friendly approach.

"I looked around at the time, and nobody was safe for work," he said. "There were, like, two safe-for-work channels on Twitch."

Cassell was not the first on Twitch to do most of these things, but he was close. More importantly, he was among the first to *systematize* both the tracking of other streamers and a workmanlike approach to the daily grind.

"He approached everything from a data-centric perspective," said Marcus "DJWheat" Graham, the livestreaming pioneer turned Twitch community champion who's known Cassell since Twitch's early days. "He was tracking things like 'I played a drum and bass song at this time and got this many viewers.' He was religious about it. He scienced Twitch. . . . I see Cassell as an incredible innovator. Not so much in his content—honestly, overall, I don't find it super entertaining—but he's a ten out of ten for how he builds his audience and shapes it and approaches games."

Cassell's newfound focus stabilized his channel. As a result of tracking other streamers, he came to realize that early Twitch was a game of positioning—swooping in at opportune times to either avoid big names or snatch up their viewers as they were logging off. Over time, he began to grow. In the years to come, many would imitate his approach, but few would be able to do it as effectively.

"That was when my actual channel started: three months after I got lucky, and then I failed," Cassell said. "That's what's gonna happen to most people. And the only reason everything picked up after that is because I sat down and was like, 'Let's figure this out. Let's figure out what the code is.'"

- - - - - - -

IN CASSELL'S STILL-IN-PROGRESS dream home there is more to his streaming room than meets the eye. To demonstrate this, he opens a door on the far side of the room, which leads into a smaller, separate room that houses multiple game consoles, numerous spare controllers and peripherals, and most crucially, the PC to which his computer monitors in the streaming room are connected.

There is a purpose to this divide: Consoles and PCs, especially, can get quite noisy when their cooling fans kick into overdrive, and Cassell doesn't want his microphones picking up any of that while he's live. Where others might accept a slight whirring in the background from time to time, Cassell has dedicated an entire room to solving the problem. The price of silence can be deceptively high.

"When we designed it, we asked, 'What is the perfect situation?'" says Cassell. "So we pulled out all the stops."

That's just the beginning. The side room also contains a grapevine of cables that link into a business-class fiber internet connection. To say that Cassell had to jump through hoops to obtain this—typically a perk of living in more densely populated areas—would be an understatement.

"It's an enterprise," Cassell says. "It's $1,500 a month and cost me $40,000 to put in. I paid for a third of it, and the internet service provider paid for $80,000. They basically dug out all the front yards of my neighbors for about fifty-five hundred feet to the cell tower. . . . I had to sign a document for the vice president of this company promising I wasn't starting my own ISP."

All that to ensure that sporadic lag or the odd disconnect doesn't ding his stream's fidelity. But what if the power goes out? you might ask (if you're really trying to poke holes in this). Cassell reveals an additional room, near his garage, that contains an industrial-size generator. The house's previous owner had it installed, but Cassell isn't complaining.

"It could not only run this house, but pretty much the neighborhood," he says. "The power has gone off twice since we've been here, and both times it kicked in in thirty seconds, and suddenly the whole house had power."

Nothing, seemingly, can knock Cassell's stream offline.

"Health!" he replies to that assertion. "Health is the biggest thing these days."

- - - - - - -

MODERN TWITCH VIEWERS tune in for a variety of reasons. Some might spend hours trolling and meme-ing in the unabashedly chaotic chats of top streamers like Kai Cenat and Félix "xQc" Lengyel. Others might want their daily dose of leftist political commentary from Hasan "HasanAbi" Piker. Others still might flip between multiple channels for gossip about the drama of the day, or for real-life collaborations between popular streamers that function almost like rapid-fire seasons of reality TV.

Amid the din of daily Twitch chaos, Cassell positions his channel as akin to the bar from eighties sitcom *Cheers*: a friendly oasis. An escape.

"I wanted a situation where people could just come to my channel, say hi, have a bunch of people say hi back, and know that all the shit they left at the door is gonna stay right where it was—that we're just gonna have a good time and escape and chill," he said.

Some might pop into one of Cassell's broadcasts and get the impression anyone can do it. All they'll see, after all, is a guy sitting in front of a camera playing video games. Cassell himself is an unflappable presence, warm and low-key even as chat flies by at blinding speed and games throw complex new mechanics at him. It all just looks so straightforward, so natural.

But this easygoing presentation belies a deceptively multifaceted operation. A high-level Twitch stream is not just a stream; it's a community of potentially millions of people across Twitch chat, Discord, Reddit, and other platforms—all of which require hands-on moderation. Twitch streamers also regularly upload videos to other platforms, like YouTube, which requires editing down eight-plus hours of footage on a daily basis. And Cassell, more than most, regularly ventures into new games, which necessitates a dedicated team member to set up guilds for fans to join and another to handle online multiplayer servers. Additional members work on various stream-optimizing apps and tools and create art to make broadcasts pop.

In this day and age, most top streamers have teams, but few are as expansive as Cassell's. Cassell's team includes a total of twenty-seven members. Of them, thirteen receive a set amount of money as regular compensation for their roles. Others—largely on the moderation side of things—either get paid a cut of donations from viewers or are in training for general moderator positions that will eventually grant them that perk. Moderators are Twitch's unsung heroes, screening a nearly impossible-to-count number of chat messages per day to ensure trolling, toxicity, racism, and issues of that nature don't get out of hand. Despite their cruciality, the lion's share of moderators are unpaid fans—not Twitch employees—and generally arise from streamers' communities. Effectively, they are volunteer soldiers manning the front lines. Most streamers, unfortunately, cannot afford to pay their small moderator armies. Cassell is one of the few who does so in any capacity.

But that's the price of sustaining an operation like Cassell's—one that is polished and, like a good DJ set, never misses a beat.

"In our channel, we have a draw because we *don't* have drama," said Tony "theboatman" Bottita, Cassell's channel coordinator, who essentially functions as the manager of his team. "We're never gonna have those #MeToo issues. We're never gonna have '[Cassell] dated and broke up with a random famous person.' We're never gonna have a chat that devolves into nothingness and toxicity. . . . And because we don't surround ourselves with that bad attitude, we don't attract people who want to be around bad attitudes."

Maintaining this is a group effort that forces Cassell and his team to make tough decisions. While some viewers might catch an hour or two of a stream and then get on with their days, others treat places like Cassell's chat as their primary source of community—like less-online folks with the fandoms around their favorite sports teams or the band Phish. This breeds a sense of closeness and comfort, one that can be disruptive in unexpected ways.

"When you have a community that is happy, helpful, and respectful like ours, where the chat is not just a toxic mess and people in general feel safe, that will attract people who [are struggling], because they feel safe," said Bottita. "They'll say, 'I'm thinking about suicide,' or, 'My cat died,' 'My mother just passed away'—any number of things."

These people do not generally mean to cause harm, and in cases like the latter two, a Twitch community might even be able to provide support or kind words to some degree. But ultimately, a streamer is not a licensed therapist, and if a viewer is too adamant about bringing their personal life into chat, then Bottita and Co. might have to (gently) show them the door.

"The best thing that we can do—and it seems like a cop out—is say, 'Here's the number to the crisis hotline,' or 'Here's the suicide prevention number. You need to call them,'" said Bottita. "Because you have to be able to protect yourself as well. You have to be able to protect yourself legally, you have to be able to protect your channel legally, but you also have to be able to protect your heart."

Numerous major streamers have adopted similar methods after initially trying to engage with chatters who'd threatened self-harm. Former Twitch star turned YouTube streamer Ben "DrLupo" Lupo, for example, was forced to push aside his impulse to lend a helping hand after a mid-stream encounter with a viewer named Davey, who said he planned to "end it all" after a 2018 broadcast.

Lupo, though distinctly uncomfortable, did his best to extend a helping hand. But when you're a streamer with millions of young fans, nothing happens in a vacuum. You can't just pinch off a parcel of time and tell everybody else to forget about it. Lupo's fans certainly did not forget about it. Instead, one of them recorded it and uploaded it to YouTube with the title "FORTNITE STREAMER PREVENTS SUICIDE DURING LIVESTREAM! (EMOTIONAL)."

It accumulated millions of views. At the time, this led to an influx of Twitch viewers who decided that they, too, wanted help from their old buddy Lupo—or, in some cases, their own fifteen seconds of viral fame.

"The next day, the number of $5 tips I got with the exact same wording was ridiculous," said Lupo. "Kids just want to troll. They want to fuck with you and try and tear you down, because they think it's entertaining. So by me helping that guy—by me responding to that guy—the amount of negative bullshit that has come from it is overwhelming." And so, not long after, Lupo drew a new line: "Now my stance is and always will be: 'I understand. I'm very sorry you're going through something. But you need to talk to a professional. I'm just an entertainer. I'm sorry.' And then I'll always block the donator from donating again."

Bottita explained that one of Cassell's moderators once quit after struggling with the emotional toll of the job. "It's not for everyone," Bottita said, adding that in such cases, he and other members of the team regularly advocate for moderators to take a step back and recover for as long as they need to.

For Cassell, striking a balance between friendly neighborhood streamer and sporadically stern barkeep is doubly important. His stream, he explained, functions as an escape not just for his viewers, but for him as well. If the tone of chat changes too much, his quiet downstairs oasis transforms into a miasma of human misery. Suddenly, his channel isn't so sustainable anymore.

"Frequently over the years people have asked, 'How are you so damn positive all the time? How is it that every day when you get on, you're smiling? You've been doing this for ten years. That's not how humans work,'" said Cassell. "And my answer is, because the stream for me is the exact same as it is for you: If I'm having a shitty day, I come here to just have a good time, to relax with you guys. It's my moment of recovery."

- - - - - - -

THE ULTIMATE EXAMPLE of Cassell's dedication to his craft is also his biggest accomplishment: In October of 2013, he resolved to stream every day for six months. He succeeded. And then he kept going. For a total of two thousand consecutive days—more than *five years*.

Cassell's half-decade-long streak played host to numerous life events: birthdays, births, and deaths. He celebrated, laughed, and cried with chat. While he did not stream from the hospital on the day of his son Roen's birth, he did still manage to briefly stream from home that day. Live or not, his viewers celebrated with him the entire time.

"Even though I wasn't online, I was getting pages of chat every minute," he said. "There were people in there chanting, 'Roen,' my son's name. It was basically just this amalgamation of good vibes that went on for almost twenty-four hours straight. It was incredible."

Roen was born a month early, which led to health scares and doctor's appointments.

"It was a really tumultuous time in my life," said Cassell. "But thankfully, my community was behind me the entire time."

During the streak, Cassell streamed through holidays and illnesses, even once bringing a camera to the bathroom with him while he helplessly vomited into a toilet. The highs were stratospheric, the lows craterous.

"I had animals die, I had people die," said Cassell. "I had horrible, horrible events happen. I had giant fights with my wife. You still just get on and smile and say, 'No, let's not worry about that shit.'"

Cassell was not on camera for the entirety of his two-thousand-day streak. He only streamed for a portion of many days—sometimes as little as a couple hours. Still, sometimes real life could not help but interfere. In those cases, Cassell attempted to be honest with his viewers where he deemed it necessary. If he showed up on stream visibly down in the dumps, he would try to explain where he was coming from—albeit without making the whole stream about it.

"With some of my animals passing and stuff, I knew that if I were to start talking about it on stream, I would have trouble handling it," said Cassell. "And that would bring the whole vibe down."

While some creators view their streams as confessionals staffed by thousands of infinitely attentive priests, that's never been Cassell's approach. On his worst days, he was able to keep the streak alive, but only by the skin of his teeth.

"There were a couple times when I just called streams," he said. "When my dog died, I streamed, like, an hour a day for a few days because I was just really not in the state to handle it."

Ending the streak, ultimately, was almost more difficult than simply allowing it to continue indefinitely. Cassell had momentum on his side. More importantly, he'd put together a team and support system that he felt could keep him afloat indefinitely.

"I had built the entire apparatus to at that point work so well that I could easily have kept it going," said Cassell. "My two thousand and first day I had to force myself not to stream. Even now, I've taken less than ten full days off [since the streak ended]."

Ultimately, Cassell decided to end the streak to spend more time with his family, which had added multiple members during his long-haul marathon.

"I got to the point where I said, 'You know what? This is no longer who

I am. This is no longer my life,'" said Cassell. "'It's time to close that chapter and see what comes next.'"

Cassell had pushed himself hard—sometimes going for as long as thirty-six hours without stopping—but by most measures emerged from his record-setting streak unscathed. Still, Twitch is a platform that systemically incentivizes long hours; more time spent live means more chances viewers will discover you, and lengthy gaps between streams translates to a precipitous drop in paid subscribers even after just a few days. This is true on other platforms to varying degrees: Iterations of the YouTube algorithm have prioritized video quantity over length, and countless wannabe TikTok stars have fallen into the trap of following up their first hit video with slight variations on the same bit, day in and day out, in hopes of striking gold again. But on those platforms, time is secondary to what is being produced. Some people can make a bunch of videos in no time at all, while others slavishly pore over every detail. Conversely, an especially ambitious YouTube video might take months of full-time-job-like work to film and edit, but those parts are effectively invisible to viewers. On Twitch, time is a large portion of the product. Creators are offering their presence. They can't cue up a bunch of videos they've already made and then quietly take a vacation. They need to be there. For hours and hours each day.

For every success story like Cassell's, or Ludwig Ahgren's star-making thirty-one-day marathon in 2021 during which his broadcast *did* stay live the entire time, there's a story of someone who took things too far. Most infamously, a thirty-five-year-old named Brian "Poshybrid" Vigneault died in 2017 after a series of sleepless marathon broadcasts, the longest of which was meant to last twenty-four consecutive hours. Vigneault got up to take a smoke break at around 4:30 a.m. during said broadcast. He never came back.

Despite this, some streamers continue to push the limits of the form, inspired by Twitch's structure and headline-generating records like Cassell's.

One, Brian "Aircool" Stern, streamed for seventy-two hours straight with as little sleep as possible in 2021. While he came away from the experience feeling proud, his body broke down on him.

"You start to hallucinate," Stern said. "I would go to the bathroom and look at the carpet, and I would hallucinate people fighting on the carpet. You just see stuff, like the wall started caving in. . . . I fell asleep live on stream and hit my head on the microphone."

It took Stern more than a week to return to a normal schedule. He tried to rest and recuperate, but his body refused to stay unconscious for longer than four hours at a time.

According to Graham, one of the first streamers to be hired by Twitch, the practice of streaming for uncomfortably long periods of time goes way back. He does not recommend it.

"We streamed the whole PlayStation 4 launch [in 2013], and I was like, 'I'm never fucking doing a twenty-four-hour stream again.' We'd shot [prere- corded video] for twenty-four hours before, but that's totally different. The stream was miserable. Fucking miserable."

Another creator, Parker Coppins, locked himself in a room-sized box for ten days in 2021 and streamed the entire thing. It might sound extreme, but this and other endeavors centered around broadcasting a creator's entire life aren't so far removed from the stunt that started it all: Justin Kan's "lifecast" on Justin .tv, without which Twitch would never have come to be. Coppins's goal was to make a statement about depression and anxiety born of isolation, and he did so with help from collaborators and the video game–focused mental health nonprofit Take This. During the stream, he measured his blood pressure and did yoga, in addition to playing video games. Nonetheless, Coppins worries that some viewers might get the wrong idea from watching streams like his.

"My biggest fear is kids that are eight years-old—or even twelve, fourteen, fifteen—are watching these streams and thinking, 'Wow, that's great. I want to do that, too,' without preparations for it."

Coppins, like Stern and many others, has attempted a sleepless marathon stream. It took an immense toll.

"I didn't mentally recover from my forty-eight-hour stream until probably a month later," he said. "That's when I could feel like my mind was fully back."

Dr. Rachel Kowert, research director at Take This, said that streamers can do even longer-term damage to themselves if they're not careful.

"There's real risks among streamers who don't take breaks," said Kowert. "There's a range of research that has looked at the effects of chronic stress on cognitive functioning, mental health and well-being, fertility issues, heartburn, heart disease—there's a lot."

In one particularly extreme case, an artist named Tim C. Inzana streamed from a single room for 128 days in 2021. He worked on camera, he ate on camera, he slept on camera. He said that his history of similarly performance-based projects had immunized him against the mental ravages of nonstop surveillance, and he outsourced his health to his audience—viewers could spend points accrued from watching his channel to make him do push-ups and other activities—to positive effect. But ultimately, real life still found a way to pop his *Truman Show*–esque bubble.

"A family member wasn't doing well and needed help," he said of his decision to end what was originally meant to be a year-long stream. "It gets into a strange space when you're doing this extreme project and then someone on a very basic level just needs people around them."

Inzana, more than many, came to recognize why livestreaming—spending numerous hours per day in a heightened state of emotion and expression in order to entertain others—regularly pushes people to the point of burnout.

"Livestreaming is notorious in my estimation for being a constantly shifting landscape of faces that come and go," he said. "That's the nature of being an extreme medium. It's physically demanding, it's mentally demanding, and that's why you see people leave."

The above streamers all nonetheless pointed to substantially increased viewership during their marathons, whether short and restless or long and (at least a little more) health-conscious.

"It's such a bold headline that I just knew doing that and using things like TikTok would be a powerful way to attract people," said Inzana.

Human beings, Inzana believes, enjoy the spectacle of sacrifice—of giving up time, freedom, and health in an era in which we both take them for granted and consider them as precious as any currency. Kowert believes that as long as platforms like Twitch and YouTube allow these behaviors to continue and regulators place few limits on new forms of entertainment, performers will keep grinding until they can't grind anymore.

"The way you combat burnout, generally, is by establishing personal and professional boundaries," she said. "There are no regulations in this new industry. Where the lines are, you have to figure out for yourself. And with this constant pressure of new content, more content, more engagement, it's becoming ever more difficult to find out where those lines are."

Cassell sees many streamers trying to marathon stream solo—or with only a small pit crew of mods—and he believes it's a fool's errand.

"Understand that you may not have the support structure to be doing this eight to fifteen hours a day," he said. "Maybe it's a group of friends, maybe it's a girlfriend or boyfriend, maybe it's family—if you're not at a point in your life where you comfortably have that system in place, marathon streaming or endurance streaming is not something you should do. You're only going to put yourself in a position where things could go wildly wrong."

For Cassell, even his seemingly extreme challenge was an exercise in creating sustainability—the kind rarely seen on Twitch, where many streamers pursue viewership at all costs.

"I did my two-thousand-day challenge because I had a support structure. I had people who were helping me," Cassell said. "It was not just to build the community and the channel; it was also a way for me to fine-tune all the mechanisms that let me do this how I want to do it."

- - - - - - -

THERE IS AN elevator in Cassell's home. It's another holdover from the previous owner, but it's also emblematic of Cassell's long-term goal: He wants to continue being a streamer for the rest of his life—or at least until he's so old that his gaming muscles have atrophied into exhausted dust. The elevator, he hopes, will buy him some extra time.

"When I'm seventy-five years old and can barely walk, I'll take my elevator down to my studio," said Cassell. "Hobble my old ass in here."

Where many streamers hardly plan ahead beyond their next broadcast or two—and others, like the aforementioned Ahgren, are building consultation/

production companies that will allow them to recede into the background in a handful of years—Cassell is looking toward the distant future.

That means constant adjustments to stay on top. Despite the old-school vibes of Cassell's stream, his team keeps him on the cutting edge with bespoke applications that, for example, monitor the top ten streamers on Twitch and YouTube, what they're playing, their viewerships, his viewership, and other metrics.

"I stare at that all day, every day," he said before rattling off a scientific analysis of why Tyler "Ninja" Blevins's September 2022 debut across all platforms at once—eschewing Twitch exclusivity—actually wasn't that impressive. ("His viewership [returning from a break] went up moderately, fifteen to twenty percent. . . . The average that a person's numbers will go up after receiving a two- to three-day ban on their return is about a hundred and fifty percent higher than that." This is because while paid subscriber numbers might drop while a streamer is away, absence makes the heart grow fonder—or at least curious to learn why the streamer in question suddenly disappeared and if they've got any tea to spill.)

The software-based backend of Cassell's broadcast automates just about everything a streamer could ever hope for, explained Barry Carlyon, Cassell's primary coder who also maintains similar infrastructures for other streamers in Cassell's circle, like John Paul "itmeJP" McDaniel and Christopher "Sacriel" Ball.

"We've got the chat bot, we've got stream overlays, we've got Twitch extensions, we've got the new mobile app, and all the integrations to Discord," said Carlyon. "We get in all the various notifications from various systems, so we've got subscription alerts, we've got donation alerts, we've got merch alerts—that all comes into the thing, and it all spits out onto the stream or into [Cassell's] reader app."

Carlyon, another programmer (who goes by the handle Kimen), and others who've come and gone have spent years building up this monolith, to the point that Carlyon believes Twitch has cribbed some notes from Cassell's stream for its own built-in features.

"Twitch used to have developer days where you could go to the Twitch office in London or San Francisco, and I was showing off what our extension did if a viewer was banned on the channel," said Carlyon. "It would say, 'Oh, you're banned. Do you want to file an unban request? Here's the form.' Here we are a couple years later, and now it's an intrinsic part of Twitch."

Recently Carlyon and Kimen even put together a program that allows them to remotely end the stream in case Cassell has to dart out early because he's late for dinner with his family.

"This was true even before [Cassell] had kids, but now it's even more," said Kimen. "Basically the number one design rule is: Anything that can be automated so that [Cassell] doesn't have to think about it makes his job and life easier."

"When I'm building things, I'm not necessarily thinking too far ahead about sustainability or future stuff," said Carlyon. "But more often than not, I build something naturally in that style anyway, so it's extendable or reusable. . . . It's just my natural way of building things."

Carlyon, however, confessed to regularly working fifteen-hour days across his gigs with multiple streamers. Long hours, it turns out, are a common feature of the Twitch world, even among those who toil invisibly in the background.

"I'll sleep when I'm dead," said Carlyon, who added that the intensity of his work ebbs and flows—and that he'll sometimes take an hour or two off in the middle of his day to do research or watch YouTube videos.

Cassell and his team are planning so far ahead that they're even gazing into the Doctor Strange multiverse shard where Twitch goes up in smoke. The past few years have seen competition in the livestreaming space become fierce, with YouTube and, more recently, a livestreaming-specific app called Kick offering multimillion-dollar contracts to big names like Lengyel, Lupo, Ahgren, and a slew of others to lure viewers away from Twitch, while TikTok cultivates its own universe of streamers. All this against a backdrop of Twitch facing criticism for eliminating a 70/30 revenue split option that favored streamers—now most get 50/50, with programs that allow a select few to qualify for a 60/40 or 70/30 split via performance metrics—and foisting lengthy blocks of advertisements on streamers and viewers alike, detracting from the viewing experience. These moves proved unpopular, and multiple rounds of layoffs and leadership shakeups at the top of Twitch left streamers feeling even less confident in the platform's future. In more recent times, Twitch has tried to improve its outreach to streamers and build more of the features they've requested, which has rehabilitated its public image somewhat. But after years of instability, there's a pungent aroma of uncertainty surrounding Twitch.

"These days we are on a path where Twitch is going to fundamentally change what it is internally and publicly," said Cassell. "It's impossible to know where Twitch is going to be in five years or even a year. They are drastically changing what it means to be a Twitch streamer. If anyone tells you they know otherwise, they are either lying or don't know what they're talking about."

For now, Cassell remains loyal to the purple-hued site that's played host to his entire streaming career, but he's more prepared than most to jump ship if need be. A big part of this is the "Cohhilition" mobile app, which anybody can download. This partially solves a major problem encountered by creators who decide to monkey bar from one platform to another: A large chunk of their viewers will just stay on, for example, Twitch and find somebody else who fills essentially the same gap in their viewing habits. It's an issue of convenience and community; people like what they already know, and they stay where their friends are.

Cassell's app collects everything he's produced—streams, chats, YouTube videos, shorts, tweets—and puts it all in one place, regardless of which platform he's on. He and his team are also adding a "Cohh-vatar" system where viewers can customize on-stream avatars with gear they've unlocked by tuning in each day. The system, based on Twitch's "drops" system—which allows game developers to reward Twitch viewers of specific games with in-game items—will also exist entirely within the app and travel with Cassell no matter where he ends up. Once again, Cassell is not the *first* streamer to have his own app, but nobody else has built one with such an eye for longevity.

"Having an application that allows me to communicate with tens of thousands of [people in] my audience instantly and send them the information I need is going to potentially be very important in the future," said Cassell. "Having systems set up so that wherever I go, I can immediately enact things to help reward people for sticking around or be able to deploy instantly bots that are able to moderate systems to what I want, having frameworks set up so I can immediately adapt to different environments—that's the kind of stuff we're thinking about these days."

GRAY CLOUDS CLUTTER the sky as rain patters on the roof of Cassell's house. The foliage-covered landscape just outside his front door takes on a mildly mournful complexion. Humans and wildlife have roughly the same idea: hide out on the porch until the drizzle passes. A flock of wild turkeys mills about, gobbling up a storm of their own. Laina, brown hair tied back after a long day of momming, begins to recount what she remembers of the beginning of Cassell's streaming career.

"What happened was, we got married," she says. "And then three weeks later, he quit his job to go back to school for game design. And while he was doing that, he would also stream raids [in online games] and stuff. It just sort of exploded. And it was really not at all what we imagin—"

Just like that, one of Cassell and Laina's sons totters into view. Cassell, previously inside, runs out behind him.

"You had one job!" says Laina in a mock-pleading voice.

"I know," replies Cassell. "I'm trying!"

Both laugh as Cassell does his best to corral his errant son. Once they're out of view, Laina resumes her story.

"The goal was, if we could get to 5K [Twitch] subscribers, I could quit my job I didn't like and take a thirty percent pay cut," she says. "I could become a zookeeper instead of working a desk job. So it allowed me to have more freedom to do something on a day-to-day basis that I actually enjoyed."

Eventually, Laina continues, she quit her job entirely, first to help out with the stream and then to raise the kids. In the years following, life became a push and pull—an effort to strike a balance between Cassell's career and the myriad responsibilities of family.

"It's been harder since we've started a family," says Laina.

Earlier in the day, when the sun was still shining outside, Cassell expressed certainty that he'd largely achieved that balance. Following his two-thousand-day streak, he said, he adopted a schedule that only really requires a three-or-so-hour stream in the morning and, sometimes, another of similar length later in the day. Anything else, he said, is "icing" and can be left off the cake if his wife and kids need him.

"I still stream a lot because nowadays it just works," he said. "I have multiple games I want to play, maybe my kids are at school, and of course I still have my Twitch hours-per-month [requirement]. But again, I prepared: When I got my most recent Twitch contract, I made sure it didn't have crazy hours like some of these other streamers."

He chalked up much to his ability to work in a way that he regards as ideal to Laina.

"I found my soulmate," he said. "The big thing I tell people about relationships is: You don't need to have a single thing in common with your significant other. You don't need to go biking together. You don't need to listen to the same music. The best people you could ever be with are the ones who respect your passions, and you respect theirs. Do [Laina and I] have friction? Absolutely. All relationships do. But at the core, we understand each other on that kind of stuff."

Back outside, as Cassell does his damnedest to wrangle kids for the duration of a conversation, Laina says she's of the opinion that her husband's work-life balance—like their home—remains a work in progress.

"I've been asking him to take full weekends [off], and I only get a half day each week," she says, a hint of exasperation in her tone. "So I feel like we're still not where I envision us being balanced."

She agrees, however, with his overall assessment of their relationship—that it's founded on mutual respect.

"Sometimes there's that stay-at-home mom where the husband doesn't feel like that's a job, right? I'm grateful he sees everything that goes into that," she says. "And while he understands, conceptually, the stresses of it, he's never been in my shoes; he can't understand what it's been like day-to-day. It's the same for me: I've never had the responsibility of being the breadwinner and making sure our family has the income to pay for what our standard of living is at the moment. I can only imagine how much that keeps him up at night or stresses him out."

Until something changes or gives, her goal is to ensure his short windows of time off are well spent—largely with her and his kids.

"I tell him, for all the marital problems people have, you're pretty lucky that the biggest one you have with your spouse is that she just wants to spend more time with you," she says. "Could be worse!"

- - - - - - -

YOU CANNOT ACCUSE Cassell of being ungrateful.

"I love what I do," he said. "Even if I won the lottery, if I had $70 million at my disposal tomorrow, I'd still be on at 8 a.m. because this is what I love to do."

In a way, Cassell has won the lottery. Many creators starting out now do not have enough money saved up to quit their job or, as in Cassell's case, a college fund from their parents, nor do they have a partner willing to support them when they decide to take that leap. Money cannot buy everything. No amount of money, for example, will ever return Twitch to the more variety streamer–friendly era from which Cassell also benefited.

Natalia "Alinity" Mogollon, who's been streaming on Twitch since 2012 and has 1.5 million followers, doesn't think she could become a big name again if she had to start over today.

"If I wanted to make it again, from zero, it would be really hard for me," she said. "I think I'd be stuck at, like, the fifty-viewer or one-hundred-viewer [range]. I don't think I'd be able to break out from that anymore. I have the advantage of having been around for so long, so everybody knows who I am. And even then, I sometimes struggle to break three thousand viewers."

But money can buy time. Given *enough* time, Cassell believes, it's still possible to climb Twitch's ranks using his method.

"My success has been because of ten years of consistent positioning. I did not get big overnight. I've just gotten a little bigger from constantly putting my channel at the right place at the right time," he said. "The second my thirteen-thousand-viewer channel goes offline, I guarantee that at least a few hundred people are going to want to keep watching the game I was playing. That's what I did for years: Find big streamers, find out what they're playing and what their schedule is. I would track their numbers, their metrics, which games are most lucrative—that kind of thing."

"But," he added, "you need to be watchable. Some people aren't, and that's the blunt reality of the situation. Same thing as if you run off to California to be an actor, right? There's no guaranteed success. But if you're a personable, energetic, interesting person, you can absolutely make it the same way I did these days."

But it's difficult to point to a streamer who does what Cassell does and is as much of an institution as he's become on Twitch. Certainly, there are popular streamers who wear the "variety" tag to varying degrees—Félix "xQc" Lengyel spent years as Twitch's most popular streamer, and most would consider him a variety streamer of sorts—but they mix numerous already popular games with ample time spent reacting to videos, engaging in drama, and hopping from trend to trend. Cassell mostly just games, and he plays what he wants. In his eyes, it's a big part of why he hasn't burnt out.

"Having somebody who's gaming every day, and they're like, 'I hate this game.' That's one of those things that happens when you find streamers who are locked into a single type of game: They burn out," said Cassell. "But it's constantly new to me, and I always stop when I'm not having fun."

Perhaps burnout sideswiped potential Cassell-alikes into a ditch before they could ascend to his level. Longtime variety streamer peer John Paul "itmeJP" McDaniel—with whom Cassell has been hosting a weekly video game podcast called *Dropped Frames* for over five years—views it as a distinct possibility.

"I don't know how he's done it for as long as he's done it," said McDaniel. "We've had talks off-stream where he's definitely had some low, low points. But he doesn't show it [on-stream], and it doesn't come through in his content."

After streaming since Twitch's early days, McDaniel hit a wall of his own in 2022, forcing him to take an entire month off.

"After two years of [contractually obligated] one hundred and sixty hours per month—and some of those months, I was streaming two hundred and twenty to two hundred and thirty hours—I burned out," he said. "And so it was the big question of 'Is this still what I want to do? Is this still where I want to find myself a year from now, five years from now, ten years from now?'"

The sort of indefinite sustainability Cassell has achieved might be out of reach even for streamers who are at least making something resembling a living on Twitch. Few, after all, can afford to buy a home and renovate it into a streamer's pin drop–silent paradise with infallible internet, a generator, and an elevator. Few have the time or money to remove every imaginable obstacle between a streamer and their job in the way Cassell has managed. You can probably count them on one hand—and maybe a foot or two.

Everybody on Twitch respects Cassell, but they also recognize the unique set of circumstances that propelled him to prominence.

"Yeah, no, that does not happen anymore," said Hasan Piker, a political pundit who's become one of the most popular streamers on all of Twitch. "[Cassell, Saqib "Lirik" Zahid]: Those guys are able to do that with their audiences, but their audiences haven't necessarily grown all that much, right? They've just kind of stayed the same size [in recent years]."

Cassell is a product of a different time, of an era in which somebody could become a top streamer by focusing on games and strategizing around Twitch first and foremost. Nowadays, to be a Twitch streamer is to be a creator across numerous platforms, engaging with all sorts of different mediums and discourses on a daily basis. On top of all of that, to truly make it to the top, you've got to have an angle or a specialty, like Piker's focus on politics, that makes you novel to other big creators—that makes them want to collaborate with you so that they can get more views out of the arrangement, too.

The jury's still out on whether creators will be able to find sustainability en masse, but one thing is certain: They will not be able to walk the same path as Cassell. They'll have to forge their own, whether on Twitch or less-calcified platforms yet to come.

Even though Cassell contends that today's crop of young upstarts can still learn from his example, he agrees with the overall sentiment: The best way to grow is on your own terms, if only because nobody's gonna tune in if you're exactly like everybody else.

"When I started there weren't a lot of people doing positioning, which is why I did it," Cassell said. "There weren't a lot of people doing safe-for-work channels; that's why I started doing it. There weren't a lot of channels focused on good vibes and community. There weren't a lot of heavily moderated channels. And so on. So when people are like, 'You can't make it on Twitch anymore,' I want to grab them by the neck and go, 'There are literally infinite things that have not been tried yet.'"

chapter six

control

Kaitlyn "Amouranth" Siragusa's Houston, Texas–based office is humming along like clockwork. A sign emblazoned with cursive lettering that spells out "Real Work" greets those who enter her company's portion of a shared workspace, though Siragusa has her sights set on buying a building of her own before too long. If anybody else said this after running a business for just a couple months, you might find it hard to believe. But by this point, the superstar streamer already owns three gas stations—each a multimillion-dollar investment—as well as an inflatable pool company and part of a plastic ball company. Purchasing an office building, in all honesty, would be significantly *less* eyebrow raising than her other splurges.

Real Work's goal is to help other creators manage their presences across platforms, thereby alleviating day-to-day busywork and improving profitability. The company employs eighteen people, Siragusa says, though just around half that number are in the office's main area, which is adorned with Halloween decorations despite the holiday still being a month away. A handful of employees silently type at their computers while others report metrics to Siragusa. One says a client's account is doing solid numbers on a subscription service that allows users to pay to subscribe directly to their favorite creators and receive benefits like exclusive posts, pictures, and videos. Siragusa seems pleased by this.

If you were a fly on the wall of this meeting, you'd probably find it to be pretty standard, albeit mildly confusing if you weren't well versed in the creator economy. Only one thing about the scene might strike a typical fly who spies on business meetings as amiss: Near the main office's entrance, an employee stares intently at his laptop screen. It's open to OnlyFans, a popular subscription platform used most prominently by sex workers. The employee's screen is almost entirely blotted out by explicit images.

In most offices, this would be a category 5 no-no. At Real Work, it's just part of the job. Real Work, after all, derives its name from "Sex work is real work," a saying often used to advocate for decriminalization of sex work and a broader understanding that it's a job like any other. Aiding those in the business of so-called "lewd" content is a natural extension of Siragusa's own history; especially on Twitch, where she spent years pushing boundaries by, for example, getting kicked out of a Bed, Bath & Beyond for pretending to "clean" it in a frilly maid outfit and, most famously, broadcasting in a bikini from an inflatable hot tub to get around Twitch's rules against sexual content. While Siragusa was not the first to deploy the latter stream format, she popularized it, to the point that Twitch ultimately created a dedicated "Pools, Hot Tubs, and Beaches" category so that concerned advertisers could opt out of having their content appear alongside these streams if they so pleased.

This tricky tightrope walk over a tub of lukewarm water has defined Siragusa's career. By many metrics, she's the most popular female streamer on all of Twitch—doubtless a draw to the platform and a boon to the Amazon-owned company's business. But she's also been suspended numerous times for breaking Twitch's ever-evolving rules, and a sufficient (though at the platform's highest levels, often quite high) number of strikes means you're permanently out.

This, in part, is why Siragusa created Real Work—and built an OnlyFans presence before any other streamer of her size (*and* became the only streamer of any size to buy gas stations): She knows the whims of the platforms that undergird her work are fickle. She knows that no online empire, no matter how smartly established, can last forever. She knows that everything can change in an instant.

"Social media is still such a new concept compared to the work options we thought we had growing up. I don't think I should put all my eggs in one basket," she says. "Doing just one thing is very risky. If you grow your following and then, boom, it's gone, you're left up a creek."

This is true not just on Twitch, but also across YouTube, Instagram, TikTok, and basically every other popular platform, where trends materialize and evaporate like dew drops under a summer sun. Nothing lasts forever, or even for long. Creators have to be prepared to pivot, pivot, and pivot again to whatever the next big game, stunt, or drama of the week is. And that's if it even lasts a week.

What matters more to Siragusa than where she ends up is what she gets up to, regardless of how others might react.

"I just think I care less inherently what people have to say about me as long as I'm doing what I want to do on my own terms," she says. "If someone doesn't like it, I just tell them they don't have to watch."

- - - - - - -

SIRAGUSA'S GAZE IS unwavering. Across numerous hours and multiple conversations, she rarely breaks eye contact. It does not take long for her green-hued stare to singe its way onto the back of my eyelids, like a burnt-in afterimage on an overused TV. Small in stature and clad in a hoodie–sweat pants combo she bought on Amazon, her presence nonetheless looms larger than life.

This is the focused look of somebody who's streamed between three and four hundred hours per month since 2018, working nine-to-fifteen-hour days on Twitch and putting what others would use as off time toward creating additional content for platforms like OnlyFans, Fansly, YouTube, Instagram, TikTok, and more. This is the look of someone who refuses to turn off, or perhaps does not know how.

But this Sauron-like tendency disguises a paradoxical truth: Siragusa, like many others in her field, isn't entirely comfortable interacting with people.

Sometimes it almost seems like she's not *sure* when to glance away, so instead she chooses not to. In that sense, socializing with hundreds or thousands of human beings in a text box is easier than talking to one in the flesh.

Siragusa says her awkwardness stems from the fact that she didn't grow up with many friends. Her parents worked a lot and socialized very little, and there was a big age gap between her and her brothers. As a child, most of her friends were dogs.

"Since I was always playing in the front yard before the internet got huge and everybody was on their phones, the dogs from my neighborhood would come up to me for belly scratches," she says. "I kind of just formed animal friends. And I didn't really have human social skills because I didn't have many examples for that. . . . I was really awkward with humans. I'm getting better!"

This canine connection led—in a less roundabout way than you might expect—to Siragusa discovering the motivation she says ultimately turned her into one of Twitch's most tireless stars.

Before Twitch came knocking, Siragusa was a Disney princess. An avid practitioner of the art of cosplay—creating and wearing costumes based on various popular entertainment and video game characters—she managed to parlay her passion into a business entertaining kids at parties and hospitals. Siragusa found the work fun and fulfilling, but in 2016, Twitch came along with a more intriguing offer.

By that point, Twitch had decided to go against the grain of its previously hard-line video games–only stance, attempting to attract creators with specialties as far ranging as visual art, costuming, robotics, and woodwork. Siragusa was one such creator. If nothing else, she figured, streaming was a fun activity from which she could squeeze an extra dollar here and there. The next year, however, brought with it a personal tragedy that changed her outlook.

In the middle of a 2017 night, while Siragusa was streaming, one of her own pet dogs died from bloat.

"It was midnight, and I couldn't get into the vet in time, so I just had to watch my dog die," she says. "That was heartbreaking for me."

Siragusa had rescued her dog from a shelter, and the pain of his passing set her to thinking about what happens to animals who are less fortunate.

"[My dog] had five good years of life," she says. "Then you think about animals that get trapped in a shelter for, like, two weeks, and then they kill them because there's just no space."

In this realization, she found her purpose: She would create an animal sanctuary, a space where animals could simply live without the guillotine-like threat of an all-too-sudden end dangling overhead. But that requires even more money than retirement following however briefly a creator can last in the internet's fickle spotlight. By Siragusa's estimate, a lot more.

"That kind of thing requires so much capital, especially if you think that social media may not always be around," she explains. "That means I have to have money going into investments that can keep kicking back money to me year after year—not only for me to live off of, but also that will pay for animals and make sure they don't have a lesser quality of life."

Siragusa, a self-professed metrics junkie both on and off Twitch, has already calculated the number. Researching a thirty-acre ranch-style rescue in Florida that allows dogs to live together in air-conditioned rooms—rather than cages—she found annual operating costs to come out to about $2 million. And that would be on top of supporting herself and an additional ranch for her own pets.

At this moment in time, Siragusa makes over $1 million per month across OnlyFans and Twitch, as well as numerous other platforms and business ventures. She's everywhere, doing everything, which puts her light-years ahead of other creators according to her former talent manager, now her business partner, Devin Nash, with whom she's worked for several years.

"I've given that advice [to diversify across multiple platforms] to so many content creators, and she was the only one and the best one that really followed it," says Nash, whose agency, Novo, now powers the portion of Real Work that provides creators with brand deals, bolstering their income. "She just went nuts and did every single thing and more. . . . She owned Instagram on multiple accounts, she owned YouTube on four channels—all while streaming on Twitch twelve hours a day."

No single platform controls Siragusa. In business as in everything else, she's got her hands on the steering wheel. But Siragusa knows her gargantuan paydays won't last forever, and she fears the end could come at any moment. She believes she's got to burn bright right now, heedless of how burnt out she might end up in the future.

"Now, while I'm young and have the momentum, I should just be trying to do everything I can to achieve that [goal of earning enough to build an animal sanctuary], because most people don't get that opportunity," Siragusa says. "I just feel like I don't want to waste it, you know?"

This means an absolutely torrid work schedule.

"For me, the average workday is, like, eighteen hours," she states matter-of-factly, as though it's simply a reality she's accepted, like the sky being blue. "I sleep about four hours."

Morgan Bancroft, Real Work's managing director, who first began working for Siragusa as an assistant years prior when she was just eighteen (she's now twenty-four), has witnessed Siragusa's breakneck pace firsthand.

"I don't know if she sees it the way other people see it, but she'll work herself super hard and then be, like, falling asleep standing up," says Bancroft. "She definitely gets tired, but she does everything she can to just muscle through it. . . . She feels like she's caught lightning in a jar, and so she needs to just do it while she has it, because you don't know when it'll go away."

Her peers, too, have noticed her tendency to work far past the point where most would collapse. Natalia "Alinity" Mogollon, a friend of Siragusa's, who has 1.5 million Twitch followers and has actually been streaming longer than her, nonetheless considers her an inspiration.

"She's so dedicated and so focused," says Mogollon. "I don't understand how a person can be so disciplined. I just don't fucking get it. I've thought before, 'Oh, she's a robot. She's not human.' I was in medical school. I've seen really dedicated people. She's on another level."

For Siragusa, vacations are exceedingly rare, even in an era where bigger streamers like *World of Warcraft* titan Asmongold (real name Zack, last name unknown) have found wiggle room to take the odd extended break amid spells of personal tragedy or unbearable burnout. In some cases, they've returned to larger viewerships than ever. Despite how much more diverse Siragusa's business is than the lion's share of her peers, theoretically insulating her against the ravages of a precarious Twitch subscriber drop, she fears that the same rules don't apply to her.

"For my content, I feel like it's not as mass market in its appeal, because I know a lot of the audience on the internet is younger, and mine is definitely older," she says, pointing to the fact that sites like OnlyFans have age requirements and often necessitate credit card usage. "It would be harder for me [to come back after a break] because my audience has lives and stuff. If they got busy while I was gone or found another creator, they're kind of just locked in because they're not as into the cycle of 'Oh, this particular streamer blah blah blah drama' that young Zoomers are."

- - - - - - -

TWITCH, EVEN IN its most modern, performatively progressive incarnation, is not a place where women thrive compared to their male counterparts. In 2022, women rarely made it into Twitch's top 100 most popular streamers (as sorted by hours watched). The only one to regularly pull off the feat was Siragusa, who banked 32.6 million hours watched in total by the year's end. That's hardly nothing, but top male streamers doubled that, with a handful crossing the 100 million mark.

At various points, Twitch has proven outright hostile toward creators who don't fit neatly into the expected box of a male, often-white gamer stereotype. In 2017, not long after Twitch's 2016 introduction of a non-gaming section called "IRL" (short for "in real life"), a popular streamer named Tyler "Trainwrecks" Niknam went on a rant directed at women that, in his mind, were using sexuality to garner views on a gaming platform.

"This used to be a goddamn community of gamers, nerds, kids that got bullied, kids that got fucked with, kids that resorted to the gaming world because the real world was too fucking hard, too shitty, too lonely, too sad and depressing," Trainwrecks whisper-shouted during a Twitch broadcast at the time. As he saw it, IRL streaming made Twitch the domain of "the same sluts that rejected us, the same sluts that chose the goddamn cool kids over us. The same sluts that are coming into our community, taking the money, taking the subs, the same way they did back in the day."

The presentation of Niknam's speech—a series of faux-dramatic lines delivered over a filmic piano track—signaled a tongue-in-cheek-ness typical of online edgelords. Additionally, Niknam later apologized for what he'd said. But the message still found an audience, primarily with men, who made up 80 percent of Twitch's user base at the time. Twitch, some believed, *had* changed. Where once a random dude could plop down in front of a camera and play video games until an audience showed up, that audience was now ignoring gamers in favor of women who had not, these men insisted, earned it.

Never mind that this was never true—as evidenced by the trials and tribulations of even early success stories like Ben "CohhCarnage" Cassell, Twitch has always required more than simple attrition—it *felt* correct to would-be streamers who couldn't hack it on an increasingly saturated platform. It was honey to those already predisposed to resent women, a simpler solution than acknowledging that platforms evolve unpredictably due to time and companies' whims. That's the kind of realization that makes people feel helpless. Anger, bitter as it is, still goes down easier than recognizing that the good old days aren't coming back, and odds are, they were never actually all that good to begin with.

In this specific case, history proves *especially* inconvenient for creators like Niknam and Twitch superstar Félix "xQc" Lengyel, who years later in 2023 would continue tugging on this cultural thread by saying that paying adult-oriented content creators is "one of the most deliberate life-backpedaling, progress-hindering, brain-rotting activities anybody's ever come up with." Sex workers pioneered many of the business models content creators rely on today, not to mention the entire concept of e-commerce.

"The porn and adult entertainment industries, and the women whose work built them, were one of the earliest to provide real-time credit card verification, establishing a precedent for models of e-commerce other industries would adopt later on," wrote *Vice*'s Sofia Barrett-Ibarria in a piece titled "Sex Workers Pioneered the Early Internet—and It Screwed Them Over." "Sex workers and porn performers essentially created, adopted, and inspired many of the technologies later co-opted by tech corporations and Silicon Valley entrepreneurs long before they reached the mainstream, and continue to do so."

On top of that, in 1996, long before Justin Kan ever thought to broadcast his life and founded what would eventually become Twitch, a nineteen-year-old college student named Jennifer Ringley began an experiment in which she rigged a webcam to snap a shot of whatever she was doing in her dorm every few minutes, inventing what became known as "lifecasting." Sometimes she'd be reading a book or browsing the internet. Other times she'd be having sex or masturbating. Eventually, she took to charging viewers for premium access via PayPal. Ringley continued to lifecast herself for seven years. She is now regarded as the internet's first camgirl, without whom livestreaming and content creation as we know them would not exist. Or, at the very least, they'd look very different. So if Niknam and others want to bicker over who was here first, it seems only right to ask who's really taking from whom.

At the time of Niknam's rant, streamers—especially female streamers—pushed back. They pointed to the fact that all the most popular streamers remained male, that women on Twitch faced constant harassment in chat simply for being. While there were exceptions, the majority of women adhered to Twitch's rules, which in 2017 prohibited "nudity and conduct involving overtly sexual behavior" as well as "any content or activity involving pornography, sexual intercourse, or adult services." Some women did, indeed, get banned for nudity, but many simply wore tops with plunging necklines or cosplay that didn't *completely* cover them head to toe, which in most cases was not against Twitch's rules.

Niknam didn't start the conversation around "titty streamers," the Twitch community's derogatory nickname for women who showed skin; it's nearly as old as Twitch itself. He simply amplified it. He also, inadvertently, showed it for what it really was.

"If all the titty streamers were gone tomorrow, does anyone really think shitty people would stop degrading and insulting women?" veteran Twitch partner Renée Reynosa said on Twitter in 2017. "Truth is, they'd just find another hoop for us to jump through."

This was hardly the end of Twitch community complaints about women, which repeatedly forced Twitch into a reactive posture. In 2018, Twitch introduced more specific, seemingly stricter attire requirements that stipulated that "attire in gaming streams, most at-home streams, and all profile/channel imagery should be appropriate for a public street, mall, or restaurant." Twitch later walked this back to a degree but attempted to maintain a purposefully vague rule set so it could justify case-by-case decisions. In many instances streamers only learned where the line was after they crossed it. This led to complaints that Twitch was erring too far on the side of caution when, in 2019, female streamers were suspended for seemingly innocuous behaviors like streaming in video game–accurate cosplay of *Street Fighter* character Chun-Li, wearing midriff-exposing gym clothes . . . to the gym, and even just drawing art of scantily clad characters. All the while, streamers complained that Twitch did not adequately explain *why* they had run afoul of the rules. Inconsistency, in their eyes, was the law of the land.

Then came 2020 and 2021 and, with them, the emergence of the so-called "hot tub meta." "Meta" is short for "metagame," a term that comes from the gaming world, for exploiting a game's current set of rules to devise a winning strategy. In the context of Twitch, the "meta" refers to the winning viewership acquisition strategy of the moment based on exploiting what viewers and Twitch's platform are rewarding most. At the time, a growing number of streamers began to realize that if the context was right, there was no rule preventing them from wearing a swimsuit during broadcasts. The most straightforward option? Stream from a pool or beach, which many had already done in years prior as a one-off or special event rather than something sustained. Most people, however, cannot afford pools or regular trips to the beach, which gave a streamer who goes by the handle xoAeriel an idea: purchase an inflatable hot tub.

"In December of 2020, I went on Amazon and purchased a blow-up hot tub," she told gaming news site *Kotaku* in 2021. "I wanted some kind of different content, and no one else was doing it. I got a couple of LED lights to go inside, and when it arrived I began streaming. Views took off pretty quickly, and my following started to grow pretty fast. A few streamers started noticing my views shot through the roof and also ordered a blow-up hot tub."

From there, streamers put their own spin on the idea. Some sat in inflatable tubs and simply talked to viewers, while others played video games or set subscriber goals which would lead to rewards like (off-screen) bathing suit changes. The trend was quickly adopted by many streamers in Twitch's hangout-specific "Just Chatting" section. It proceeded to spark off blowback, which ignited further blowback, which exploded into nuclear blowback. Tweets and Reddit posts lambasted the state of Twitch, implying that the platform had been completely overrun with hot tub streams. It hadn't. Sometimes only a single-digit number could be found anywhere near the top of "Just Chatting."

But some women were enjoying increased success as a result of hot tub streams, mirroring the rise of platforms like OnlyFans, where women could cut out middlemen and monetize sex appeal, personality, or some combo of the two on their own terms. On Twitch, this gave rise to a familiar refrain: Women, who hadn't played by the rules, were stealing views from more deserving gamers. Moreover, they were doing so while *wearing swimsuits* on a platform whose audience skewed younger (though, notably, where more than 70 percent of users are between the ages of eighteen and thirty-four).

Some streamers who took part in the trend noted that wearing a swimsuit is not inherently sexual—especially when a man does it. Counterarguments also pointed to everything else on Twitch, also viewable by young people: inappropriate language, violent video games, and other games that sexualized women.

"We live in a world where it's okay for men to sexualize women in media all the time," streamer and cosplayer Hillary "Pokket" Nicole wrote on Twitter at the time. "The minute a woman owns her own sexuality, it's somehow . . . *gasp* immoral!"

Even after weeks of discourse, Twitch had not banned the hot tub trend. It was at this point that Siragusa waded into the proverbial bathwater, previously wary of a potential suspension or ban. By this point in her Twitch career, she'd become known for cosplay, dancing, and ASMR, a form of hyper-delicate sound meant to produce an "autonomous sensory meridian response," aka a tingling sensation that begins at the top of the head. She'd already amassed a legion of over 1 million followers largely by pushing boundaries. While she did not incorporate adult content into her Twitch streams, she did use her channel as a "funnel" into a separate subscription service called Patreon, through which she offered "naughty" pictures and cosplays. This put her in an ideal position to become one of the first big Twitch streamers on OnlyFans once the service began to explode in popularity in 2020, climbing to nearly 100 million users. Other streamers, noting how much it boosted her income in Twitch's otherwise male-dominated space, followed suit.

"She paved the way on OnlyFans," says Mogollon, Siragusa's friend and fellow streamer. "I remember looking at it [before I started using it] and being like, 'Oh, I would never do that. Yuck. What are people gonna think? What is my family gonna think?' Because of [Siragusa], a lot of the judgment went away. Now it's so common. . . . I made in my first two months on OnlyFans what I made in ten years of streaming."

Prior to the pandemic, Siragusa had also flirted with on-stream disaster in a handful of ways, making jokes that were not always in good taste and, during various IRL streams, getting kicked out of a salon, a gym, and the aforementioned Bed, Bath & Beyond. She'd also suffered an accidental wardrobe malfunction in 2019 that got her temporarily suspended from Twitch. Insofar as one who's about to enter a hot tub can be, she was on thin ice.

But given how much she'd already popularized the idea of a Twitch streamer who moonlights as a lewd content creator, she couldn't just sit on the sidelines and watch opportunity pass her by.

"When the hot tub meta started, I was like, 'Oh fuck, I have to get in on this,'" she recounts from the Real Work office in 2022, saying that she'd intended on taking a break beforehand but decided to push those plans aside. "I was like, 'If I don't get in on it, I'm gonna lose that momentum in my audience.'"

So Siragusa fully immersed herself in the hot tub craze, upping the ante in ways that were uniquely her. She added a gargantuan floaty of Pickle Rick from the popular Adult Swim cartoon *Rick and Morty* to the mix. She proceeded to regularly straddle it while floating in her hot tub, creating a piece of immediately recognizable visual iconography that landed smack in the middle of captivating and confusing. This is Siragusa's strength: She can't resist making things weird. Eventually, at the behest of a Twitch viewer who'd donated money to her, she sliced open her Pickle Rick floaty and donned its plastic remains like the skin of a slain animal. "I'M PICKLE RIIIIIICK," she shouted at the top of her lungs while wobbling back and forth in knee-deep water.

"She's always been quirky and funny," says AustinShow, a popular streamer who hosts live comedy game shows on Twitch, on which Siragusa has guested at various points over the years. "She's, like, an icon. You don't just become an icon for sitting there and looking pretty. There's more to it than that."

"She's not afraid to be herself," says Youna "Code Miko" Kang, the comedic VTuber who's streamed with Siragusa on numerous occasions. "She's funny because she is just naturally herself and silly, and [she] doesn't care what other people think of her."

Needless to say, Siragusa managed to stand out, even among a growing sea of hot tub streamers. Thanks in part to her prior popularity, she quickly became the face of the movement. After more than a month of watching her income soar, however, she attracted the exact sort of negative attention she'd feared—but with a twist. Twitch did not suspend her. Instead, in a previously unprecedented move where big-name streamers were concerned, it indefinitely suspended advertising on Siragusa's channel. This meant she could no longer make money off ads run before or during her streams, a chunk of revenue she deemed "significant" in terms of her overall take from Twitch.

"This is an alarming precedent," Siragusa said on Twitter at the time, "and serves as a stark warning that although content may not ostensibly break community guidelines or terms of service, Twitch has complete discretion to target individual channels and partially or wholly demonetize them for content that is deemed 'not advertiser friendly,' something that there is no communicated guideline for. This leaves open-ended the question of where the line is drawn."

After a few days of pandemonium within the Twitch community, Twitch explained itself in the form of a blog post announcing a new, self-contained "Pools, Hot Tubs, and Beaches" category. This category, notably, allowed advertisers to opt out if they found the content within objectionable, with Twitch explaining that "on Twitch brands get to decide where and when their ads appear" and "in rare cases, [we] will suspend advertising on a channel at the advertisers' request." The company admitted, however, that with Siragusa it messed up, at least where communication was concerned. "Our creators rely on us, and we should have alerted affected streamers to this change before it happened—it was a mistake not to do so," the company wrote. "We're working with individual creators to address their specific situations and restore ads."

Marcus "DJWheat" Graham, who departed Twitch less than a year after the incident, found it to be a symptom of Twitch's larger troubles at the time, the ones that ultimately led him to make for the door: "I think the hot tub [meta] and a lot of the sexually suggestive stuff, it all boils down to communication," he said. "I came to a point in 2021 where I realized that there was a complete lockdown on communication from Twitch."

In finally explaining its rationale, Twitch ended up singing a different tune around sexual content than it ever had previously.

"While we have guidelines about sexually suggestive content, being found to be sexy by others is not against our rules, and Twitch will not take enforcement action against women, or anyone on our service, for their perceived attractiveness," the company wrote. "Under our current Nudity & Attire and Sexually Suggestive Content policies, streamers may appear in swimwear in contextually appropriate situations (at the beach, in a hot tub, for example)."

With that, hot tub streams no longer lived in a gray area. They were explicitly allowed, which effectively normalized the form after years of stigma against women's sexuality on Twitch. Siragusa would go on to receive a couple more Twitch suspensions in 2021—one for unknown reasons, another for an ASMR stream in which she suggestively posed in tight yoga pants . . . and a horse mask—but believes her relationship with Twitch was at least moving in the right direction.

"I mean, they did give me a meet and greet at TwitchCon, which I guess is a positive sign," she says. "Earlier this year, I was able to secure front page placement for [a game show I hosted]. And occasionally they'll be like, 'You might have broken a rule, here's a warning,' which is nicer than a direct suspension right away. But they still don't really communicate. Like, *which* line did I cross, so I know what to correct?"

Siragusa believes, though, that livestreaming—whether on Twitch or elsewhere—will remain a key part of her content creation arsenal no matter what. Other platforms allow her to paint a near-flawless version of herself, but streaming completes the picture.

"Livestreaming gives you a more genuine experience," she says. "Like, 'This person, they're not perfect either. They also make mistakes. They don't look their best every single day.' I feel like it humanizes you a lot more. Whether that's better for a career based on looks, I'm not sure. . . . But I think it's more personal. I think people are just after that personal experience, especially in a world that's moving so fast, that's so digital that we don't feel like we get those often."

- - - - - - -

IN A SMALL podcast room next to Real Work's main office, Kayla, a student who's been with the company since its grand opening earlier in summer 2022, explains how she and other employees try to create online interactions that *feel* personal. When employees manage the accounts of creators on platforms like OnlyFans, they often end up posting for them and even responding to their direct messages. That means pretending to *be* them, more or less.

"We'll post a story, send out a video or something like that, and then keep up with DMs and the personal relationships these people already had with their fans," Kayla explains in a nervous tone. "Just emulate their voice as much as we can so that it doesn't really seem like they have a management company."

With growing confidence, she proceeds to dive into the minutiae: "I have someone in my account who doesn't use capital letters," she says. "They don't use punctuation—things like apostrophes. *I* am a very precise typer. I love capital letters and complete sentences. I type a sentence [for a client's post or DM], and I'm like, 'Damn, I have to go back. First letter, make it lowercase, take out that apostrophe.'"

In the digital era, when many creators necessarily communicate at and with hundreds, thousands, or millions of people per day—and still wind up exhausted and burnt out—is personal even possible? Or is it just a well-crafted illusion no matter who's pulling the strings? And if so, are fans paying for what they perceive to be real, or do they know, deep down, that they're getting a distant echo of their idol—a hologram projected in some cases by somebody else entirely? Does it matter so long as all involved agree not to break the illusion?

Perhaps it matters more when money is on the table. In a November 2021 lawsuit written about by *Insider*, two former staffers from a firm called Unruly Agency that ghost-wrote responses for OnlyFans creators claimed their employer required them to "intentionally lie to, dupe, and mislead fans." Others at the company, *Insider* wrote, believed this to be the key to their success: "Some Unruly insiders said they believed that if the illusion that the fans were always chatting directly with the influencers were shattered, the money would stop flowing." The suit further alleged that fans divulged their "deepest and innermost personal secrets including sexual fantasies and fetishes," something they would not have done if they realized they weren't actually talking to their favorite creator. (Unruly denied these allegations.)

Kayla clarifies that individual Real Work employees don't run creators' accounts entirely in a vacuum. There are group leads at the company who show them the ropes, and in cases where creators get angry comments, especially, employees generally reach out and ask if the creator in question would like to suggest a response or step in directly. "Anything we can do to either emulate how that person would respond or let them respond so that we can respond like that in the future," she says. "But we don't get too many [angry comments]. Most people are pretty nice to the people that they pay."

Kayla—the actual person, rather than the invisible account operator—isn't a big fan of social media. If she posts anything to her own accounts at all, it's usually a picture every couple weeks or so. A job at Real Work just happened to fit her schedule. She's studying to become a funeral director and embalmer. That's where her real interests lie. Despite the gloomy subject matter, she lights up as she describes the circumstances that led her down the path toward a job in some ways more personal than any other.

"I've always really loved anatomy," she says. "And then my mom passed away a few years ago. That was the first funeral I'd ever been to. I just found it really interesting: the embalming aspect, the restorative arts. I really love the idea of restoring somebody's face and body to be viewable for family because I know losing a loved one is a top-three hardest thing you're ever gonna go through in your life. I love the idea of being able to help someone through that."

- - - - - - -

SIRAGUSA PICKED HER hires with an eye not toward histories working in social media or specialized skill sets, but because she needed to be able to trust them. For the most part, she explains at her office in 2022, it all began with Bancroft, an assistant originally from an era during which both were significantly younger and Siragusa's operation had yet to start raking in millions.

"I don't have a huge social group of streamers," she says. "Mostly it's been [me being like], 'Morgan, your friends at first, and then your friends know other trustworthy people.' And then there were some old high school friends I reached out to like, 'Hey, you were a good person. Come over here and work for us if you need a job.'"

This means employees' backgrounds run the gamut from retail to restaurants to mortician school. While some, like Kayla, see Real Work as a pit stop on their career path, others are pretty satisfied with where they've wound up.

"[The restaurant industry] is rough," says Parker Ray, who previously worked in said industry and now handles client onboarding and strategy at Real Work. "I've got scars and burns all over my hands from it. Coming into this job [at Real Work], nobody's yelling at you. We're working together towards deadlines that are feasible—stuff like that. Complete culture change for the better."

As for the pace Siragusa keeps, it either does or doesn't pressure her employees to similarly overwork themselves, depending on who you talk to. Ray characterizes himself as highly engaged while on the job but able to maintain a healthy work-life balance outside it. He believes that's key, considering that Real Work's purpose is to help creators keep their own digital houses clean.

"A lot of these people that come to us, they have issues with work-life balance," says Ray. "So that's one of our biggest hurdles."

But Bancroft, Siragusa's assistant turned managing director, cannot help but get swept up in Siragusa's maelstrom—both in terms of schedule and mindset.

"My physical office hours are generally Monday to Friday from ten a.m. to seven or eight p.m.. And then we go home and do more work," she says. "I try to find time on the weekends to do [non-work] things, but we're busy a lot on the weekends. . . . I feel like when you're in your early twenties you think that's your time to be young and whatever. But I feel like I can do things in my thirties. I would rather grind it out right now and be investing and putting money away."

- - - - - - -

PULLING PEOPLE FROM numerous walks of life and training them up from scratch is preferable, Siragusa says, to what could happen if somebody with an ax to grind went rogue: "There's always the fear that these people want something or will try to exploit girls, since we work with very sensitive personal content."

Siragusa's fears are far from unfounded. Reports by the *New York Times* and *Rolling Stone* outline instances in which OnlyFans managers—essentially, third party entities that offer similar services to Real Work—scammed creators out of hard-earned money or failed to impersonate them so disastrously that fans whipped out their pitchforks and torches.

"Despite her own success, however, [a popular creator named Autumn Nelson] cautions OnlyFans newcomers against hiring someone to outsource their content management off the bat," wrote *Rolling Stone*. "Prior to hiring her current manager, she says, she had a bad experience with a former manager who coerced her into videos that she 'wasn't comfortable with at all,' which ended up being posted on the website ManyVids without her consent for additional profit. The manager, she alleges, also sent photos to her family and tried to sell foot fetish videos to a private client."

As with the organizational pratfalls Real Work seeks to remedy, Siragusa's understanding of the dangers creators face online is also born of personal experience. Over the course of her Twitch career, Siragusa has dealt with numerous forms of online harassment: sexist language in chat, death threats in DMs, and such regular swattings—weekly attempts, in some cases—that she's on a first-name basis with local law enforcement. Even so, the latter remains a potential tinderbox.

In some instances, Siragusa's most dedicated detractors have taken things further. In 2020, somebody shot fireworks at her house under the guise of Fourth of July festivities. In 2021, garbage—and a small portion of her home—caught fire, with police at the time suspecting arson. In 2022, she dealt with a stalker who she says flew all the way from Estonia to Houston, Texas, where she lives.

"He was in Houston for a month or two," she says. "Every day he would do IRL streams of himself walking around. My assistants were actually able to track what hotel he was at based off his streams—to make sure he didn't come to the house."

Then, one day, a viewer in chat provided the stalker with Siragusa's address—swatting incidents meant it was out there for those who knew where to look—and he attempted to enter her home.

"He was trying to knock on the door, jiggle the handle, tap on the windows, get into my house," she says. "We had to call the cops. But the problem with streamers is that since we get swatted so much, now the cops in our area don't take it seriously all the time. When we call in, they think it's a prank. . . . It took them, like, thirty minutes to get there even though the station is five minutes away."

If these incidents rattled Siragusa, she doesn't show it. She maintains a collected, occasionally amused air even while describing experiences that would keep others glancing over their shoulders for years. But Siragusa is rarely one to display big emotions when she's doing her thing: talking into a camera or, in this case, a recorder. Sure, you can find clips of her on the verge of losing her cool from her younger days—for example, when, in 2018, the staff of a local gym from which she was streaming forced her to leave due to privacy concerns. But even then, she only fired back at staff with a snippy tone rather than a raised voice or sustained outburst, muttering, "I'll go to a gym [that] is more understanding of their members' careers," before trudging away.

Siragusa—especially the current, more mature (and perhaps less entitled) version—rarely lets the mask slip. She presents herself as flawed and more than a little goofy, but in a manner that feels calculated. The performer and the persona always eclipse the person.

One of the only notable exceptions to this rule took place on somebody else's stream entirely. In 2020, she guested on a Twitch broadcast by Dr. Alok "Healthy Gamer" Kanojia, a psychiatrist who performs public therapy-like sessions with creators, which have raised ethical concerns despite his organization's claims that he informs all guests of the non-private nature of the conversation and always stops short of a diagnosis or prescription. In Siragusa's case, Kanojia certainly knocked something loose. By the end of the session, his insistence that Siragusa was neglecting herself in favor of an endless work grind brought her to tears.

"I think you've gotta let go of your dream," Dr. Kanojia said over an hour into the session. "I'm not saying you shouldn't pursue it. But there's no such thing as long-term happiness. The very idea is false. This is like the pot of gold at the end of the rainbow."

He provided the example of an investment banker who worked their way up the ladder to wealth and other material markers of success, only to look down and realize they were old, had barely ever taken a break, and had gotten divorced three times. Happiness deprioritized temporarily, he explained, often becomes happiness delayed indefinitely. He then asked Siragusa how making progress toward her long-term goals felt.

"It's like a light at the end of the tunnel," she replied. "It's like, 'Oh, I'm almost there,' and then I can feel the peace. But then part of me is like, 'What if I get there, and I'm so fucked up that I can't even find that happiness?'"

Not long after, she began to cry. She insisted, however, that she was not sad.

"I don't even know why I'm crying," she said. "It's not that I'm sad. It's just that my system is physically overwhelmed."

In response to this, Dr. Kanojia suggested that perhaps she was experiencing a disconnect, a suppression of Kaitlyn, the person, so as not to hold back Amouranth, the burgeoning empire. Siragusa agreed with this assessment. The situation, the idea of it, she explained, is what made her cry.

"It sucks that I'm losing myself," she said. "[I'm feeling] sorrow for my personality, I guess. I'm not a sad person. It's just a sad thing."

"I'm sure there's a lot of people who make content who feel similarly," she continued. "Like the grind is taking away part of what made them them before the social media grind began, and they just don't know how to talk about it, or who to talk to, or if they even can because they'll sound like ungrateful little bitches."

Dr. Kanojia went on to suggest that things didn't have to remain that way. Siragusa could, as starting points, begin seeing a therapist and take a little more time to herself during each workday.

"Just gotta work on it," Siragusa replied.

- - - - - - -

TWO YEARS LATER, on a sunny September afternoon in 2022, the grind continues. Siragusa insists that shortly after the Dr. Kanojia stream, she did *try* to adopt better habits.

"The beginning of 2021 was actually a big burnout point for me," she says. "I had just bought a horse in February, and I was like, 'Now I want to relax with my ponies for a bit and have more of a work-life balance.'"

But then the hot tub meta came along. As a result, Siragusa's daily stream hours remained sky-high. She, with assistance from her team, continued to produce content for OnlyFans, Fansly, Patreon, and numerous other platforms besides. Also she launched a whole company.

When asked how she maintains a schedule that's all tunnel and no light, Siragusa lets out a tired chuckle.

"Willpower and Adderall," she says. "Vyvanse, in my case. And lots of caffeine. I guess because I haven't really taken breaks, I'm kind of in the routine now. I feel like if I were to take a vacation for a month, I would totally wreck my cycle because it's harder to come back into the grindset when you take a break. So my solution is to just not take breaks."

She notes that she hasn't taken a whole week or more off since she started streaming—in 2016.

"Typically I stream holidays, too," she adds. "So I really don't take a break from it."

Is she burnt out? Even she's not sure anymore. But money helps.

"We pushed past a million dollars a month," she says. "So that kind of, I guess, resolved my burnout."

- - - - - - -

JUST A COUPLE weeks later, in the middle of October 2022, Siragusa decides she's had enough. During a stream from her bedroom, framed by purple-hued mood lighting and flanked by Pokemon plushies, she broadcasts to tens of thousands of viewers a phone call with a man she claims is her husband. His name, per police records, is Nick Lee.

"Why did you say you were gonna kill my dogs?" Siragusa asks, referencing an earlier conversation.

"Leave the house," Lee replies in a venomous tone.

"OK, I can leave the . . . actually you know what? I shouldn't leave the house because my dogs are here," says Siragusa.

"Well, take the dogs and leave," he retorts. Then he begins to yell: "I'm telling you, you're asking the question, I'm telling you, and you're interrupting my fucking . . ."

"What are you saying?" Siragusa asks. "You were just telling me you were gonna kill dogs if I didn't do a twenty-four-hour stream!"

Lee accuses her of being a liar and then begins to yell again. This causes Siragusa to cry. He goes on to claim he only said "something terrible"—about hurting dogs—to prove that when something is "very important" to Siragusa, she doesn't listen to anything else he's said. He spends the next few minutes repeating variations on this argument and screaming over Siragusa when she tries to interject. Then he threatens to publish a tweet from Siragusa's account—which he has access to—claiming that Siragusa is trying to get him swatted. He follows that with additional threats: He's going to get her OnlyFans banned, he's going to sue her for "every fucking dime," he's gonna spend the night "disassembling" Siragusa's "entire fucking empire."

"You're about to lose your entire life in terms of what's been built because you're too obstinate to just accept, merely accept, that you didn't hear a thing," Lee yells.

The two argue back and forth for a few more minutes, with Lee claiming he "built" Siragusa's empire even as she points out the reality of the situation: "I've literally been the one streaming for all these years."

Eventually the call concludes. Siragusa's husband texts her and tries to call again.

"No," she says into her webcam, "I'm not gonna answer your phone call now that you know I'm streaming it and you're like, 'Oh, fuck.' Yeah, you piece of shit. . . . I'm so tired of shit."

Despite rumors over the years, this is the first time Siragusa has publicly spoken about having a husband. She says she's taken calls from him during numerous streams, but that she's always gone off-screen while doing so.

"I've been wanting to tell people," she says to her viewers. "'Let's just stream together. Just tell them we're fucking married.' Because it's, like, our relationship would be better if we just streamed instead of fighting all the time. But [he's like], 'Noooo, don't say that because it's going to ruin the business model. It's not time yet.'"

She goes on to show a series of texts from a prior incident in which Lee repeatedly calls her a "dumb fuck" and threatens to dump her luggage off a hotel balcony, delete her social media presence, shut down Real Work's bank account, and harm her animals.

"That's just, like, a typical day at the office for me," she says while wiping away tears with a tissue.

She also accuses Lee of forcing her to broadcast sometimes against her will, telling her to "commit to the grind because it was a good financial opportunity."

"The hot tub meta, he was pushing me to stream every day," she says. "I needed to be in the hot tub for twelve hours, fifteen hours, and then in September we'll fucking have a day off now. But then September came, and guess what happened? Didn't get days off."

Toward the end of the stream, one viewer in chat types that the whole thing "seems fake."

"I wish it was," replies Siragusa as she works to secure her various accounts. "I really wish it was."

Shortly after, her husband returns home. Just as he opens the door, she ends the stream.

- - - - - - -

THE NEXT DAY, Siragusa goes live from her bedroom again. This time, it's just her—and two of her dogs.

"As you can see, doggos are safe," she tells her audience. "Big one is outside, in case crazy people show up."

She goes on to say that she's regained control of her accounts and finances and is seeking "legal and emotional counsel" following years in an abusive relationship. Her husband, meanwhile, is away "getting help." Despite her attempts at recording previous blowups and outbursts, she says he had never really been confronted with his own behavior before. Reached prior to the publication of this book, Lee verified Siragusa's account of events but declined to comment further on the record.

"I think when he heard himself on that call, it sunk in how much of an asshole he really is," she says. "It's like, you never even realized, idiot?"

Still, she's bracing herself for the worst: "It's just gonna be really messy, I fear. But, you know, the alternative, keeping it hidden, was messy, too. So, I guess, choose your mess."

But she recognizes that even in this dire situation, she has a lot to be grateful for. Following the on-stream phone call, fans—and even haters—offered her assistance up to and including offers of legal support.

"I didn't think that many people would give a shit, to be honest. It's kind of crazy," she says. "Even haters are like, 'Damn, I fucking hate Amouranth, but you know what, I hope she's OK.' That's so nice."

At times she sounds like she hasn't slept in days, but not for the reason she's regrettably used to. She slumps in an office chair, reddened eyes wandering, mind lost in thought. Her expression flits between exhaustion, deflation, and elation.

"I'm positive about the future," she says weakly. "I'm happy I'm free. It's just still a lot."

Other upsides slowly but surely bubble to the surface.

"I don't have to wear cleavage every day," she says at one point. "I can wear clothes!"

"I get to sleep for eight hours tonight, for once," she says at another.

"I actually feel like I can have friends again," she says later.

When individuals become brands, enterprises, and empires with tight control of their own communication channels, at what point do traditional means of extracting information—interviews, "behind-the-scenes" deep dives, etc.—cease to usefully reveal the truth of a situation? Should we even expect them to when the information in question is so delicate, so personal, despite sending shock waves through a multimillion-dollar operation that employs dozens of people and attracts millions of viewers? Who, at that point, has a right to know? And how do we obtain that information if the small handful of people involved aren't interested in sharing it for years, or potentially ever?

But truth has never been a single moment, a big reveal. It's always had a way of seeping out over time, like a leak in a roof that keeps drip-dropping on your forehead until you can't ignore it anymore.

The two top comments on the YouTube recording of the Dr. Kanojia interview—originally posted in 2020—are from October 2022.

"Looking back on this interview with everything from the past couple weeks makes everything she talks about make more sense," reads one.

"I feel for Amouranth right now," reads another. "I can't believe she's been through this much."

- - - - - - -

A COUPLE DAYS later, Siragusa announces on Twitter that she's going to take a break from streaming. "Taking a break," she writes. "Not sure when I'll be back."

By this point, the news about her abusive husband has already rocked the streaming world—and it continues to. A handful of streamers, including Mogollon, Siragusa's friend who considers her an influence, check with her and local police to make sure she's safe.

According to public records from the sheriff's office of the county in which Siragusa lives, police are dispatched to her residence multiple times the morning following the Twitch broadcast of the call between her and Lee. First, they respond to an early morning call placed by one of Siragusa's Twitch moderators who knows where she lives due to previous swatting incidents and who warns of Siragusa's dogs. Police make contact with Siragusa and Lee, but find that they do not "require police action." Around noon of the same day, Alyssa Jordan, Real Work's chief of media operations, reaches out to police saying she hasn't heard from Siragusa since 4 a.m.. Police check Siragusa's home again but do not receive a response upon knocking. On the same day, Mogollon and a man identifying himself as Siragusa's uncle also call to express concern. The next day, police are once again dispatched to Siragusa's residence, at which point both Siragusa and Lee state that "no assault or threats were made" and that they had just been arguing over business.

Numerous streamers spin the content mill into overdrive. By this point, it's a full-on news story. Big names like Imane "Pokimane" Anys—another one of Twitch's biggest female stars—Hasan "HasanAbi" Piker, and AustinShow are sympathetic, albeit surprised. They all know Siragusa, having collaborated with her at various points over the years. But they had no clue this was brewing in the background.

"Just by nature of being connected with so many people, you just kind of hear things, but I still had no idea," Show tells me after the fact. "Not to a point where I really had any suspicions nor was it something I really thought about because I respected whatever she wanted to tell people."

The fact that she didn't tell people sooner quickly becomes a major point of contention in the immediate aftermath. Some creators and viewers argue that female content creators effectively lie to men by appearing single when, in reality, they're not—and, in so doing, take advantage of them. But others poke holes in this rationale.

"The idea that female entertainers must be perpetually single virgins so their parasocial male fans can indulge in the fantasy they might one day have sex with them is fucking insane," Clara "Keffals" Sorrenti says on Twitter.

"Amouranth never said, any of these girls never said, 'Oh, if you donate money to me, you know, there's a higher chance of you getting acknowledgment or recognition from me, and I'm single,'" massively popular *World of Warcraft* streamer Asmongold says during a broadcast. "I have no sympathy for [people who think like that]. . . . You're not going to get me to say, 'Oh, they got taken advantage of!' No. They're stupid and they're weird and that's what they get."

"People just hate women, and they hate sex workers," says Hasan "HasanAbi" Piker during a stream at the time, in response to a viewer's comment that people seem to be blaming Siragusa for her husband's actions. "And the hatred of sex workers is often tied to the hatred of women—and stems from wanting to police women's bodies."

YouTube livestreaming star Rachell "Valkyrae" Hofstetter sees the fact that there's even a debate at all as a symptom of a much larger problem.

"Literally this is the exact reason why abuse victims have a hard time coming out," she says during a broadcast. "Because of how people are reacting online."

- - - - - - -

SIRAGUSA RESUMES STREAMING just five days after announcing her hiatus. For the most part, her broadcasts from then on and well into November see her playing video games like *Overwatch 2, Call of Duty,* and *Just Dance.* Every couple of weeks, she does a hot tub stream. It's a major change of pace, something she trumpets in response to repeated criticisms that nothing has really changed.

"Weird L take that my content hasn't changed," she writes on Twitter in November while posting a graph of Twitch categories she's streamed into over the course of the month. "Ninety days ago I was doing fifty percent or more hot tub. Now it's, like, sub-ten percent? . . . I played more *Overwatch* than I did hot tub. That's NEVER HAPPENED."

"That rebrand worked out," snarks one user in response, evidently doubting the veracity of her abuse situation.

"Not about rebrand," she replies. "I literally don't care. I get to do what I want, and I still make [seven figures] money a month. Life is better."

However, she continues to stream *a lot*. In total, she streams 311 hours in November 2022—significantly more than she did in October and just 5 hours less than in September, before the phone call that changed it all.

"Been cleaning house and moving forward with an eye towards prioritizing hires that have strong cultural fit and align with my values," Siragusa says on Twitter, noting that she intends on sticking with all the projects she began prior to the recent seismic shifts in her life. "There will be some staffing changes that reflect my renewed priorities and focus.... Some points of contact will change, but I've always kept a strong pipeline of talented employees and will continue to use the best person available for each role."

However, months later, in January, creators express publicly that they're having trouble getting ahold of anybody at the company.

"Is this site still active?" writes one in response to a tweet from Siragusa. "All of my emails and Discord messages have gone unanswered."

"Is this company still available?" tweets another. "I talked to them on the phone and [through] Discord. I've been waiting to sign contracts and start working together but they have been MIA since December."

Siragusa does not publicly reply to either.

- - - - - - -

DESPITE SIRAGUSA'S REASSURANCES on platforms like Twitter, the following months see fans continue to express concern. In a highly upvoted Reddit thread posted at the end of December, one asks what's going on with Siragusa after they notice an uptick in hot tub streams: "I don't know if all she's doing is the same sex appeal stream[s]," they write, "but the few times I've checked it has been that." Numbers back this up: In the first three months of 2023, Siragusa spends 59.2 percent of her time on Twitch—or 419 hours—streaming into Twitch's "Pools, Hot Tubs, and Beaches" category.

Others in the Reddit thread point out that Siragusa has also gone on sporadic one-off "dates" during a handful of broadcasts, but even so, they're unsure if anything has truly changed behind the scenes. While some flippantly suggest that she should just take her millions and walk, others discuss how difficult it can be—both psychologically and materially—to exit an abusive relationship.

In interviews about the evolving nature of abuse and technology's impact on it, experts back up more sympathetic fans' thinking.

"We, as survivors, did not get into this situation because we enjoy abuse," says Ruth Glenn, head of the National Coalition Against Domestic Violence. "We got into it because we loved somebody or cared enough about somebody. So when this happens, you question yourself. You may even leave and still question yourself. At the same time you probably have the abusive person calling you, sending you flowers, sending you cards, or saying [something like], 'I'll kill you if you don't come back. I know where to find you.' And particularly as we're talking about technology, 'I know *how* to find you.' . . . Oftentimes, because of all these factors, it's just easier to go back."

"It could be financial. There could be threats. It could be emotional blackmail, if somebody coercively controls. [A victim] is gonna feel pretty reliant on their abuser," says Dr. Lisa Sugiura, a researcher of cybercrime and gender at the University of Portsmouth's School of Criminology and Criminal Justice. "In having these conversations, some of the onus or responsibility is placed on the victim. They don't have the power. We need to remind ourselves of that: Who's pulling the strings here?"

In Siragusa's inner circle, some speculate that she has not fully extracted herself from Lee.

"I don't think that anything's changed," says one of her friends under the condition of anonymity. "And I know that getting away from an abusive relationship takes a lot of time and many, many tries and a lot of work."

"What she told me is that they're pursuing a divorce. But I haven't seen anything material from that," says Nash, formerly Siragusa's talent manager and now cofounder of Novo, which in addition to handling brand deals for Real Work, also negotiates some for Siragusa herself. "There was so much link in bank accounts [and] financials that it would be very difficult to untangle," says Nash.

True separation, at least, would indeed seem to be a difficult process. Records from the Texas Secretary of State's Office show Nick Lee as a "managing member" of Siragusa's limited liability company, Isolani Media, which means he's a co-owner of her personal business. The filing has been updated since the events of October 2022, but Lee's status remains untouched as of March 2023. According to the filing, he's been a managing member since 2018.

"I usually tell people that the business divorce is the only thing that is as messy if not messier in some instances than an actual divorce," says Ryan Fairchild, an attorney at Odin Law, a firm that specializes in video game, digital media, entertainment, and internet businesses. "Even if it's smaller, if you have a creator who's been successful and probably diversified and [is] doing a lot of different, interesting things—even though it might not be at the same scale as a giant company—it could have complications just disappearing depending on what positions it holds, what contracts it has, and ongoing obligations."

Real Work, on the other hand, belongs solely to Siragusa. The filing lists her—and her alone—as manager. This, Nash says, makes sense: Siragusa has proven to be extremely business savvy.

"That's not to say she was not heavily involved in this shit," he says. "She could vibe with me for four hours on a podcast talking about [minute details of business]. She was in it. But [Lee's] involvement in the business was really material."

Siragusa stands atop an empire that has been assailed from inside and out. Since her channel's inception, Twitch tried to limit her creativity, and her husband tugged at the strings more and more forcefully until she eventually snapped. Despite appearing to be in control of her own destiny, she certainly didn't feel that way. Even as she raked in millions, control slipped further out of reach. Now, finally, she has an opportunity to take it back, even if mopping up the mess might make it look bigger at first.

- - - - - - -

AFTER A SERIES of scheduling snafus, Siragusa is ready to talk to me again in early February 2023. Around this same time, the Real Work Twitter account begins posting again. It appears that things are back to some form of business as usual.

Over a call, Siragusa refuses to comment further on the status of her marriage.

"I can't really talk about that at all," she says. "The things of it are still true, but I can't legally say more than what I've said on stream."

"I'm trying to move on from all of that," she adds.

She goes on to explain that she continued to specialize in hot tub streams and other, more overtly NSFW content on platforms like OnlyFans because an immediate one-eighty would've required her to let go of numerous staffers. Instead, she took her time, transitioning many over to Real Work and ultimately finding new positions for "every" staff member. Only one, she notes, opted to leave.

"I can't make them do new stuff right away because it's not a stable business," Siragusa says. "It'd be slowly changing content over time, and I'm already starting to do that. I just hosted a birthday party [stream] and invited a lot of big streamers. I've been doing animal shelter streams. I've been doing a lot more IRL streams, a lot more collaborations. So things are moving in a good direction."

She imagines that in the coming years, she'll still produce at least "some" adult content. But beyond that, time will tell: "It depends on the way the industry goes in the next several years," she says. "Is it still mainstream, as like a better, more reliable source of income, or is [the industry] shifting away from that? . . . But eventually I want to spend most of my time doing passion projects rather than grindy work ethic stuff."

The grind, Siragusa insists, isn't breaking her down at a molecular level this time, even if it doesn't seem like all that much has changed. After the dip in October, Siragusa's stream time rebounded spectacularly in November and December—up to 311 hours and 320 hours, respectively—before falling to 175 hours in January and 234 hours in February. Still, by most streamers' standards, that remains an insurmountable workload. Now, though, Siragusa says she's in control, and that makes all the difference.

"[Control] is not just turning off the camera," she says. "It's also knowing that [my life] is not always going to be monetized, and there will be a day that comes in, like, twenty years where I'm like, 'Man, I wish my time was worth as much as it was in my twenties,' and I'll regret not doing more with it if I don't make the most of it now."

"I know there's an end to it eventually, so make the most of it while you can," she adds, echoing the mentality she previously espoused under very different circumstances. "I don't feel like I'm missing that much. The world's kind of a mess. It's barely non-pandemic-y."

Still, she's making up for lost time where she can—for example, with the aforementioned birthday party stream.

"I never really had a birthday party since I started streaming because I don't really have the same friends I used to," she says. "I've been kind of lonely, I guess, these past few years not really having anyone to celebrate with. It was nice to finally just invite some friends over."

responsibility

The air is thick with anticipatory tension. There's a vibe, a tingle, a sensation in the pit of everyone's stomach. It's like gazing upon a lightning rod during a thunderstorm, or standing at the bottom of a hill that's about to be crested by an opposing army. Something *big* is about to happen. Something so big that it's commanding the attention of hundreds of people in a room otherwise devoid of focal points. The walls are a blank, purgatorial white, as though to drive home the notion that what's to come in mere minutes matters far more than what is happening now.

A nondescript-looking young man, clad in a hoodie and a baseball cap, emerges from a door in the back corner of the room and strides onto a ramshackle convention stage. Shrieks arise from the crowd—ear-piercingly loud, endlessly blaring, almost otherworldly. In the following days, several people who are in this room will Google "tinnitus symptoms" for the first time in their lives. They will not be pleased with what they find. One by one, additional young men walk onto the stage. Each is met with louder and louder screams, a ferality devoid of self-consciousness. These fans are fully submerged in the moment. The world around them has fully faded from view. They're living a . . .

Dream, at long last, steps onto the stage—the A side, the man of the hour, the ring leader of this crew of wildly popular creators. "DREAM, I LOVE YOU," an already hoarse voice cries with every ounce of fervor it can still muster. It is quickly drowned out by hundreds of others sounding like thousands of others. Dream, tall, lanky, and wearing a plaid shirt–black beanie combo that would make him impossible to pick out of a crowd, penguin-waddles onto the stage. It is instantly apparent that he's never had this many eyes on him before—at least, in real life.

This TwitchCon appearance in an overstuffed convention hall conference room is Dream's first, ever. Mere days prior, the *Minecraft* sensation finally revealed his face to the internet. Despite an explosive rise to fame that began in 2020, Dream always wore the game itself as a mask. Fans spent years listening to his voice as he and his friends put together increasingly viral *Minecraft* challenge videos on YouTube, which they parlayed into millions of followers on Twitch. They followed this up with their magnum opus: Dream SMP, a *Minecraft* role-playing server that mixed meticulously written lore with real-time improv to construct grand narrative arcs. But viewers never saw hide nor hair of Dream's real-life body. Then, in October, after years of mystery and speculation, he finally dropped the figurative (and literal) mask in a video simply titled, "Hi, I'm Dream." The video has over 62 million views.

Dream, whose first name is Clay and whose last name remains undisclosed, after many years of mystery ended up looking like a pretty normal white dude. Brown hair, green eyes, light stubble—a twenty-three-year-old who did not appear out of place among the trendy YouTuber and Twitch streamer crowd, but who also wouldn't have seemed out of place anywhere, really. And yet, his facial features threw the online discourse machine into overdrive. In countless other videos posted by Dream's friends and stars from every corner of the creator-verse, people reacted to their first sight of Dream's scruffy mug. Fans on YouTube, Twitch, Twitter, TikTok, Instagram, and every other platform known to man chimed in with their takes, as well. Dream, some said, was ugly. His chin protruded too much. His eyes were too far apart. He had the features of a dishonest person, or a bully. Others, often posting in all-caps on Twitter, thirsted after him, drawing attention to his smile, his jawline, the way he gestured with his hands. He was gorgeous and kind-eyed—the picture of wholesome innocence. Whatever people had previously felt about Dream, they projected onto the suddenly far-less blank canvas that was his face.

At TwitchCon, though, you wouldn't know anybody thinks him less than a god. All throughout his panel, intended to celebrate the Dream SMP server, young female fans howl in delight at every word. If you closed your eyes, you'd assume you were at a K-pop show, not in a sterilely lit conference room listening to gamers answer questions about impenetrable lore. But in many ways, this is a new breed of pop star, and as Dream—and his legions of fans—will soon learn, that carries weight.

DREAM SMP DOES not, at first glance, come across as a natural celebrity incubator—at least, in the traditional sense. It doesn't spotlight its stars in ways we're used to, with physical talents and characteristics glammed up on a stage or screen. But look closer, and it becomes abundantly clear why modern teenagers and twentysomethings regard it and its stars with a similar—or even greater—level of enthusiasm.

In *Minecraft*, players can create their own servers, on which they are able to build to their hearts' content, with their creations persisting between play sessions. The appeal of the game itself, then, is not unlike that of Lego blocks, except at a scale constrained only by players' imaginations. Some have poured years into their own cities and planets, as well as re-creations of Middle-earth from *Lord of the Rings*, the *Titanic*, and Manhattan from, you know, Earth. But while many—Dream and his crew included—once saw *Minecraft* first and foremost as a playground, a growing number of players now view it as a stage.

Dream SMP takes place in a world constructed by Dream and his fellow creators, but with a twist: During broadcasts, players are in character as fictionalized alter egos, drawing on a mixture of in-game improvisation and prewritten lore that they collectively come up with in writing sessions that take place outside the game. As a result, they're able to have their cake and eat it, too: Fans of labyrinthine world building find plenty to slice open, dissect, and endlessly speculate about on Reddit or across fan-assembled wikis—as they would with a lore-heavy TV show like *Game of Thrones*, movie series like *John Wick*, or video game series like *Five Nights at Freddy's* (yes, seriously)—but lighter, looser, character-driven moments ground the whole enterprise.

On top of all that, you never know quite what's going to happen. A creator might make something up on the spot that changes the course of the story entirely, or becomes a new, foundational element of the lore. In 2020, a major election plotline was born of the fact that a key player slept through a session, forcing his running mate to spin up a new political party with a different player. They won the election, ushering in a new era in the fictional country of L'Manberg. This followed a saga that included rallies, flashbacks, and the fall of an autocracy, which culminated in 220,000 players voting on which party should win.

It was large-scale, interactive live theater that viewers could follow from the perspective of whichever participating creator they chose by simply tuning into their Twitch or YouTube channel, whose individual communities, in turn, have their own objectives and in-jokes. This is the appeal of Dream SMP: As characters bond and betray, kingdoms rise and fall, and memes recount it all, viewers don't just watch; they participate. They might not be in the game, but they still get to say, "I was there." They still get to feel like, without them, the situation might have played out a little (or a lot) differently, both in and outside the game itself.

Minecraft is hardly the only popular video game to have spawned a role-playing culture along these lines. *Grand Theft Auto V*'s role-playing scene is a never-ending mash-up of slapstick comedy and reality TV trailer trash that's turned the aging crime caper into a mainstay of Twitch's top ten most popular games. *Rust*, a lesser-known but still popular survival game, has inspired unexpected collaborations from top streamers across countless cliques. Unsurprisingly, role-playing in these games received a big popularity boost in 2020, when the pandemic prevented streamers from meeting up in real life, forcing them to huddle together (from a distance) in virtual spaces instead. *Minecraft*, however, produced far and away the biggest stars. Part of this is a factor of age; though *Minecraft* first came out in 2011, it appeals strongly to (and is marketed toward) kids. It's also brightly colored rather than grim and gritty, more focused on creating than destroying. This has led to an audience more diverse along gender lines than that of, say, *Grand Theft Auto*.

Moreover, stuck at home during the pandemic, teenagers had ample time for non-schoolyard crushes on their favorite creators to develop into obsessions. On platforms like Twitter, the Dream SMP fandom grew into a force, regularly causing quotes and phrases from the server to trend—in all caps, naturally—as tens or hundreds of thousands of fans tweeted them out in unison. Devotion and thirst became accepted (and in many cases encouraged) languages in creator-focused *Minecraft* communities. Again, the K-pop community functions as a parallel—if an all-caps phrase or name trends on Twitter, it can be hard to tell, at first glance, if it's from the K-pop community or the *Minecraft* community. But it's often one of the two.

To some degree, this behavior has always existed in pop culture—think the classic image of Beatles fans screeching and mobbing as the band disembarked from a plane. But now it persists online and shapes digital culture, creating new languages of expression. In her book *Everything I Need I Get from You: How Fangirls Created the Internet as We Know It*, internet culture writer Kaitlyn Tiffany explains that Twitter and other modern platforms were destined to become megaphones for fandom, noting that early virtual communities, dating as far back as the 1980s, functioned as gathering grounds for Deadheads. This pattern gave way to fan sites in the nineties, where fans once again functioned as early adopters, establishing thousands of pages on Yahoo's free web hosting service, GeoCities, that catered to every interest imaginable. What fans talked about—and how they talked about it—helped define the feature set of social platforms to come. At a more atomic level, as Tiffany puts it, "early adopters innovated the idea that the internet might be organized by affinity." Years later, fans did this with Twitter, as well.

"[In 2009] Twitter had not yet decided what to be," Tiffany writes. "These early Twitter-using fans often came from the cultural powerhouse of Black Twitter or from insular fandom spaces like LiveJournal or Yahoo Groups, and initially found themselves in small, tightly knit clusters, discussing the movements of their heroes in circular conversations. They came up with the internet-age semantic convention of using an abstract plural pronoun even when speaking alone. As in, 'We have no choice but to stan.' As their circles grew, they realized they could disrupt conversation and funnel attention at will, taking over the Trending Topics sidebar whenever they had a whim to. Eventually, they settled into a rhythm—Tumblr was the confusing and therefore secluded site for longer-form conversations and strategy sessions, while Twitter was the faster-paced site for a public-facing display, where they showed off their numbers and their no-limit capacity for posting."

"Stan" is a term derived from a 2000 Eminem song of the same name about an obsessed fan sending the rapper increasingly deranged letters. For a time the term carried a negative connotation online, but in more recent years, hyper-dedicated fans have taken to wearing it as a badge of pride. This has resulted in no small number of think pieces and videos that suggest fans—especially female fans—have finally gone too far. But Hannah Ewens, author of *Fangirls: Scenes from Modern Music Culture*, argues that over the course of decades, little has changed except the speed of interactions and the sheer volume anybody can see if they so choose. Fans and stans are ultimately people just like the rest of us: messy, complicated, and prone to mistakes born of impulse and emotion. They're not always going to put their best foot forward.

"As well as the more joyous stuff—meet and greets, following around artists to their hotels and venues, documenting their work in zines or blogs— the impulses we're essentially now cordoning off as potentially problematic have always been acted on," she writes in a piece for *Crack* magazine titled "Stan Culture Is as Old as Pop Music Itself."

There is nothing intrinsically wrong with standom or other forms of intense fandom, but they can lead to negative outcomes—especially at massive scale—whether that means endlessly self-reinforcing echo chambers, a tendency to defend creators who've done indefensible things, or harassment of individuals both inside and outside a particular fan community. The Dream fan base demonstrates all of these characteristics and more. It's made up of millions of people, thousands of groups, and hundreds of factions.

With all of this in mind, fans and former fans see it as perfectly natural that their digital continent borders that of the K-pop realm.

"Overlapping fan bases share the same kind of structure," says Daisy, a former Dream fan who spent two years running a large fan account on Twitter. "It's the interest [in] certain content too popular to be niche, not popular enough to be mainstream, being enamored with the people creating the content, having people who share the same demographics, young people, and pop culture in general."

It's such a natural overlap that many fans haven't even thought to question it.

"Honestly I'm not sure why so many people in this community are also K-pop fans," says Rosh, who straddles the line between *Minecraft* and K-pop fandoms. "To me it just makes someone cooler."

- - - - - - -

IN PERSON, IN the confines of an otherwise pin drop–silent interview room instead of a cacophonous panel, Dream comes across as easygoing but confident. He states, matter of factly, that the face reveal was always a matter of when, not if. It was the final step in a plan to move in with two of his best friends, fellow *Minecraft* stars George "GeorgeNotFound" Davidson and Nick "Sapnap" Armstrong, and create content together—some of which would naturally include their real faces. Davidson, originally from the UK, had been waiting to move to the US, but Covid threw a wrench in those plans. The year 2022 proved to finally be the Dream team's year.

"It was only two weeks after [Davidson] got his visa that the face reveal happened," says Dream. "So now he's here and moved in, and we're all living together. That was the 'when.'"

Despite popular conceptions to the contrary, Dream does not believe himself to be a private person relative to other content creators.

"I'm really not," he says. "I feel like my friends would laugh at that: If someone was like, 'He's a private person,' they'd be like, 'He tweets out what he had for breakfast in the morning.' I've always been open about everything that I do. I feel like that's why my friends have connected with me so much. They feel like they know me, really. . . . I think that's a big part of me, even though I am faceless—well, *was* faceless."

He also feels like hiding his face in some ways made it more difficult to hold on to his final scraps of privacy, not less.

"I think I probably experienced way more [people prying]—like maybe a hundred times more than the average creator even of my size," Dream says, "because there was that secret of 'Oh, we need to keep digging. We need to find out. We still haven't found his face.'"

In this moment, Dream is clearly riding high. He's the talk of the internet, and he's just faced down hundreds of fans who were freaking out externally as much as he was internally. As far as he's concerned, the future is all roses. Potential downsides of a more public persona don't faze him.

"Realistically, revealing your face doesn't do anything about swatting," he says, as an example. "[You don't have someone going], 'I recognize that guy. He's my neighbor!' That's not usually how it happens. . . . It's one of those things where it's a negative of being a content creator or being in the public eye in general: There's gonna be people that do horrible things."

"Negative consequences can't stop me from living my life," he adds. "I feel like my best life is being able to make content with my friends and being able to go out in public and just go get coffee. Actually, I don't like coffee."

He also says he was unfazed by the online furor following his face reveal, in part because he's no stranger to controversy. In fact, if there's one thing that follows him more reliably than throngs of faithful fans, it's dark clouds of controversy. Most notoriously, in 2020 he was accused of cheating in a *Minecraft* speedrun—a challenge in which players race to complete a game as quickly as possible—by installing modifications that would make certain items appear more often. This resulted in a very public war of graph-filled, math-heavy statistics reports with *Minecraft* speedrun moderators, followed six months later by Dream confessing that he *had* cheated—but only by accident. Critics were, naturally, skeptical about that last bit.

Internet denizens have also mined Dream's past for controversy, digging up old videos and Reddit posts that suggested more conservative, in some cases bigoted, points of view than his wholesome online image would suggest. In 2021, in an on-stream conversation with Twitch politics king Hasan "HasanAbi" Piker, Dream explained those things by saying he used to hold "way more conservative views" back when he was sixteen and "an idiot kid growing up in Florida, in a red area, going to online school." Still, a new set of values more befitting of his star status among the generally progressive, pro-LGBTQ *Minecraft* community did not stop him from slipping up. Piker took Dream to task for releasing a video featuring Markus "Notch" Persson, *Minecraft*'s original creator, whose conspiracy mongering and racially insensitive rhetoric caused current owner Microsoft to remove all mentions of him from the game. That, said Piker, was "significantly fucking worse" than having once held different values. Dream agreed and ultimately deleted the video featuring Persson.

Dream and Piker wound up discussing the internet's tendency to keep a record of everything creators have ever done—even before they became creators—and how that can be useful, but only up to a point. There still needs to be room for the idea that people can change, they agreed.

"I understand that a lot of younger *Minecraft* stans or *Minecraft* Twitter people have almost idealistic expectations of their own content creators, and they want to hold them accountable—and in certain instances, it is good," Piker said at the time.

"I've been criticized a lot of times for things I didn't deserve criticism for," said Dream during the same broadcast, "but I've also been criticized for tons of things I deserved criticism for—even recently."

In 2022, at TwitchCon, Dream says these experiences have helped him learn to roll with the punches, even in the face of comments about his, well, face.

"This is almost exactly how I expected things to go," he says. "I got a lot of texts from people who were like, 'Dude, are you OK? Don't listen to the haters.' I was like, 'Every single day, this is happening.' . . . I guess to most people, it feels more real when you're calling a real person ugly. That's not any different than somebody saying you're a horrible, crappy person—the same thing that has happened before and will continue to happen."

Dream found some reactions to be memorable, however—often when they were overly positive, to a degree he found "very creepy."

"It's like, 'Thank you for the compliment, but you're talking about my inner eyelid,'" he says.

But this genre of reaction was also far from unexpected. Some would argue that, over the years, Dream and his closest colleagues have even encouraged fans to behave this way.

- - - - - - -

YOU'D HAVE TO throw a lot of rocks into a lot of different crowds to finally hit a creator who'd say they don't love their fans. It's basically a given, at least when it comes to the truly loyal fans, or the longtime stalwarts at the heart of a creator's community. The real question at the heart of most creator-fan interactions, rather, is what kinds of behaviors a creator brings out in their beloved fan base—and vice versa. Some of this is incidental; when you have millions of eyes on you every day, you can't possibly be held accountable for every act of petty indecency perpetrated by groups claiming to represent you. But big creators do, unavoidably, control the direction in which the winds are blowing. If they repeatedly approve of one thing—or fail to disavow patterns of pernicious behavior—fans notice.

In the livestreaming world, this becomes dicey when parasocial relationships are involved, which is basically all the time. True diehards spend hours watching their favorite creators every day—and potentially more interacting with fellow fans, vacuuming up videos and other ancillary content, and creating memes and additional neon-lit "NOTICE ME" signs in hopes of garnering love kernels from their streamers of choice. This, for some fans, leads to the impression that they truly *know* a streamer, that there's a friendship or relationship brewing even where the actual dynamic is 100 percent one-sided. But attachment is a strange thing. We, as humans, are terrifyingly skilled at hand-waving away rejection if it means protecting our own feelings. It is not uncommon, then, for streamers to end up with thousands of viewers who are functionally that one person in the friend group nobody really likes, but who is able to stick around because everyone else lacks the heart to tell them.

A central criticism of Dream and other members of the Dream SMP is that they've spent years reeling in these sorts of fans, stringing them along with stunts and messages and, at least in some cases, defending them against warranted criticism. For example, shortly before the face reveal in 2022, Dream began selling a USB drive that, according to its official product description, contained "baby pictures, some chapters from Dream's old books, childhood emails, old gaming screenshots, pictures/memes from Dream's camera roll, and more." That's awfully personal stuff! It would not be hard, if you were a particularly devoted fan, to scroll through that collection of keepsakes and imagine Dream himself revealing them to you, his dear friend, one by one. At the time, detractors accused Dream of crossing a line, while defenders said it's not all that uncommon for celebrities to release books and other promo items containing similar material. The truth, perhaps, is that online creators are far from the first winners of the social lottery to profit off other human beings' intrinsic need for connection; they've just streamlined the process to the point that it's harder to ignore how uncomfortable it all is.

Others in the anti-Dream camp have taken shots at the Dream SMP crew for seeming all too happy to hint at the idea of romantic relationships within the group despite the apparent lack thereof. Similar accusations have been leveled against pop stars like Taylor Swift and Harry Styles, the latter of whom has pushed back against the notion that he's projected any specific sexuality. "I think everyone, including myself, has your own journey with figuring out sexuality and getting more comfortable with it," Styles said in an interview with *Rolling Stone*. While certain subsets of fans took aim at Styles for his gender-fluid fashion sense and decision to play a gay character in a movie, Dream critics see queerbaiting in the group's tendency to make flirty, seemingly longing comments or kiss each other at events. This sends fans—many of whom are young and, again, pro-LGBTQ—into a tizzy. As a result, fans are especially keen on the idea that Dream and Davidson are secretly together. They write fan fiction and make fan art about this pairing. This has fueled the accusations that Dream and his friends are queerbaiting, a practice in which the creators of generally fictionalized works hint at but do not actually depict same sex or other forms of queer representation for the sake of publicity or marketing. A small handful of streamers, veteran comedy streamer Kacey

"Kaceytron" Caviness chief among them, have openly criticized Dream and others in his circle for this perceived practice.

"[It] just seemed like profiteering off the LGBTQ audience," said Caviness. "After I commented on that, I was really, like, attacked. It got a lot of the fans upset. I got a deeper glimpse into what his fan base was like."

But in more recent times Dream has spoken openly about his own sexuality—saying in a 2022 tweet that he's "not gay" and mostly finds women attractive but thinks "some men are OK too, I guess"—and has at various points as far back as 2020 explicitly denied dating his friends. The question then becomes: How many times should he have to repeat it?

"I joke with my friends because I'm comfortable [with] my sexuality, and so are they," Dream wrote on Twitter. "There's lots of LGBTQ+ members on the SMP and even in the Dream Team. I have no need to 'profit' off of 'pretending to date [Davidson],' we're not dating and have no plans to, and we've said that."

Other streamers who've proclaimed themselves straight—like Piker—have kissed friends at events and during broadcasts and received significantly less blowback. But those creators don't have Dream's overwhelmingly young, intensely parasocial fan base. There are different levels of responsibility involved. That, to Dream's critics, is the difference maker.

"I think that people who do have younger fan bases should take greater measures to protect those fan bases," said Caviness. "But then a lot of the time, the creators are younger themselves. Maybe they don't realize the kind of [influence they have]."

In videos and arguments with other creators, Dream has repeatedly espoused a live-and-let-live stance.

"If someone wants to ship [Davidson and me] because for one reason or another them picturing us dating makes them happier, then why do you care, and why should I care?" Dream wrote. "Who cares. I'm glad that the LGBTQ+ community can feel safe enjoying mine and my friends' content, that's it!"

Lynk, a fan who enjoys drawing fan art of Dream and Davidson as a couple, says that as long as the creators in question are OK with being shipped in fan works, they don't see the issue: "For me personally, if two or more real people are OK with it and have stated multiple times that they are comfortable with being shipped together, it's OK to ship them together," they explain. "If it leads to unrealistic expectations for some fans, it's unfortunate. But to my knowledge, most shippers understand that their ship is just that: a ship. Not reality. It may be fun to speculate, as long as it's not hurting anyone, but at the end of the day these are real people."

In a video released in 2020, Dream defended his personal stan army and balked at the idea that stans are all cut from the same cloth.

"Like who you like, don't like who you don't like, but don't generalize stans," Dream said in the video. "Let people look up to who they want to look up to. It shouldn't bother you, but if it does, that's fine. Just ignore it and move on like you would if someone said they liked ketchup on their broccoli."

"Almost every single thing that I see brought up regarding stans is just completely false or very, very out of context," he added. "I don't agree with everything my fans do, obviously, and if they overstep boundaries, I tell them. . . . When I tell them, they stop, because they genuinely look up to me and care about me. And why would they want to make me upset?"

But Caviness and others see that as part of the problem. Dream probably doesn't mean harm, nor is he doing things light-years outside the bounds of what other creators are doing; he's just a young person overseeing an online community of even younger people—one as populous as an actual nation. That's a recipe for trouble.

"Being a creator in the Twitch space, it so often feels like there are no adults in the room," said Caviness. "With the Dream situation, especially with his fandom, it's just *Lord of the Flies*. There's no adults, no adult opinion. Whenever you don't have adults supervising what's going on to a certain degree, it's just like, 'What's going on here?'"

- - - - - - -

TO REACH THE TwitchCon press room, you head through the main entrance, past the main hall, up an escalator, past an additional hall, past a multitude of rooms where panels are held, and down a lengthy secluded path that just screams, "You're going the wrong way." But at this particular moment, an army of attendees stands right outside it, fully blocking the path back to the rest of the convention. There are over fifty, maybe a hundred.

They are, of course, screaming.

A lone convention security guard—assisted by their loyal but overtaxed stanchion—keeps the group from progressing any farther. These fans wait in a state of rapt, near-breathless attention. One explains what's going on: They all thought they saw Dream go this direction, and now they're waiting to catch him on the way back. This is not a special event, or an event at all, and yet it has more attendees than some TwitchCon panels.

Throughout the weekend, other popular streamers put together impromptu meetups that draw similarly large crowds, but nobody else at Twitch-Con watches, waits, and swarms in quite this fashion. Dream fans are in a class of their own.

- - - - - - -

THE DREAM SMP TwitchCon panel largely went off without a hitch. From the moment the panel's moderator asked everybody how they were doing and Dream's grunt of "good" elicited a maximum-decibel response from the crowd, it was clear the Dream team could do no wrong. These fans were like pigeons in a park ready to go absolutely ham on a handful of crumbs. Some were in Dream SMP cosplay. Others used precious mic time to compliment each other's Dream SMP merch. But even though there were no wrong answers to fan questions like "What's your favorite *Minecraft* block?," "Can you do your best lore line in your lore voice?," and "Do you like my shirt?," Dream felt an immeasurable pressure.

"It was like being in a dream," he says during an interview a couple hours after the panel. "I wasn't thinking, 'Oh, I feel like I'm in a boy band.' I was just thinking, 'What is this? How is this real? How are these people screaming for me?'"

The reality of the moment really hit him, he continues, only after he got back to his hotel room.

"I got taken back to my place, and I was just sitting there for a while—literally just laid flat on my bed, on my face—like, 'What was that?' Then my mom came in the room and asked, 'Are you OK?' And I started just bawling my eyes out.' . . . She asked if I was stressed, if it was all the people, and I said, 'No, I don't know what it is. I'm just feeling something!'"

Online fame exists across numerous spectrums and sliding scales. Tens of thousands of channels on YouTube and Twitch have over 1 million followers. But that's not the same as having over 30 million, like Dream does—not even remotely. Thirty million is a few tiers of notoriety up from what most *big* creators can comprehend. (To put things in perspective, Taylor Swift's YouTube channel has 56 million followers—not that many more than Dream's—and she is one of the most famous people on the planet.) It is, to put it succinctly, the difference between revealing your face to adoring masses within your own bubble and, well, everyone. At that point, too many eyes are on you at all times for you to reliably maintain a bubble. You never know what might leak out and become the next big controversy.

But in some ways, even all of that pales in comparison to seeing just a thousand of those fans' real faces and bodies gathered in the same place, filling a room and spilling out into a hallway.

"It's one of those emotions that probably doesn't have a word," says Dream. "It's something I feel like humans aren't made to experience. There's so many people on social media. There are millions of people watching you, and you have a thousand people in front of you. It genuinely is indescribable. I still don't know how to describe what I was feeling or why I was crying or what was going through my head."

There are different levels to this for fans, too: Some fans view individual creators as resources or light entertainment—appreciated, sure, but not beloved by any stretch. They might go to a panel hosted by a creator and experience a mild thrill at the prospect of having their question answered. But it's unlikely that they'd scream. The Dream SMP crowd, on the other hand, was full of kids wearing their hearts on their sleeves, tearfully professing how much Dream SMP meant to them and offering handmade gifts to their favorite creators. Dream, though new to the real-life version of this, remains firm in his position from 2020: Stans are not an intrinsically negative phenomenon, nor are they even all that new. He also believes that gender plays a role in the perception of his stans, in particular.

"When you see it with a bunch of teenage girls, people like to kind of make fun of it. But when you see it with a grown man or anybody [else], it's like, OK, what's the difference?'" he says. "I've always related it back to my childhood watching football. I was definitely an obsessive stan of football players. You wear the jersey, and you get the hat. You run up and try to get signatures, and you cry when your team loses—that same kind of emotion."

"Obviously," he adds, "that is something that [can] easily be taken advantage of by people, if they have negative intentions. . . . I'm very conscious of it. I want to have a good impact on the world."

- - - - - - -

IN A STREAMERS-ONLY hotel lounge near TwitchCon, Karl Jacobs, another member of Dream SMP, rifles through his bag. After a moment, he produces a book with a purple-and-yellow cover and a swirling blue sigil in its center. It appears, at first glance, to be the work of a professional. Jacobs immediately dispels that notion. The book is a gift from a fan, says the twenty-four-year-old, whose painted fingernails gleam as he flips through its pages.

"I have a series that's associated with this book," Jacobs says, explaining the book's meticulously constructed cover. "So [this fan] wrote out a transcript of the series."

Two of Jacobs's friends, fellow SMP members, and podcast cohosts (not to mention, Dream's housemates), Davidson and Armstrong, sit next to him and examine the book. Both appear impressed.

"They put more effort into this than I did in school," Armstrong chuckles.

"That is so true!" Jacobs exclaims. "That is so true."

For Jacobs, especially, it's been an almost-overnight rise—at least, in internet time. After he linked up with the Dream SMP crew in 2020, his follower count skyrocketed.

"One August, I had twenty thousand followers," says Jacobs. "The next January, I had two Twitter accounts with over a million followers. It was that quick. It really was."

Fame struck these creators like lightning bolts, and now they're learning how to weather the storm. But even as they face criticism in cases where their audiences have, for example, dogpiled on other creators, they feel like they already have a pretty good handle on how to manage audiences that dwarf any gathering of people they'll ever see in real life.

"Oh yeah, now our favorite part is attacking people," Jacobs says in a dryly sarcastic tone. "Drama is so boring to me for content creators. I think it's cringy and lame. . . . There's opportunities for us to get engagement out of it, and we could have reaped a lot of benefits from joining the drama, but I feel like any attention you get from drama is always really weird. So we stay clear from that."

In the eyes of Jacobs, Davidson, and Armstrong, the best thing a creator can do to avoid drama—a convenient catchall that can be used in reference to everything from spats with other creators to harassment mobs—is set firm boundaries.

"They're their own people," Armstrong says of fans. "We don't have access to their computer. We can't tell them, 'No Twitter for a week.' We can set our boundaries, and then there's only so much we can do. We can condemn the bad things, and we have."

Jacobs says he's repeatedly told his audience that if they're going to take up arms—read: keyboards—against creators or fans, they should leave references to him out of it. That means no pictures of his face as their Twitter profile pictures, otherwise a common practice among Dream SMP fans. He thinks his fans have gotten the message.

"The community does a really good job of self-policing," Jacobs says. "I've seen somebody use my profile picture attacking another content creator, and then another person responded, 'Yo, Karl doesn't like it when you do that.' They do that a lot."

As for other activities creators might view as boundary pushing—for example, the act of pairing up real people, like Dream and Davidson, as though they were fictional characters—Jacobs, Davidson, and Armstrong just don't see the harm.

"A lot of people assume we'd think it's weird, but I just don't really care," Davidson says. "I don't find it bad. I don't think it's weird at all. And if I do, then I would just say something, and then people shut them down. It kind of holds people in the community accountable."

"Calling the fan base weird for stuff like that is weird to me," Jacobs adds. "First of all, why do you care? Second of all, imagine what other bad shit they could actually be doing [instead]."

On the surface, at least, some Dream SMP fans do seem to nominally value boundaries as a core principle. If you read profile cards they've written for themselves, they'll often have some variation on "violating creators' boundaries" listed as a dislike, suggesting that Dream team creators' messaging is having an impact. But words and actions don't always align, and assigning responsibility in those cases can be tricky. The years-long lead-up to Dream's face reveal is a good example of this: Dream noted that fans tried to dig into his personal life—in some cases invading his privacy—even more so than with other creators because they were always chasing that final mystery. This dynamic clearly got to him, leading to a handful of angry responses in cases where fans (or critics) thought they'd unearthed a picture or biographical fact about him. However, before revealing his face, he chose to sell baby pictures and other assorted childhood mementos to fans, which is not exactly the kind of move that dissuades people from trying to turn up additional details. Boundaries, in Dream's parasocial world, are ever shifting.

But that's also precisely why Jacobs viewed the outcry around Dream selling those photos as "the dumbest controversy ever": Streaming is, to him and others like Dream, Davidson, and Armstrong, *unavoidably* parasocial. Creators from previous generations, like Caviness, are uncomfortable with that idea. They try to discourage parasocial relationships where possible, because it's impossible to be everybody's friend. But members of the Dream team, who grew up on those sorts of connections with creators they looked up to, have embraced parasociality.

"I think it was an interesting angle to continue to monetize the successful marketing campaign that was his face," Jacobs says of Dream's baby picture

USB drive. "I can hear the angle [critics are coming at it from]. I just think people are looking too deep into it."

"I don't think there's any problem with it," Davidson concurs.

Jacobs, Davidson, and Armstrong also agree with Dream's assessment of this strain of fandom: In their eyes, it's not so far removed from the arena-shaking passion of sports fans. But, Jacobs adds, it *is* a new evolution of fandom. Online fandom leads to stronger, more personal bonds, and livestreaming creates stronger, more personal bonds still.

"It's different because there's streamers, right?" he says. "Streamers really do hang out with chat, for better or worse, for hours. That is just going to harbor a parasocial [element] with every single person watching. Every single person watching is going to feel like to an extent they understand this person's life way better than you would if you just watched a ten-minute YouTube video, right?"

At TwitchCon, even with hordes vying for their attention on all sides, Jacobs and other Dream SMP creators have felt this connection: "They watch us for, like, six hours at a time," says Jacobs. "So I think it's easier to get along with them."

- - - - - - -

EVEN THOUGH DREAM and his friends blew up when they were barely out of their teenage years, there's an obvious savviness to their operation. In other words, their success was far from an accident, though time and place certainly played a role. They put immense thought into not just lore, but also marketing, video packaging, making their streams feel like can't-miss events, and now, how to keep their group dynamic fresh by adding a real-life element. Additionally, they have numerous irons in the fire: other series, podcasts, books. Theirs is a bona fide multimedia mega-venture that's making millions.

It can be hard to square this with the idea that they are also, in other ways, flying by the seat of their pants. Even if you're scrupulously studying blueprints laid down by more traditional entertainment industries, you'll find few courses in online community management or growing up on the internet such that, by the time you're in the limelight, you'll have a miraculously spotless record. The latter, one could quite reasonably argue, is also something no one should *need* to learn how to do. Childhood is for making mistakes.

Dream has a self-admitted tendency to leap to his own defense before looking, but he harbors no delusions that he's done everything perfectly. At TwitchCon, surrounded by starstruck fans, his hope is that he can lead by example.

"Being able to have any impact on future generations—anyone who's younger now and is impressionable and is learning—I want to make myself a good influence," he says. "That's why I've always tried to do my best to be caring and loving and appreciative and apologetic and willing to admit my mistakes: to show growth and to try to include everyone."

"I'm not always gonna be the best I can," he adds. "I'm gonna make mistakes. As long as I respond to it well, [my fans] can learn that everyone makes mistakes. It's OK: You can learn and grow from it yourself."

- - - - - - -

AROUND A WEEK after TwitchCon, a new hashtag trends: #DreamIsAFreak. It stems from a thread posted prior to TwitchCon, but which was initially lost after its user made their account private. On an anonymous account, however, somebody else publicized the thread for all to see. In it, a Twitter user accuses Dream of grooming her—that is, establishing an inappropriately emotional or sexual connection with her—back when he was twenty and she was a minor. She posts Twitter DMs in which the two seemingly discuss her age ("18 soon," she says, meaning she was 17 at the time), her dislike of school, and Dream's wariness of conversations leaking and being blown out of proportion, leading him to prefer Snapchat (where messages auto-delete). She also tweets what she claims are screenshots of much more overtly flirty texts with Dream, in which he jokingly proposes the idea of meeting up during Covid quarantine and alludes to the idea of sex. The "worst" flirtations, she adds, took place on Snapchat, but the platform deleted them.

Dream responds to these allegations the same day they're reposted, describing them as "disgusting false accusations."

"My heart goes out to actual victims who get questioned in their hardest moments because of stuff like this," Dream writes on Twitter. "Fuck you if you abuse concern around horrible real issues out of spite. It's sad to see the trend that whenever there's something big going on for me or for friends of mine, people try and use those moments to spread negativity and lies."

The next day, another user posts similar allegations on Twitter and Tik-Tok, claiming that a series of DMs between Dream and her on Instagram escalated to sexually explicit messaging on Snapchat. This took place, she says, when she, too, was seventeen. In one video of a message she managed to save, the person she claims is Dream calls her "gorgeous as fuck." She goes on to say that they at one point made plans to meet up while she was visiting Florida—and that during that trip, Dream intended to use "a chest full of sex toys" on her.

"I thought that I was genuinely building a bond with my favorite YouTuber, and, boy, was I wrong," she says in a video. "That's what grooming is: Content creators make you feel important and take stuff out of you because they know you're not gonna do anything. The only reason I'm speaking up about this is because someone else did, or else I never would be posting any of this."

The day after the internet grabs hold of the second set of allegations, Dream posts a much longer response to both sets. He lends credence to some parts of both stories, saying the Twitter DMs from the first set of accusations are real, but that "there are no inappropriate comments whatsoever." He also claims her Twitter bio said she was eighteen at the time, and just to be safe, he asked her age. He goes on to claim she faked the flirty text messages.

He casts the second set of allegations in a similar light: The initial Insta-gram messages, he says, are real, but constituted a "friendly normal conver-sation" and "nothing inappropriate." He again says the accuser told him she was eighteen at the time of their communication and that all her other claims are "completely false."

"I have almost completely stopped replying to DMs from fans, random people, and old friends due to situations like this and out of fear from stuff that has happened in the past to my friends and those close to me," Dream writes. "My team has had access to my social accounts [for] as long as I could remember, in an effort to always stay on the side of caution given the size of my platform and inevitable, falsely spread situations like this."

He goes on to say that from this point forward he plans to "pursue legal action towards people using my name to spread disinformation or those that are misrepresenting facts, lying, faking things, or falsely abusing my name and image."

Dream also takes a moment to once again ruminate on the nature of parasocial relationships, this time singing a more cautious tune than before.

"Having such a deep obsession towards someone to look deeply into their family, friends, and personal life, or making up relationships or friendships in your head is one of the biggest reasons parasocial relationships can become so dangerous," Dream writes. "It's also one of the reasons why creators need to be as responsible as they can be and be careful when they interact with anybody."

- - - - - - -

DREAM IS FAR from the first streamer to face accusations of this nature. In 2020, following a full-blown #MeToo reckoning in which over one hundred streamers and industry professionals were accused of abuse or misconduct, Twitch banned five and commended women who came forward for demonstrating "incredible strength, vulnerability, and bravery." The YouTube space is also no stranger to such allegations: In 2021, immensely popular beauty YouTuber James Charles admitted to sending sexually explicit messages to two sixteen-year-old boys. "I fully understand my actions and how they are wrong," he said in a video at the time.

Closer to home in this case, *Minecraft* YouTuber and streamer Carson "CallMeCarson" King—whose SMP Live project served as a predecessor to Dream SMP—was accused of grooming a minor in 2021. Numerous creators proceeded to cut ties with him, at which point he disappeared off social media for several months and later returned saying that he "learned a lot" and was "not seeking forgiveness," nor was he "looking to make excuses."

Around the time of King's return, Imane "Pokimane" Anys, one of the biggest female stars on Twitch, attempted to make sense of the actions of King and other creators accused of similar infractions.

"A lot of people, because they're so good at content and gaming and whatever, it's because they've spent a lot of their young formative years only on this one thing, which means it's likely that they are kind of lacking in social experience," Anys said during a stream at the time. "So when they are inundated with all of this online attention and girls worshiping them and wanting to do anything for them, it's an unfortunate combination. And a lot of the time it ends in inappropriate or egotistical behavior, because they don't know any better."

But that doesn't absolve creators of guilt, she added.

"Not that it's not their fault or they shouldn't take responsibility for their actions," Anys said. "This is a . . . multi-level problem, for sure."

- - - - - - -

IN THE MONTHS following the accusations against Dream, fans divide themselves into camps. Many, upon Dream's denial of wrongdoing and allusions to legal action, decide the issue is being settled by suits in a back room somewhere, and until then it's out of sight, out of mind. But others come to regard Dream with suspicion or outright contempt. At various points in late 2022 and early 2023, hashtags like #DropDSMP and #DropDream—and even one imploring Spotify to remove references to music associated with Dream SMP—trend on Twitter, with ex-fans and longtime critics imploring Dream's faithful flock to find a new shepherd.

Those who defect from Dream's camp find it difficult to leave behind a creator who felt like a friend. But in their eyes, it's the right thing to do.

"For the first few days after hearing of the allegations, I remember being pretty devastated and generally depressed," says a former fan named Adrian, "not only because I felt betrayed by my favorite YouTuber, but because it was really frustrating seeing all the victim-blaming narratives other Dream stans were spreading on my timeline."

Adrian, nineteen, had been a self-described "huge" Dream fan for two years, but in hindsight, he believes it was all a parasocial spell. Now the spell's broken.

"When I was a stan, I didn't really see the problem with this," says Adrian, "but it's clear now that this kind of parasocial relationship really helps him in times like this. When fans see you as a friend, even if they don't know you personally or how you act in private at all, they want to defend you like you're their friend and want to believe every word you say."

"A lot of people in the fandom saw his actions as normal, like saying, 'I love you' to his fans after a big controversy or not having strict boundaries with his fans," agrees another former fan who goes by the handle Rosh. "It's hard to realize when you're indulged in the community."

But fans who stuck around view Dream's interactions with fans through a less jaded lens.

"He has expressed in the past that it was exciting for him to have a new fan base, just like it would be for any content creator, which gave him inter-actions and DMs from people who started looking up to him and wanted to talk to him," says a nineteen-year-old fan named Leah. "I remember there was one time where someone on [Twitter] was going through a hard time and posted something that implied they were going to end their life, and Dream sent them a message in private saying that he would miss them. Dream does not know that person, but he might have saved their life that day."

Another fan, Lynk, twenty-five, believes these issues are not exclusive to Dream. He just takes the most flack for them.

"I do feel some fans tend to get a bit overly parasocial and obsessive about his personal life, [but] I feel that's a big issue with a lot of content creators, not just Dream," they say. "I think his handle of parasocial relations has gotten better as he has gotten bigger as a creator."

Remaining fans say they want to believe victims and their stories—a common refrain in progressive circles—but in this case, they don't believe the evidence adds up. They feel like sans indisputable proof of malfeasance, this amounts to a bad-faith attack on Dream.

"People who do not currently support Dream and the people who have just always hated him are the ones to have [escalated] the whole situation," says Leah. "They claim to support victims, but hurt victims by saying, 'Yeah, but you support a groomer,' in their [own] defense at every given opportunity. . . . People just like to use it as some sort of 'gotcha' moment. They don't actually care and never have."

In the eyes of those who defected, however, the problem isn't necessarily whether or not Dream behaved inappropriately with minors. Even if Dream denies that part, they say, he still—at least for a time—made a habit of interacting with young fans over whom he, by way of his status, held tremendous power. Imagine Timothée Chalamet or Zendaya sliding into a random fan's DMs. It's basically unthinkable. There is no version of that interaction that could play out normally. Admittedly, Dream inhabited the same spaces as his fans; the leap from YouTube comments and Twitch chat into a person's DMs didn't seem so far compared to a movie star descending down from Hollywood's heights. But the power differential was similarly undeniable. That's enough to put former Dream fans off, at least for the time being.

"There is a healthy boundary between content creators and fans," says Daisy, the ex-fan who spent two years running a large Dream fan account on Twitter. "This also applies to any celebrity or well-known person, and several times Dream has allowed his fans—made up of mostly teenagers and young people—to cross those boundaries."

Lynk, who remains a fan, agrees that Dream should have exercised more caution at the time.

"I don't think he should've continued entertaining that conversation," they say. "I think there is a time and place for fan interaction, and DMs is not it. Dream interacts with a lot of us by liking our fan art, letting us talk in his spaces or podcasts, and meeting fans in person when he's out. I think that fan interaction should stop there for him, personally. It should stop there for everyone."

In the months following the accusations, Dream refrains from speaking on the subject at all and is silent in the face of multiple requests for comment. Other streamers within Dream's circle largely keep quiet on the matter, though two, popular *Minecraft* content creators, Thomas "TommyInnit" Simons and Tobias "Tubbo" Smith, end up embroiled in community controversy after Simons jokes that he's "not gonna add you on Snapchat" to Smith during a lighthearted on-stream exchange in January. Fans take this as a reference to the controversy around Dream and pounce with claws out. Simons and Smith quickly apologize.

"I wasn't joking about any of the current Dream controversy," Simons says during a follow-up stream. "As you can imagine, [I] can't believe I didn't connect those dots before making the joke, because I am a dumbass. I also assume you all know that I wouldn't joke about serious stuff like that, but in hindsight, I can totally see how it did look like it."

"It was a terrible thing to do, and I didn't mean it like that at all. It was a stupid joke," says Smith during a similar stream of his own. "I didn't even connect the dots in my head when I laughed."

Both say that despite loud and repeated requests from fans, they don't feel comfortable speaking about their feelings on Dream's situation in public, even as they continue choosing to associate with him.

"Don't get me wrong," says Smith, "it involves me because I'm on the [Dream SMP *Minecraft*] server and stuff, but . . . if legal stuff is happening and stuff like that, I feel like I'll get in the way. I don't want to cause any problems. But I one hundred percent take everything that any victim has said at face value, and I completely understand the importance of trusting at face value—and believing and acting accordingly."

When young creators invariably cultivate young audiences, how can we ensure they do so responsibly? If a young creator does harm in word or deed, should audiences treat them with more grace than an older creator who, one would figure, should know better? Should younger creators get more second chances? And which, if any, infractions should be absolutely beyond the pale, no matter who's responsible? With Twitch and other platforms opting to largely remain hands off and norms differing wildly across communities, concrete answers remain elusive.

Daisy says she began to take issue with her then-favorite creator during other controversies. The allegations were just another straw atop a camel whose back was already looking mighty creaky. She doesn't regret the time she spent in the fandom, however.

"I am still friends with the majority of the people I met through the community, despite having very different interests . . . and I feel extremely lucky to have met such lovely strangers through my teenage lockdown obsession," she says. "I now spend most of my time interacting with fans of my favorite bands and singers. I'm not as involved in stan culture as I would have been a few months ago; it isn't really my type of scene anymore."

Adrian was worried that departing the Dream fandom would leave him without many friendships he'd come to cherish, but he, too, has found connection removed from the *Minecraft* monolith.

"All my close friends on Twitter from the Dream fandom, many of whom were relatively large accounts, got into arguments with me after I was vocal about my support of the victim. The others simply blocked or unfollowed me after seeing that I was open about calling Dream out," he says. "I'm lucky I had both my sister and some other newly turned former-Dream stans to find comradery in. I started a group chat with them on Twitter so we could vent to each other about our feelings on the situation. That connection helped me a lot to come to terms with it all."

- - - - - - -

IN SOME WAYS, 2023 is an eventful year for Dream. Dream SMP concludes its grand tale, and the stars it created log onto their shared *Minecraft* server for one last, tearful play session. Afterward, some continue to collaborate via projects like QSMP, a multilingual *Minecraft* server from popular streamer Quackity that translates what players say to one another in real time, while others go their separate ways. At almost the same time, Dream announces a similar multilingual *Minecraft* server called USMP, which leads to conflict between Dream fans and Quackity fans. Dream goes on to say that he and Quackity hadn't spoken in a while and, effectively, that left hand and right hand failed to meet while tinkering away at their respective projects. Eventually, the conflict dies down.

But Dream is unusually quiet on YouTube and Twitch for most of the year, releasing just a handful of videos and only streaming sporadically. He takes some unexpected detours, however, temporarily deleting his face-reveal video and posting a tongue-in-cheek replacement in which he calls himself "ugly" and says he will resume hiding behind the mask forever. What happens next seems to at least partially explain that eyebrow-raising, headline-grabbing stunt: In the fall, Dream drops his debut EP, *To Whoever Wants to Hear*, and goes on a brief tour of the United States to support it.

At TwitchCon 2023 the month after his tour, Dream explains himself. The facetious face un-reveal, he says, was a branding exercise.

"It was related to the visual identity for sure," Dream says. "It was like 'Hey, this is still Dream. Dream still has the mask. Dream still wears the mask even if you know who is under the mask.' I've always talked about superheroes and stuff. It's a good analogy: Even if you know it's Peter Parker that's Spider-Man, he's still Spider-Man."

Dream has plenty to say about the evolution of his not-so-secret identity and newfound interest in flexing his creative muscles outside of *Minecraft*. But the secluded TwitchCon interview room—like any room Dream enters these days—houses an elephant: the allegations, which continue to follow him wherever he goes. He addresses them warily, admitting that he could have handled his initial public reaction better.

"Coming right after my face reveal, there was a lot of difficulty to that," he says. "I've dealt with so many things people think about me over the years, always hot topic things like racism or transphobia or homophobia or very serious things. So I had definitely had experience with people saying things that are not true about me. But I think, that being my experience, my initial response was like, 'This is ridiculous.' Very similar to what I would say to anything else where it's like 'Oh, you're racist' or whatever. But [this is] a different kind of thing, so you can't respond the same way."

He goes on to repeatedly suggest that an interview is not really "the avenue to discuss specifics," but he maintains his innocence.

"Obviously, it's misinformation," he says. "It gives people who don't like me a reason to be like, 'Well yeah, I don't like him because of this.' But you didn't like me before. . . . I think it's a very common thing in the community."

In his eyes, what actually happened is that he used Snapchat to interact with a variety of people—mods, editors, fans, old friends, random people he met in the enormously popular competitive shooter *Counter-Strike*—which led some of them to feel close to him, or like he owed them his attention. In the lead-up to the face reveal, he began to reconsider his approach to socializing. This, he says, culminated in the creation of a new Snapchat account, causing him to abandon the old one and many of the people he kept in touch with through it. This, he believes, bred resentment among those lost contacts, though that was not his intention.

"I think [that] was a big kind of catalyst to what ended up happening," he says.

After ostensibly incensed Snapchat connections came out of the wood-work, some of whom made allegations, Dream says he decided to take a step back and a look inward.

"That certainly had a massive impact on my content and my decisions I made after that. I did definitely step away from it for a bit," he says. "My perspective definitely changed in terms of parasocial-ness. Not in a negative way. . . . I think it's more in [a] one-on-one [sense]. You have to be very, very careful about one-on-one interaction, and with me it's kind of with anybody because whether somebody is a fan or not a fan, when you're at the size that I am, almost everybody has some knowledge of you or who you are, or could have ulterior motives. It was a wake-up call to be like, 'You've gotta be really careful about who you talk to, who you trust, what you say, who you say it to—especially with fans.'"

But the saga's not over, and Dream knows it. Fans still don't feel like they have the full story.

"It's definitely something I'll talk about more," he says.

- - - - - - -

AT THE TAIL end of 2023, Dream talks about it more. A lot more. In December, he releases a nearly hour-and-a-half-long video titled *The Truth*, which—according to its description—covers "important and serious topics." All pro-ceeds from the video, says Dream, will go to the Joyful Heart Foundation, an organization that seeks to eradicate sexual assault, domestic violence, and child abuse.

In the video, Dream devotes separate sections to an exhaustive range of topics including (but not limited to): claims that he posts thirst traps on

Snapchat, his decision to sell a flash drive that included baby pictures and other assorted personal artifacts, the time he lied about a photo of himself as a kid that leaked before his face reveal so as not to spoil the surprise, 2023 drama that involved a drunken Uber ride with Nicolas Cantu, the voice actor of the titular character from the hit Cartoon Network show *The Amazing World of Gumball,* and the 2020 *Minecraft* speedrun cheating scandal—a saga with which this new video rhymes in its attempt to dispel all doubt by performing obsessive comprehensiveness.

Eventually, Dream makes his way to what he calls "the really important stuff," aka the allegations. For the most part, he reiterates the same denials he's made before, albeit in greater detail. He posts what he says are full Instagram message logs that read as largely innocuous and even somewhat obligatory on his part, with him waiting days or weeks to reply to an enthusiastic fan's repeated inquiries. He calls out contradictions in what he says are faked screenshots of texts from one fan making grooming claims and Snapchat sexts from another. He repeatedly talks about how suggestions that he revealed his face to them ring false because he was "paranoid" about anybody getting a clear look at him before the face reveal. He even interviews his mom about it. She says that between 2021 and the face reveal in 2022, Dream left the house just five times, mostly for dental and medical reasons. She calls her son's approach to exiting the house "crazy."

"I pulled into the garage, shut the garage door," she says. "You'd get into the backseat, way back, of the van, with a blanket over yourself, and you wouldn't come out from under the blanket until we were on the highway."

Every window in their home, she adds, was also covered.

Dream goes on to say that he had his legal team search for claims against him, which yielded no results. He says they even called a specific police station where one fan supposedly began the process of seeking justice, which they identified by obsessively pouring over the details of a single screenshot the fan posted of their entryway. Nothing there, either. Admittedly, this is not necessarily proof of anything. The justice system often mistreats and casts aside victims. Dream's accuser could have gotten cold feet. But for the purposes of a video like this—an exploration of criminal matters from a content creator who normally posts about *Minecraft*—it carries the appearance of ironclad evidence.

Dream repeatedly accuses the two fans behind the original set of allegations of lying. He also takes aim at a third who made distinctly more spurious claims in 2023, suggesting that Dream sent a video of himself moaning in a sexually suggestive fashion to an underage fan. (This claim was ultimately shot down by the supposed victim on behalf of whom it was being made.) At times, Dream's tone borders on sanctimonious.

"This isn't online drama," he says after completing his takedown of one set of allegations. "This is real-life stuff. There are real victims that have been manipulated, abused, and taken advantage of. You are hurting actual victims. You are diminishing the very real trauma that victims of grooming and abuse have gone through. You are making it harder for real victims of abuse to come forward. You are not a victim. You are not doing a good thing. No matter how terrible you think I am, or that the ends justify the means, you are hurting victims. Just in case this video isn't enough for you to realize that, check your mailbox."

It never becomes entirely clear what he means by that last part, one of the video's many small strangenesses. Near the end, to demonstrate how easy it is to fabricate evidence of malfeasance, Dream displays a doctored set of sexually implicit DMs with Félix "xQc" Lengyel, punctuated by an audio file meant to sound like Lengyel moaning suggestively. It is not clear if Lengyel gave him permission to do this. Dream also posts a doctored DM in which Imane "Pokimane" Anys seems to call her fans "stupid AF" and admit to a debunked conspiracy theory that her newly launched snack brand is just a massively marked-up version of a preexisting product.

"You get the point," Dream says. "I made all those pieces of evidence in ten minutes with only free programs. What's stopping anyone from going and making a fresh account, faking evidence, and then accusing a person they hate of something vile? Be careful what you believe and ask questions. Believing real victims is important, but not believing fake victims is very important for real victims, too."

Toward the end of the video, Dream cops to a degree of culpability.

"I'm probably in this position because of myself," he says. "People that made these claims undoubtedly had unhealthy parasocial relationships with me, and that's why it's gotten to this point. . . . My view on fans has shifted slowly over time, jumping massively when I face revealed and actually got to meet fans in person, which made things much more real and changed my perspective. I think it's incredibly unhealthy to be obsessive with someone, and I also think it's clear to anyone that's stepping back and looking at these situations that people obsessively hate me and are making up lies about me—which is also because of parasocialness. Parasocial love turned to parasocial hate."

He then takes a moment to clarify his boundaries, which after too many public slipups to count, he realizes are overdue for a seismic shift. Going forward, he says, he does not support any sexually explicit art of himself or his friends. He explains that while it "never bothered me personally," it's "just weird, especially if you're a minor." He similarly discourages emotional investment in shipping.

"I've always found it funny being shipped with [Davidson] because we're not dating, and we're friends," Dream says. "But if you genuinely think that we're dating and it's part of your personality, or you obsess over it, you need to get off the internet. That is not healthy."

(A few months after Dream publishes his video, Davidson is accused of sexual assault by another content creator. He denies that he intentionally assaulted her but admits to physical contact at a party. Ultimately, he apologizes, saying that his lack of ill intent "does not change the fact that you were hurt.")

Bringing things full circle, Dream says he deleted his 2020 video defending stans, which he no longer "necessarily view[s] the same way now."

"That doesn't mean that I don't appreciate you as a fan, but again, just be normal," he says. "Be the passionate fan—not the stalker, obsessive fan."

- - - - - - -

HINDSIGHT IS 20/20, but if you ask those who attended the TwitchCon Dream SMP panel in 2022—at least, those who weren't so caught up in the moment as to be consumed by the screaming crowd—they'll tell you they,

too, were struck by a sense of anticipatory anxiety. But the line between ex-
hilaration and apprehension is a thin one, and this feeling fell decidedly on
the latter side. Something *big* was about to happen—not when Dream and
his friends took the stage, but after. Maybe years down the line, or maybe
just a week. When young creators find themselves surrounded on all sides
by even younger fans desperate for their attention, hard lessons are bound to
follow. The internet at large continues to grapple with these lessons. Whose
responsibility should it be to ensure that these kinds of situations never arise
in the first place? Platforms are inconsistent at best and negligent at worst
when it comes to gray areas and their biggest stars. Communities can effectively police themselves at smaller scales, but if you're talking about a creator
with millions of rabid fans—like Dream—the inevitable end result is messy
inter-factional conflict. There is, as of now, no simple, agreed-upon answer.

Creators are clearly culpable to some degree, as they are modern celebrities who wield power, same as any celebrities from any other era. But we
again find ourselves in murky waters. If we're dealing with young creators
coming up via less traditional pathways than, say, Hollywood and with less
oversight, where do we draw the line when they misstep? How do we allow
young people necessary room to make mistakes and learn from them while
minimizing harm? And where is the point of no return? How many times
can a young creator step in it—and proceed to fling the muck every which
way—before audiences cut them off for good? Is there even a "we" here at
this point, or have audiences grown too fragmented for there to be any larger
set of standards that fans adhere to? The emergence of platforms like Kick,
where stars banned from Twitch for egregious behavior have found great
success, suggests that some viewers just don't have a line—or that they delight in watching creators cross other people's lines. It appears, then, that as
long as there's money to be made and advertisers don't mind too, too much,
accountability will remain a secondary (at best) concern online.

At the time of TwitchCon 2022, Dream had no way of knowing what
was to come, but the subject of difficult lessons was top of mind. He felt like,
after countless other controversies, he understood why online communities
routinely held his feet to the fire.

"Whenever you have somebody that is in such a public space," he said during an interview, "you want to make sure they're a good person and make sure that they have good values—and that they support people that are good and [have] values that are good, right?"

Just as crowds fail to convey much beyond big, blunt feelings, they are also not the most elegant tools when it comes to meting out accountability. But often, in the face of few other options that *feel* effective, even a disorganized collective effort is something. Dream has reached a level of fame where not even a community schism can displace him, but he still speaks the language of the crowd. He still feels an urge to answer its call.

He just hopes the crowd will give him a lot of chances.

"The most I can do for certain things is say, 'Oh, I don't believe in this now,' or 'I did this thing, and I'm sorry for it; I was a kid, I was fifteen,' or whatever. And then move on from it," Dream said. "And then if you don't want to accept that, then you won't accept that, and I'm fine with it. I actually genuinely am OK with that. Just like a friendship in real life, it wouldn't have worked out."

chapter eight

- -

survival

Clara "Keffals" Sorrenti is in bed. It is not her bed. She has not seen her bed in months, after being forced from her home in the middle of 2022 by a harassment campaign ring-led by a notorious online hate forum. Instead, the raven-haired Twitch streamer leans back against the headboard of a hotel bed in San Diego, surrounded on all sides by open suitcases. Clothes litter the floor. A table has been shoved between the room's two beds to support a smattering of soda cups, Red Bull cans, and medicine bottles.

One of Sorrenti's collaborators and close friends, a curly haired young man named Jay, half-snoozes in the second bed, so entangled in a mass of pillows and blankets as to have become one with them. Another, Aaron Barnett, sits on the edge of the same bed, wearing a plain T-shirt and shorts. There is no pretense here—no flash or show. Everybody is wiped.

TwitchCon 2022, taking place in the nearby San Diego Convention Center, has been something of a reprieve for Sorrenti after a summer spent first drawing the ire of—and then acting as a lightning rod for the worst impulses of—Kiwi Farms, the aforementioned online hate forum, which specializes in digging up personal information and figuring out targets' real-world locations. The ensuing harassment forced Sorrenti to leave her home and eventually flee

196

to another country. Now, with hired security trailing her at a distance, she's making a public appearance at a convention. She's peeking her head out to see if the coast is clear.

But it never really ends. There's always a new crisis just a tweet, text, or Discord message away: Kiwi Farms denizens trying to figure out where she's staying during the convention, the possibility of stalkers showing up on the show floor and picking her out of the crowd, online death threats culminating in real-life violence.

Immediately after TwitchCon ends, Sorrenti plans to fly back to Canada—her home country—and move into a new apartment the address of which harassing mobs do not have. But a thought gnaws at the back of her brain stem, making its way to the forefront of every moment she tries to enjoy: Can things ever return to normal? Or is this just her life now, no matter where she goes?

"I'm nervous," she says. "I'll be living there alone and returning to normal, trying to just go back to streaming. I'm excited in some ways, but it also feels like a big question mark, about exactly what's going to happen in the next couple of months. I didn't foresee anything that happened in the last two. . . . Every time I tried to let my guard down, something bad happened."

- - - - - - -

SORRENTI, WHO IS trans, got her start on Twitch in 2020 playing video games, but in early 2022 pivoted to more politically oriented broadcasts that attracted a small legion of young LGBTQ fans. Instead of sussing out impostors in *Among Us* or fabricating labyrinths in *Minecraft*, she began discussing news articles, videos, and tweets in a style popularized by political pundits like Hasan "HasanAbi" Piker.

She chalks this formatting change up to a wave of United States legislation attacking trans rights—and specifically, a letter Texas governor Greg Abbott wrote to health agencies in February 2022 which said that providing gender-affirming medical treatment to transgender youth "constitutes child abuse" and which required nurses and teachers to report parents who assist kids in receiving care of that nature.

"I started covering that, and as that progressed, more and more anti-trans bills started happening all across the US," Sorrenti said. "Being someone who's not only trans, but who came out when I was a minor, it was really terrifying to witness because it's targeting children. They don't have a way to stand up or fight back against that."

Research has found that gender-affirming care—alongside support from the families—can lead to a reduction in suicidal ideation in trans kids. It's a dynamic with which Sorrenti has firsthand experience.

"I was getting bullied at school," she said of her pre-transition youth. "My parents weren't talking to me, and my friends also stopped talking to me. I ended up attempting suicide. That was when my family actually came around because they realized this wasn't a phase, and unless they were there to support me, I wouldn't get any better."

"They made this one-eighty," she added, "from a point where my dad once said, 'No son of mine is going to grow tits in my house,' to marching with me in a Pride parade in a shirt that said, 'I heart my transgender daughter.'"

Sorrenti's parents also ended up getting her interested in politics by taking her to a Pride march her dad's union was a part of in 2014. There she found out about the Communist Party of Canada, which—following the 2016 election of Donald Trump, whose anti-Muslim stance alarmed her—ultimately led her to run for provincial office in 2018 and a federal position in 2019 as a member of the Communist Party. She lost both elections, however, and left the Communist Party behind due to a series of disagreements over stances she didn't believe in. Suddenly, she was without a community. Then she found Twitch.

"I ended up moving into a place of my own, and it was only, like, two months after that Covid started," Sorrenti said. "So I was living on my own for the first time, there was a pandemic, and it was around that time I started to find out about Twitch. I saw there were a lot of debates going on and a lot of streamers. I had no idea what it was about, but it made me decide to start streaming because I missed that aspect of having a really tight-knit community. I was so used to having that [in the Communist Party]. Not having it made me feel incredibly isolated."

In pivoting to political broadcasts after initially streaming video games, Sorrenti's goal was to marry the more entertainment-oriented style of punditry she saw from streamers like Piker with her own history as a politician and activist. She began with events like charity streams—in which streamers set goals to encourage viewers to donate to causes—to support trans youth in the United States south. She managed to raise hundreds of thousands of dollars and, over the course of a year or so, grow an audience larger than most trans streamers had ever managed to find on Twitch.

"If you're just sitting and watching all this coverage, and you're not doing anything, what's the point?" Sorrenti said. "Why do you need to tune in every day to watch as the world burns if you're not planning on actually trying to do anything about it?"

The activism element, in fact, came easier to her than being an entertainer—at least, initially.

"I rubbed people the wrong way a lot because it felt like there was this invisible rule book [to being a Twitch streamer]," she said, "and I did not know any of the rules."

This is not to say Sorrenti was afraid to rub people the wrong way. At times, she courted controversy on purpose. She regularly took shots at conservatives and liberals alike, saying, for example, that "[democratic] centrism is a disease" in reaction to Disney's March 2022 decision to continue funding "Don't Say Gay" bill sponsors even as it produced ostensibly pro-LGBTQ content.

Moreover, Sorrenti quickly garnered attention by meeting detractors where they were at, whether that was in the comments of a post about her at the top of the one-million-strong r/Conservative subreddit or beneath the tweets of numerous conservative figures she mocked. It did not take long for "ratio-ing"—that is, creating situations in which the replies to a tweet outnumber its likes and retweets, suggesting people disagree with it—to become Sorrenti's calling card. She weaponized this tactic against conservative influencers like Candace Owens, Lauren Southern, and Tim Pool, devout centrists like Steven "Destiny" Bonnell, and notable figures with anti-trans stances like *Harry Potter* author J.K. Rowling.

This dogged combativeness, while admired by supporters, attracted harassers as well. A public feud with Bonnell, said Sorrenti, led to a notable uptick in bigoted harassment against her and, eventually, a thread about her on Kiwi Farms.

"They doxxed my mom on the first night [of the thread's existence]," Sorrenti said. "I had to call her in the middle of the night to get her to delete her Facebook account."

Bonnell denied that his spat with Sorrenti—about which he published multiple YouTube videos and, ultimately, a lengthy written "manifesto" full of accusations—fueled her Kiwi Farms thread.

"The idea that I'm responsible for her thread being posted on [Kiwi Farms] is unbelievable to me," he said in an October 2022 statement to NBC, noting that his style of political discourse brings him into disagreement with many different kinds of people. "There are plenty of trans people, and trans activists, on Twitch and YouTube who don't catch their attention. The only reason Sorrenti is noticed so much is because of her insanely aggressive behavior online."

But Bonnell and Sorrenti agree on at least one point: Kiwi Farms regularly trades in transphobia, pursuing trans targets with unique virulence. This stems from the forum's history: Before it was known as Kiwi Farms, it began as a series of forums dedicated to documenting the actions of, stalking, and harassing autistic vlogger and webcomic creator Christine Weston Chandler, who ended up coming out as trans after the harassment began. Kiwi Farms later took to describing itself as a "community dedicated to discussing eccentric people who voluntarily make fools of themselves," which in members' eyes often meant women, people of color, LGBTQ people, and people with severe mental illnesses.

Numerous publications, like *Vice*, *USA Today*, and *The Hill*, have linked the forum's sustained harassment tactics to the suicides of a handful of individuals, including David Kirk Ginder, a game developer who went by the online handle "Near." The day before Ginder, who was nonbinary, died in 2021, they attributed their mental state to Kiwi Farms: "Kiwi Farms has made the harassment orders of magnitude worse," they wrote on Twitter. "It's escalated from attacking me for being autistic, to attacking and doxing my friends, and trying to suicide bait another, just to get a reaction from me. . . . It's too late for me, but I pray that someone, at some point, will do something about that website."

Sorrenti knew what she was up against. After Kiwi Farms began targeting her, she said, she asked her brother to request that police in her home of London, Ontario, earmark her as a potential future victim of swatting. That way, they would know to handle her situation with care ahead of time. Meanwhile, even as harassers spread rumors that she'd leveraged online platforms like Discord in the name of pedophilia, forcing her to constantly be on the defensive, she decided to focus on improving her stream.

"I started building up this whole infrastructure for the team where everyone knew what they were doing. Everyone had a role. There were mechanisms in place," Sorrenti said. "It was supposed to launch on August 5. And then I didn't come online."

"[My team] had no way to contact me," she said, "because I was in a holding cell."

- - - - - - -

IN AUGUST 2022, Sorrenti woke up—in her own bed—to the sound of loud knocking on her front door. London, Ontario, police officers stood on the other side. As far as they knew, Sorrenti was armed and dangerous; online trolls had sent a message impersonating her to city councilors saying she was in possession of an illegal firearm, had killed her mother, and planned to go to city hall and "shoot every cisgendered person that I see." The message also mentioned her deadname, the name which she'd abandoned when she transitioned.

"My ex opened the door," Sorrenti said of the morning police showed up at her home. "They pointed an assault rifle at [my ex], asked them to identify themselves, and pulled them out. . . . They were shouting at me to get up. I had no idea what happened. I honestly thought it was, like, a fire or an emergency. I got to the doorway and saw the gun, and I immediately screamed. I thought I was going to die."

The police ended up arresting Sorrenti and, in some cases—for example, on bags used for storage of her possessions—using her deadname instead of her real name. Uncertain of what would happen next, Sorrenti spent the next many hours alternating between crying and fending off panic attacks.

"I'm in a holding cell for, like, eleven hours," said Sorrenti. "And for the majority of it, I have no idea what the fuck is going on. Apparently [the police] call my mom's work to do a wellness check on her, and they're addressing me as her son and using the wrong pronouns."

By that point, Sorrenti had at least an idea of why she'd ended up in jail, but it wasn't until her mother got her a lawyer and she spoke to the officer in charge of the investigation that she was able to finally explain to the police how internet trolls had thrown everyone for a loop.

"They didn't understand," said Sorrenti. "They were like, 'How would someone get all of this information?' And I just said, 'It's all on Kiwi Farms.'"

Contrary to their shadowy reputation, online hate groups like Kiwi Farms don't necessarily hack databases of sensitive information or employ other techniques off-limits to ordinary people. Sorrenti believes Kiwi Farms got ahold of her deadname by simply scrolling all the way back to the beginning of her mom's Facebook page. They found other information like her mom's address, meanwhile, by digging up her dad's obituary and then searching through his memorialized Facebook page until they came across an image of her mom standing outside her house. Persistence and numbers drive these groups, rather than preternatural proficiency.

"All they had to do is take the street number to Google Maps," said Sorrenti.

Sorrenti was ultimately released from police custody with no charges, but they held on to possessions like her computers and phone, which they'd obtained with a warrant. That put Sorrenti in a bind.

"Streaming was my only source of income," she said. "They basically made me unemployed."

To counteract this, Sorrenti started a GoFundMe campaign with the intention of moving immediately, crowdfunding her continued existence for as long as she did not have access to her devices, and building a legal fund to "protect my rights." Thanks to online outrage at the way Sorrenti had been treated, fans and sympathizers collectively contributed over $100,000 to her cause.

"Trans folk, and especially trans activists, deserve the freedom to make themselves heard," tweeted Jagmeet Singh, leader of Canada's New Democratic Party. "Not to be doxxed and swatted, arrested at gunpoint and deadnamed repeatedly. No one deserves this."

Police later released a statement acknowledging that Sorrenti had been the victim of a swatting. The police promised to investigate Sorrenti's swatting with the goal of identifying the person or people responsible.

"I acknowledge that for the average citizen, having heavily armed police officers attend your residence would be traumatic," wrote London, Ontario, police chief Steve Williams. "At the same time, the safety of our officers and members of the public cannot be compromised when responding to occurrences of this nature. I am thankful they effected the arrest without physical injury to anyone."

For larger streamers—and even some smaller ones, like Sorrenti—swatting is a sadly commonplace issue. During the same one-week span in which Sorrenti got swatted, so did three other prominent streamers: Twitch star Adin Ross, Call of Duty–focused Twitch streamer Nadia Amine, and YouTube streamer Darren "IShowSpeed" Watkins. In a video released in the aftermath, the former described his own experience as "traumatizing" and added that "it's a sick, cruel world we live in." For other streamers in this book, like Kaitlyn "Amouranth" Siragusa, swatting has become a fact of life. During a 2021 interview, she said it happens to her "multiple times weekly," to the point that she's on a first-name basis with local police.

Those creators—and numerous others—have legitimate cause for concern. In 2017, a swatting led to the death of a twenty-eight-year-old man, Andrew Finch, after a dispute over a Call of Duty match. The player responsible for the swatting, Casey Viner, was sentenced to fifteen months in prison; the man who made the call at his request, Tyler Barriss, received twenty years. Nonetheless, laws around swatting remain inconsistent and difficult to enforce due to the ease with which harassers can use software to spoof phone numbers and IP addresses, allowing them to call far outside their own localities and obscure their identities. Swatting is also a uniquely visible tactic, giving harassers the power to dramatically interrupt broadcasts such that viewers and streamers can't help but take notice. This makes it especially appealing to trolls who go after streamers, specifically.

Hasan "HasanAbi" Piker, the hugely popular news streamer from whom Sorrenti takes inspiration, did not even want to cover Sorrenti's swatting due to the aforementioned dynamic—one with which he has personal experience. During a stream shortly after, however, he relented in the face of audience pressure. But even then, he minced no words in explaining why he didn't plan to linger on the topic for long.

"I don't like to address this sort of shit ever," said Piker during his broadcast. "There's no way to deal with it, as the cops basically are admitting, even though it does take up resources from law enforcement, and they personally hate it. It doesn't matter. These [harassers] are extremely online, and they will do everything they can to continue making her life a living hell. Half of the places where they exist are places where they celebrate trying to get trans people to kill themselves. And the reason I didn't want to cover it is that this only galvanizes those people. They celebrate this as a fucking [win]. . . . It's a very weird predicament to be in, but the only way to get away from this sort of thing—this sort of mass-cyberstalking, mass-harassment campaign—is by hoping they move on to the next person. There's just no other way. That's it."

In their statement about Sorrenti's swatting, London, Ontario, police also addressed the issue of deadnaming, attributing it to the existence of prior records that referred to her by her old name. Williams said that though he was not privy to conversations that occurred when she was initially arrested, he reviewed footage of the time she spent in holding cells and did not find any instances of deadnaming. However, officers did use her deadname in relation to her possessions.

"It appears the bag in which Ms. Sorrenti's personal property was held was labeled with her deadname, for tracking purposes," Williams wrote. "I recognize this explanation will not please everybody. This situation highlights for us the need to develop a mechanism to ensure accuracy in our recordkeeping, recognizing that, as in Ms. Sorrenti's case, anything otherwise can be hurtful and disrespectful, which was never our intent."

In a later internal review, Williams reiterated his belief that officers "acted appropriately" given the information they were initially provided. He added that following Sorrenti's swatting and the resulting public outcry, London, Ontario, police implemented a system to "flag locations or persons who have been the subject of a previous swatting" as well as another to help officers when dealing with individuals who have legally changed their names.

That was far from the end of it, however. In the immediate aftermath of the swatting, Sorrenti moved to a nearby hotel, fearing for her safety in her own home. To let supporters know she was safe, she posted a picture of her ex's cat sitting on a hotel bed to her Discord channel. Harassers, she believes, used that image to figure out which hotel she was staying at. This time, instead of menacing her with police, they sent pizzas.

"They figured out from the stripes on the bedsheet what hotel it was, and pizzas started arriving in my deadname," said Sorrenti.

Sorrenti moved to another hotel under a pseudonym. This provided a brief reprieve.

"Getting two days to breathe and not have them on her trail did feel like [a lot]," said Barnett, who helped moderate Sorrenti's Twitch chat and aided in numerous other tasks while she attempted to flee from Kiwi Farms. Barnett was not alone: Grim as it might sound, fleeing from online harassers—like so many other elements of livestreaming—is a team effort. Sorrenti was aided on a regular basis by Barnett, Jay, friend and fellow creator Ellen "Ellen-FromNowOn" Murray, and a journalist named Arif Hasan. They moderated all her various public channels and, most crucially, kept an unflinching eye fixed on what Kiwi Farms and other doxxers were up to.

"To help with enduring the psychological damage of having to read that stuff, we created from our exec team a specialized team to follow [the Kiwi Farms thread about Sorrenti]," said Barnett. "We had our own Signal chat that Clara wasn't in because we wanted to freely post stuff from the thread, discuss it, analyze it, and filter the final thing if she needed to know something."

It was grueling work.

"The period of August 5 to August 24 was insane," said Sorrenti.

"It felt like six months," said Barnett.

During this span, said Sorrenti, Jay, and Barnett, all of Sorrenti's moderators got doxxed, somebody unsuccessfully attempted to swat Jay, and perhaps worst of all, another, more sophisticated doxxing group called Doxbin got involved. Doxbin proceeded to hack Sorrenti's Uber account, ordering over $100 of food to the second hotel she stayed at as a cheeky prank while using information contained within those accounts to obtain numerous addresses and phone numbers.

Sorrenti was backed into a corner, and the walls were closing in. Moreover, moving around repeatedly made it difficult for her to stream regularly, further endangering her income even after it had been temporarily bolstered by the GoFundMe campaign. At that point, she took stock of her life, and she didn't like where it seemed to be headed.

"I started feeling like no matter what happened, as long as Kiwi Farms was up, this was going to be my life," she said. "I had nothing else to fall back on, so I would have to accept that this was it."

"Or," she continued, "I could fight."

- - - - - - -

WHILE KIWI FARMS had sporadically attracted mainstream attention prior to 2022—most notably for being blocked in New Zealand in 2019 after republishing material related to the Christchurch shooting and refusing to comply with police requests—it largely benefited from existing on its own little slice of the internet outside the modern platform tapestry. Victims might make noise, but their cries remained quiet enough that those with the power to do something could just tune them out.

This goes part of the way toward explaining why Cloudflare—an online security provider whose services protected Kiwi Farms and made it load faster for users around the world—was able to bulwark the site while facing little pushback. The other part of that equation stems from how regular, non–terminally online people interact with the internet: Most of us might have a passing knowledge of what tech giants like Google, Facebook, and Amazon are up to, but underlying service providers like Cloudflare remain out of sight, out of mind. This despite the fact that, according to Cloudflare's own estimates, its services protect nearly *one-fifth* of all internet traffic.

By late August, Sorrenti's plight had garnered sustained interest from both press and concerned onlookers. It was around this time that Barnett came up with a plan.

"I woke up one morning, and Kiwi Farms was already trending [on Twitter]," they said. "I went into our Signal chat, and I was like, 'I don't think we're gonna get Cloudflare to drop them, but we can get attention on a hashtag right now.' I proposed #DropKiwiFarms and #CloudflareProtectsTerrorists I think was the other one."

Sorrenti, who had already tried directly asking Cloudflare CEO Matthew Prince via Twitter to cease doing business with Kiwi Farms, preferred #DropKiwiFarms. An hour later, she and her team were leading a campaign to get Kiwi Farms booted off Cloudflare—and any other service provider that would listen. Both hashtags ended up trending on Twitter.

But Sorrenti also had another, unstated goal: use the same combative brand that had riled up so many online personalities to draw out Kiwi Farms' worst tendencies. Sorrenti would act as a lightning rod, from which others could only look away at their own peril.

"With the swatting thing," said Sorrenti, "I thought I was gonna die anyway, so I was like, 'OK, bring it on. If they actually try and hurt me again, all I have to do is talk about it. I'll just use it as fuel in order to get other service providers to drop them.'"

She and her team did not, however, expect the viciousness or consistency of their retaliation.

"From when we started #DropKiwiFarms on August 24, the post rate in the thread [on Kiwi Farms about Sorrenti] sped up by, like, five times," said Barnett. "They went from, like, one thousand to two thousand pages in the space of four or five days."

By this point, Sorrenti had leaped countries entirely and fled from Canada to Northern Ireland, taking up residence in Murray's home. A mere forty-eight hours after Sorrenti's arrival, however, doxxers, likely from Doxbin, figured out Murray's address, seemingly by way of an unreported data leak from a business to which Murray had provided personal info in the past. They proceeded to drop a link into Sorrenti's Twitch chat that led to a picture of an unidentified individual standing outside of Murray's apartment holding a note referencing numerous near-indecipherable anti-trans memes, which prompted Murray to try to get ahead of a potential swatting by calling the police to explain what was going on.

According to Murray, thirty minutes later, a trio of police arrived at her apartment. Fortunately, the situation did not escalate, and Murray and Sorrenti were able to explain the situation to them with relative ease.

"Five or ten minutes in, [the police] were playing with my cats," Murray said.

The police, she said, agreed to flag her address and put extra patrols on duty in the area to be safe. Paul Bloomer, communications director for LGBT Police UK and an officer with the Northern Ireland police service, provided aid where he could, having briefly worked with Murray in the past on a project to help improve trans people's access to justice. He reached out to Murray's neighborhood inspector, with whom he'd also previously worked, to inform him about the situation. "[I told him], 'This isn't just some flame war on the internet,'" Bloomer said. "'This is quite serious.'" Bloomer was impressed by the degree to which the inspector had already "done his homework," resulting in increased patrols in Murray's area and officers who were briefed on the situation.

Days later, however, more police showed up at Murray's door, this time, apparently, because one of Sorrenti's harassers made a call through the Metropolitan Police in London, England. So Murray and Sorrenti explained the situation again—this time more quickly because they had experience, for better or worse.

"That got us an international flag on the apartment," said Murray.

With police both local and international aware of what was going on, additional swatting attempts on Murray's apartment proved fruitless. So harassers got creative. One day, when Murray was wrapping up a stream, she said she was going to try some poutine in Belfast, Northern Ireland.

"[A harasser] found all the places that sell poutine in Belfast and said they had planted bombs," said Barnett.

Bloomer also voiced awareness of this incident: "There was a bomb threat made," he said. "The guy who rung in the threat was a local guy. . . . Police I know did take action against him."

In response to threats both physical and virtual, Sorrenti expanded her support network even further. While in Ireland, she secured the services of Chelsea Manning, the trans whistleblower who was imprisoned from 2010 to 2017 after leaking classified US military and diplomatic documents to WikiLeaks: "I hired Chelsea Manning's security consulting firm," said Sorrenti. "It was so fucking surreal. We were both sitting on [Murray's] couch. She was [securing] my laptop when the BBC announced that the Queen died."

Within the same time frame, Kiwi Farms also evidently decided to pick on a high-profile target of an entirely different sort: United States representative Marjorie Taylor Greene, a far-right conspiracy theorist so infamous that said designation is, word-for-word, part of her Wikipedia entry (with multiple sources to back it up). Greene called for the site's removal after being swatted by somebody who claimed to be associated with Kiwi Farms. (Following the incident, the police said they received a call from a person using a computer-generated voice who said they attempted to swat Greene because of her stance on "transgender youth's rights.")

"Isn't it concerning that such a website exists?" Greene said in an interview with *Newsmax* at the time. "That website needs to be taken down. There should be no business or any kind of service where you can target your enemy."

In late August, Cloudflare CEO Prince and vice president Alissa Starzak published a lengthy blog post justifying the company's decision to continue providing services to Kiwi Farms and sites like it. While critics pointed out that Cloudflare had previously revoked security services from neo-Nazi site the Daily Stormer and notorious message board 8chan, Prince and Starzak said that "authoritarian regimes" ended up trying to convince Cloudflare to terminate services to human rights organizations using similar justifications. Ultimately they concluded that "the power to terminate security services for the sites was not a power Cloudflare should hold."

"Just as the telephone company doesn't terminate your line if you say awful, racist, bigoted things, we have concluded in consultation with politicians, policymakers, and experts that turning off security services because we think what you publish is despicable is the wrong policy," Prince and Starzak wrote. "To be clear, just because we did it in a limited set of cases before doesn't mean we were right when we did. Or that we will ever do it again."

However, just a few days later, in early September, Prince did a one-eighty, evidently recognizing what had been true all along: Kiwi Farms wasn't only trading in bigotry; its users were making violent threats.

"As Kiwi Farms has felt more threatened, they have reacted by being more threatening," Prince told the *Washington Post* at the time. "We think there is an imminent danger, and the pace at which law enforcement is able to respond to those threats we don't think is fast enough to keep up."

Following this decision, users of any Cloudflare services who tried to visit the site were greeted by a Cloudflare block page and a message: "Due to an imminent and emergency threat to human life, the content of this site is blocked from being accessed through Cloudflare's infrastructure."

At the time, Kiwi Farms effectively went offline, and Sorrenti and her team declared victory.

"The campaign is over. We won," she wrote in a statement on Twitter. "Many sites that have faced pressure campaigns to be deplatformed, like 8chan and Daily Stormer, are still online. They are nevertheless completely impotent. Whether or not we are able to completely remove Kiwi Farms from the internet is irrelevant to the fact that the goals of our campaign have not only been achieved, but have achieved more than we could have ever expected."

But this, still, was not the end. Nor did the end come after Kiwi Farms fled into the embraces of other service providers, like Russian company DDoS-Guard, only to be turned away following outcry from the #Drop KiwiFarms campaign. Nor did it come when the Internet Archive, which allows users to visit long-gone iterations of webpages, removed multiple instances of Kiwi Farms. And it certainly did not come around a month later, when Kiwi Farms found hosting and security services thanks to two companies notorious for keeping far-right sites afloat: VanwaTech and Epik. It is hard to know if the end will ever come. As of fall 2023, a group of online activists continued the fight against Kiwi Farms despite it being what the *Washington Post* called a "Sisyphean battle."

"Over the past year, their little group of internet sleuths, trans engineers, and activists has methodically chased Kiwi Farms across servers and networks around the globe, successively persuading more than two dozen companies to drop the site," wrote the *Post*'s Nitasha Tiku in a piece titled "The Endless Battle to Banish the World's Most Notorious Stalker Website." "Despite this laborious undertaking . . . the site has endured, showing up for months at a time, sometimes as a 'mirror' of itself on an entirely different URL or as a foreign domain in countries such as Poland."

- - - - - - -

IT'S OCTOBER 2022, and Sorrenti is at TwitchCon. Numerous crowds intersect and disentangle in the towering halls of the San Diego Convention Center. Some attendees walk at a leisurely pace, chatting with friends en route to an event or panel, or perhaps simply lunch. Others frantically follow their favorite creators, like ducklings waddling their tiny tails off to keep up with their mother. Sometimes these tiny worlds—pocket dimensions born of parasocial bonds—threaten to collide, bringing all foot traffic around them to a standstill. The space itself is open, but navigating it is akin to moving through a labyrinth. The walls are other people.

Sorrenti and her friends walk toward an escalator, down toward the show floor. Just before she gets on, however, a TwitchCon attendee pulls her aside. They recognized her through the crowd, they say, and they want an autograph. Initially taken aback, she decides to fulfill their request and send them on their way. Sorrenti, who began streaming near the peak of the pandemic and whose following only recently experienced exponential growth, is not used to this kind of treatment. Coming from a political activism background, she never expected to become a star.

Mild awkwardness, however, is much better than the alternative. Even at this moment, she moves around TwitchCon trailed by a security guard provided by the convention. Potential danger lurks around every corner. Kiwi Farms, even in its diminished state, remains a concern.

"She hung out with some smaller streamer friends at their Airbnb," says Barnett. "There was a video posted to her alternate Twitter account, and they assumed that's where she was staying. They said they could probably figure out where she was."

Their cyber-stalking never panned out, however, because Sorrenti did not divulge her real location—a nearby hotel—and doxxers wasted their time on a red herring. Even so, you might wonder why, after months of running, Sorrenti decided to make an appearance at such a public event. Isn't that asking for trouble? Sorrenti and her team don't think so. In a twisted sort of way, TwitchCon is just about the safest place on earth—for someone who is, specifically, at risk of getting swatted.

"Because it's Twitch, stalking, harassment, and swatting is something they're used to on the platform," Barnett says. "Immediately, you could reach out to them and say, 'This is the situation.' They understood and got security detail anytime she's in the venue."

But with threads on Kiwi Farms and Doxbin about her continuing to grow, the threat still feels present—as it has for months. Indeed, most users on sites like Kiwi Farms don't want their targets gone. They want to play with their prey.

– – – – – – –

"CAN I SHOW you my favorite one?" asks Sorrenti from her hotel bed, referring not to kind messages from supporters, but to a library of mean-spirited songs Kiwi Farms denizens have written about her. Unlike the more direct abuse and threats she's endured for the past few months, she finds these songs legitimately funny.

"Kiwi Farms can be really funny sometimes in the way they make fun of me," she says. "If they didn't dox me, I never would've gone after them."

"I love this song," Barnett adds with a chuckle. "Our brains are broken."

They play the song, an acoustic guitar ballad with surprisingly decent production and lyrics like "They all call him Keffals, the Twitch streamer tr***y. He's a massive Twitter addict." In response, Sorrenti chuckles and says, "So true." The song touches on pretty much everything Kiwi Farms uses to justify going after Sorrenti: that she's trans—which in their eyes means she's a groomer—that she used to be part of a Discord server called "Catboy Ranch," that ratios bigots online ("because he has no real-life skills"), and other, more vulgar observations. As the song plays, Sorrenti, Barnett, Jay, and Murray all laugh and quietly sing along.

"We've heard it a lot," says Barnett.

Sorrenti explains that Kiwi Farms users have created numerous "tributes" to her along these lines—memes, songs, videos, and works of fan fiction and fan art. In many ways, they act just like a fan group would, observing her every move and turning her life into the axis around which their entire community orbits. More so than even some of her biggest fans, they watch all her streams. Some of their more elaborate projects have clearly taken hours of work, if not days. The person who posted the song in question took time out of studying for exams to write and record it. It's akin to the way Dream's most obsessive stans rally around him, treating his every word and deed as gospel to be documented and added to some holy tome. Increasingly, hate mobs on platforms like Twitter, Discord, and YouTube behave almost indistinguishably from fans. There's a grim incentive structure underlying all of this: Coming together and assembling what feels like a big, important project is fun. Surrounded by like-minded individuals, doing so can even confer meaning. In a world that constantly deprives people of agency—of a chance to do anything other than work a boring job and try to make it through each gray day—it begins to resemble purpose.

But these aren't fans.

"It's weird," Sorrenti says. "It's, like, parasocial hatred."

Why, though? Why band together to torment somebody with such relentless dedication? Barnett believes it's because extremist online pipelines—platforms, videos, and creators that persuade people to embrace hateful ideology—often lead to lonely places.

"They get ostracized from everywhere," says Barnett. "This behavior on Kiwi Farms was the first thing that got them socially rewarded. That pulls these kids in. So like, the sixteen-year-old who did the song . . . just wasn't finding a home, but finally found a home with people who would accept him for this. And then he had to keep doing it to keep getting that same level of community acceptance. That's how groupthink happens."

There are also gimmick Twitter accounts, like one that keeps track of Sorrenti's hairline because some of her haters are convinced she's balding. Another Twitter account briefly pretended to be her (now-deceased) dad.

"It would post these deranged ramblings about how he was in hell," says Barnett.

"His penance was having to masturbate to me," says Sorrenti. "I was super upset at that, at the start."

When harassment was at a fever pitch, this dynamic led to a vicious cycle: Sorrenti, mentally and emotionally exhausted, would make a factual error or blow up at somebody on stream, and then Kiwi Farms would use her behavior to fuel the fires of their harassment. In effect, they would argue that she deserved it—even though *they* put her in a state that caused her to slip up or act out in the first place. Even things as simple as tweaks to her recounting of the day she got swatted became evidence that she deserved the harassment campaign.

"They'll say that initially in a video, she said that she woke up with a rifle pointed in her face," Barnett explains. "Then later she went into more detail and said the police came inside, barked orders at her, she walked out of her door, and right away there was a rifle pointed in her face."

Sorrenti's detractors position this as evidence that she's exaggerating or speaking disingenuously. She says it was just an expedited telling of a story with the same basic facts.

"Even in the other [less detailed] recounting, I still have a gun pointed at me," Sorrenti says.

At another point Sorrenti encountered another streamer scrolling through her Kiwi Farms thread on stream. She ended up chewing him out in front of a live Twitch audience.

"I was just always in this heightened state, like constantly on edge," says Sorrenti. "And people started portraying me like I'm insane because of it."

But now, a couple months later, she can laugh at songs that milk her entire history for pithy one-liners. It's the kind of turnaround with which victims of sustained harassment are sadly familiar: Eventually, to cope with the constant ugliness of it all, you just stop being able to feel anything beyond grim resignation and mild amusement.

"I'm fucking numb to this shit," says Sorrenti. "This is just normal. This is life."

- - - - - - -

SORRENTI WON A battle against Kiwi Farms, but the jury's still out on who's winning the war. Kiwi Farms remains online, albeit in a diminished state. Finding it through ubiquitous means like Google is significantly more difficult now that it's on less reputable infrastructure and has lost algorithmic placement in search results to countless articles about its own demise. But it continues to exist, as do arguably more unscrupulous, less easily baited sites like Doxbin.

"In the aftermath of the #DropKiwiFarms campaign, I know that while Kiwi Farms was down, it ruined a lot of their [search engine optimization]," said Erin Reed, a trans activist and legislative researcher who's been targeted by Kiwi Farms in the past. "As of now, my Google search results do not bring up Kiwi Farms unless you search a variety of specific things. That being said, I've heard from other people that were targeted that that's coming back and changing again."

Even taking into account the #DropKiwiFarms campaign's success, we're left with a question: Was it worth the cost? Natasha Tusikov, an associate professor of criminology in the Department of Social Science at York University in Toronto, does not think these sorts of public campaigns are a sustainable means by which to contain the internet's most virulent ills. Kiwi Farms—like 8chan and the Daily Stormer before it—managed to operate for years sans intervention, causing unquantifiable harm in the process. Moreover, when it came time to confront the beast dwelling in the internet's basement, the responsibility fell to its victims.

"There can be a good outcome: At least Cloudflare acted in the end," said Tusikov, who's written multiple pieces about the relationship between online hate and the structural forces that quietly enable it. "But it could have very easily ignored [the #DropKiwiFarms campaign] and just kind of ridden this out. And then what happens? There's this kind of small, ragtag group of people who, along with their other jobs and staying safe and producing content and feeding their families, also have to fight for their safety and lives."

"I had a friend who was targeted by Kiwi Farms [in 2015] and she asked me to monitor the Kiwi Farms thread on her," said Jack "Riverboatjack" Gardner, a trans Twitch streamer and acquaintance of Sorrenti. "And so I stayed up through the entire night watching in real time as these people picked apart a complete stranger's life in order to try and ruin it. It was horrifying. I think a lot of people kind of knew abstracts about Kiwi Farms before [Sorrenti] came around. It wasn't until she made herself a lightning rod that people were forced to look and reckon with what Kiwi Farms was actually doing."

Tusikov pointed to the way this situation echoed back to discoveries made by activists about PayPal, Airbnb, and other companies in the wake of the 2017 "Unite the Right" rally in Charlottesville, Virginia, which resulted in the death of a woman named Heather Heyer.

"It was revealed that many of the tech companies were pretty happy to take white supremacist money as long as they didn't suffer reputational damage," Tusikov said. "[For them] it was worth it when no one cared, but now it's no longer worth it."

The internet's history, she believes, is a natural origin point for this troubling dynamic: "The United States government preferred a very private sector–led commercial approach," she said. "You have early internet adopters and scholars and groups like the [Electronic Frontier Foundation] today taking very much a multi-stakeholder approach where the government should play a very light-touch role—that NGOs, especially American NGOs, and businesses should cooperate together."

"But," she continued, "what happens when companies themselves are the problem?"

Regulators, activists and online denizens have argued, must take a more prominent role in mitigating these issues.

"The answer to Kiwi Farms is not more speech, but . . . actually enforcing criminal laws against harassment and doxxing—and incitement to violence and death threats," said Tusikov. "I think this is one of the things we see whenever there's a move to regulate internet platforms: the fundamental conflicts between people who are arguing for a light touch, industry-led, civil society–led approach and people who argue that there needs to be more direct government intervention, even when that means government intervention into regulating speech."

Other victims of Kiwi Farms agree that trying to blanket the flames of doxxing and harassment with more speech simply isn't working. As an example Reed offered up another entity that made headlines around the same time as Kiwi Farms: a Twitter account called Libs of TikTok, which regularly (and baselessly) characterized specific LGBTQ programs at schools, hospitals, and other locations as on-ramps into grooming and pedophilia. This, especially once the account's posts gained traction within the right-wing news ecosystem, led to harassment and phoned-in threats at those locations, including bomb threats at Boston Children's Hospital and Children's National Hospital in Washington. On Twitter, however, Libs of TikTok persisted.

"I also think it's important that tech companies be held accountable for actions committed on their platforms and for hate speech that thrives on their platforms," said Reed. "The biggest example of this right now is Twitter itself with Elon Musk and how to treat accounts like Libs of TikTok that target LGBTQ people, hospitals, school administrators, etc., who receive violent bomb threats, death threats, and actual action. . . . We've seen some companies take a stand on this, but we've also seen some companies take a stand in the other direction—sites like Shopify have come out in favor of selling 'groomer' merchandise from Libs of TikTok, we've seen Elon Musk himself jump into Libs of TikTok's comments and replies."

With companies failing to consistently act in situations like these—despite real-world harm, in the cases of both Kiwi Farms and Libs of TikTok—it's clear that the responsibility cannot lie solely in their hands. But despite calls for change, Reed has yet to come across evidence that regulatory bodies in the United States view it as a pressing concern.

"I'm worried that no action is going to be taken," said Reed. "I'm worried that there aren't going to be anti-doxxing measures proposed in legislatures. We haven't seen much movement. . . . I haven't seen much activism around it in terms of legislative lobbying or anything like that."

Tusikov again believes that United States cultural norms hold stronger sway in this area than many of us realize. Germany, for example, enforces much stricter rules around how social media companies must moderate hate speech and threats, and even in Canada, as Tusikov explained, freedom of expression is a charter value—applied on a case-by-case basis—rather than "an absolute right."

"When we talk about the internet and some of these norms that big US companies like Cloudflare take, they have a very US-style footprint in terms of their legal and technical understandings," she said. "This conflicts with other preferences, like keeping people safe, respecting people's privacy, or protecting people from hate speech."

Gardner noted that despite a popular view of the internet informed by the First Amendment, specific elements of it are nonetheless heavily governed by laws—specifically, copyright laws and laws against sexually explicit conduct involving minors.

"All of us agree that there should be *some* type of regulation of speech on the internet," she said. "This is why we have agencies that will investigate and prosecute sites that distribute child pornography. . . . I feel like arguing that there's a slippery slope from [protecting trans and marginalized people] to some kind of internet surveillance state is nonsense. A slippery slope fallacy is not a reason to avoid protecting people who are being targeted with violence."

Tusikov believes the rusty gears of government are turning slowly, but they are turning.

"The interest is at least higher now," she said. "I think there's greater sensitivity among public policymakers. That's partly because, every few months, we're wracked by scandals, whether it's Nazis, whether it's Kiwi Farms, whether it's Twitter, or the implosion of cryptocurrency. We're seeing how these tech platforms are precarious, that they are interconnected. And as they collapse or implode, they take important parts of society [with them]."

- - - - - - -

IN FEBRUARY OF 2023, Sorrenti has settled into her new place. It took some time, she says. You don't just go back to feeling safe and sound in your own home—or any home, for that matter—after being trailed for months by a eplatforming days are over: "I don't feel like the main point of me making ontent anymore is feeling like I'm gonna change the world or something," he says. "Because I realized that if I do anything that serious again—if I try to et bad actors deplatformed in any way—people are going to just start up the ame thing that I went through, and I don't ever want that to happen again."

Sorrenti's guiding light of righteous fury has been replaced by a new an-mating force: bitterness. She feels betrayed even by members of the trans :ommunity, who in her estimation did not stick up for her when she stuck ner neck out. "But I had to keep moving forward, and I had to figure out how ι would move forward, so I ended up shifting away from covering anti-trans legislation," she explains. "Like, I want things to get better, but I don't think I'm going to be able to do it, and I don't feel like putting myself at risk."

Now she views herself less as a crusader and more as an entertainer, albeit one who still has a foot in the political arena. She's begun verbally sparring with political debate streamers for the drama it produces rather than for the purpose of achieving any lasting end. Where once she reviled so-called "debate bros" like the aforementioned Bonnell, now she at least understands why they create content the way that they do. To a degree, she's become part of their world.

"The algorithms reward me for fighting with people, and I have no way of getting out of that cycle. I basically have replaced getting into fights that I think are meaningful with getting into pointless slap fights because they're funny," she says. "I feel like I've gone from being an activist who streams to trying to be a soap opera character or something."

This edgier approach rubs some in and around Sorrenti's community the wrong way. In January and February, she has on-stream conversations with creators whose values seem to conflict with those she previously espoused—most notably Daniel "Keemstar" Keem, the infamous (but massively popu-lar) host of a show called *Drama Alert* on YouTube. In years prior, Keem had advocated in favor of causes like banning trans athletes from women's sports and echoed often baseless anti-trans narratives, but in January he announced that he would be boycotting a new *Harry Potter* game in light of author J.K. Rowling's transphobic stances. Sorrenti's conversation with Keem proves controversial even as she attempts to make him answer for his

militant mob. But now she at least has solid ground beneath her
in a perverse sense, that the worst case scenario has already co

"They already doxxed me, yeah," she says over the phone f
home. "I went live without putting up a room divider, and they
and [at another point] a bathroom mirror selfie. They were a
together based on the door and the mirror [the location of] th
that I live in."

But so far, nothing has come of it.

"It's a very secure building," she continues. "I also never [pub
about it because the funny thing is, the site's still up, but for th
they don't even care about me anymore. They've moved on. I'm
them attention, and there are other people they can target that a
get a rise out of. I'm so used to people constantly attacking me tha
really faze me that much anymore."

That's a glass-half-full perspective on what's not exactly a story
ing, and Sorrenti knows it. Ideally, there'd be something more a pe
do to escape pervasive online harassment than develop thick skin
the means to move into a secure building. Not everybody *can* d
this, for the time being, is the online ecosystem in which we live.

"This is how things are," Sorrenti says. "There's no way, on an i
level, to change this without the entire system burning."

Sorrenti has moved on from the idea of burning down the wh
herself. She's too worn down to bear the weight of the torch. For tw
following the Kiwi Farms saga, she says, she struggled to go live witho
a panic attack. At various points, she found herself drawn down the wl
corridors of self-destruction.

"I struggled with opiate addiction before, and [after getting ba
TwitchCon] I was in this fucked situation where I was depressed, I v
matized, and I had a lot of disposable income," Sorrenti says. "I was li
know what? I'm gonna do heroin.' My friend got so upset that they
flew up from Minneapolis and stayed with me for a month just to mak
was OK. I didn't end up doing heroin, which is good. Heroin is not very

That experience firmly front of mind, Sorrenti's rough and

checkered past, with Keem largely defending prior actions ranging from insensitive jokes to his treatment of Desmond "Etika" Amofah, a young gaming YouTuber who committed suicide in 2019 following prolonged mental health struggles. Shortly after, Sorrenti publishes a facetious YouTube video titled *I'm sorry. I will do better,* in which she pokes fun at the pervasive notion that she'd "platformed"—or given a meaningful viewership boost—to someone who "already has a platform that is a hundred times larger than mine."

"I'm looking over what the people are saying, and it seems that people really just want bigots to be able to say whatever they want. I didn't expect that from the trans community obviously, but I love you guys," she says in the video. "You're my community, and I want to do right by you. So I'm going to take accountability for my actions. From now on, I'm an entirely new Keffals. I promise you that."

Longtime fans find this funny, while other viewers take it as evidence that Sorrenti no longer has their back—that she collaborated with an individual as noxious as Keem to get a viewership boost of her own and feels no remorse about it.

Despite all of this, she seems confident in her new direction when we talk just a couple weeks later.

"There are a lot of ways everything affected me," she says of the Kiwi Farms saga. "But in some ways I feel a lot better. I don't feel like I have to prove anything to anyone. . . . I actually really enjoy what I do every day, even though it's less impactful. My day-to-day now is playing video games while I'm reacting to stuff and just hanging out and riffing with my chat. That's a lot more fun than just going through every fucked up thing that's happening to trans people on a systemic level every day."

- - - - - - -

AT THE END of February 2023, Sorrenti publicly announces that she's checking herself into rehab.

"In the next few days I will be admitted to rehab," she writes on Twitter. "I will be off social media for 30–45 days while I work on getting better. Thank you to all my friends, fans, and supporters for staying by my side and for all the kind words. To all the people who were harmed by my actions: I am deeply sorry. . . . I am a hurt person who was hurting other people, and I think it's time for me to break this cycle."

After wishing Sorrenti well via DM and receiving a short message of gratitude in reply, I don't hear from her again until the end of March. In a brief text back and forth, she says rehab served her well—not just in the sense that it helped curb her substance dependency, but also because she saw a therapist while there and was diagnosed with post-traumatic stress disorder, aka PTSD.

When we hop on a call in early April, it's clear that she's still in a delicate state. Her breathing is shallow. Her voice shakes as she describes what she's learned about herself over the course of yet another unprecedentedly tumultuous month—par for the course for her these days, but something to which one never fully adjusts.

"My friends convinced me to go to rehab because they found out I was planning to kill myself," she says.

She goes on to explain that she hadn't realized the degree to which PTSD pervaded every crack and crevice of her existence, nor did she understand its origins. Certainly getting swatted and stalked by an online mob played a role, but so did multiple abusive relationships going back to when she was a teenager, which she had not fully interrogated. She describes a years-long pattern in which she'd feel threatened and immediately enter a figurative combat stance, ready to come out swinging at the slightest sign of danger.

"I think I made a lot of the things that happened last year worse for myself without even realizing why or what was happening," she says. "The stuff with Kiwi Farms was a domino effect, all starting with getting into a fight with [Bonnell]. And I didn't need to get into that fight. . . . I definitely provoked him. And then when I found out that [Kiwi Farms' founder] was talking about me on his podcast, I provoked him, too."

"The way I'm seeing it now," she continues, "is if you get into a fistfight with someone and they pull out a knife and stab you, you're still the person who started the fight, even though they obviously did worse."

Even after Sorrenti's harassers allowed the mercurial winds of indiscriminate shittiness to blow them down a new path, she remained in fight-or-fight-harder mode. This led to the increasingly erratic behavior of late 2022 and early 2023 that put off some of her supporters.

"It never felt like conflict ended for me, and I just kept going and getting into fights with people for all sorts of fucking stupid reasons, just because nothing makes sense otherwise," she says. "If there's no conflict, then the way that I am doesn't feel like it makes any sense. . . . I just turned it around on my own community and my friends, and it was really stupid."

From a personal standpoint, it was Sorrenti's darkest hour. But perversely, her career had (almost) never been better: "That month that led to me going to rehab, I was doing coke and meth and Xanax and ketamine. It was a fucking mess," she says. "That was the second-best month I ever had financially from streaming. All my friends were turning against me, yet I still had people throwing a shit-ton of money at me and cheering me on. I was being incentivized to destroy my own life."

These days, everything is content. Sorrenti articulates this in the early goings of a year that would eventually see, among other things, large portions of the Twitch community on the edge of their seats watching Félix "xQc" Lengyel move between multiple cities amid a messy divorce and faltering mental health. If you're wondering where the line is, there isn't one.

Sorrenti is not ready to return to that world yet. But at least this time, she *recognizes* that she's not ready. "Before you called, I was trying to put out some sort of update for my fans," she says. "I spent two hours trying to record this four-minute video, but even briefly touching on the things that were happening, my heart was racing. I was freaking out. I'm just not ready."

In the meantime, she's doing her damnedest to turn a corner. Even out of rehab, she's in therapy twice a week. She's considering a future further removed from the immediacy of livestreaming: Perhaps, she supposes, she'll get into prerecorded video essays on YouTube. Or, if she resumes streaming, she'll plan out her broadcasts rather than doing her best Hasan Piker impression and grabbing links as she goes, an approach she deems "unhealthy" for herself. In the meantime, she's just looking forward to the next couple weeks. Her friends from the #DropKiwiFarms campaign are flying out to her city for a get-together, and then a handful of days later, she's beginning the process of another move—this time to Ireland. She's now in a relationship with Murray, her #DropKiwiFarms collaborator and close confidant, and she's en route to what she hopes will serve as a new beginning.

She still has one fight ahead of her, though: Later in April, she and her lawyer will file a human rights complaint against the London Police Service, which she contends has not made sufficient changes since the swatting in 2022. Her hope is that LPS will change its record management procedures to accommodate trans people and require personnel to undergo human rights training with a focus on the trans community and wear body cameras while interacting with trans civilians. She's also asking to be awarded $75,000 in damages and $50,000 for loss of income, according to the complaint.

"I've spent tens of thousands of dollars just on my own mental health," she tells me, saying that rehab alone cost $24,000. Paired with legal fees and money she lost while streaming sporadically or not at all, expenses quickly added up.

"Maybe if I was in a better place in my life, I could have thought of some sort of alternative," she says of her costly trip to rehab. "But I wasn't . . . Watching how bad my financial situation has gotten—especially post-rehab— scares the shit out of me. But I can't go back."

While the Sorrenti of old might have looked forward to this conflict in part for conflict's sake, the Sorrenti of now hopes she can keep legal fireworks to a minimum: "That's something I'm afraid of with coming back: I don't want my trauma to be content. I feel like that's a huge fucking trap to walk into," she says. "I'm just hoping I can rebuild my life in Ireland and the cops settle out of court. . . . I'm putting a lot of faith in the people I care about that things are going to be OK."

- - - - - - -

THERE IS A problem with Sorrenti's story. The broad strokes of it—she got swatted, deadnamed, and arrested; online trolls hacked her and tracked her around the world; she collected $100,000 from supporters hoping to help her fight the good fight; she lapsed into addiction and had to do some serious soul-searching before she was ready to return to the public eye—are measurably true. These events happened. Other people experienced them with her. There are receipts online, many of them left by those who tormented her.

But over the course of a couple years, the particulars of the story shift with each telling. Some of these things, like Sorrenti's recollection of the swatting, are relatively minor. She now claims to have purposefully truncated the tale to blow through the bullet points as quickly as possible. Does it really matter exactly how it started if she still ultimately wound up with a gun pointed at her? It's impossible to deny the whole unjustly-apprehended-by-police part, because even the police—rarely willing to publicly admit fault—fessed up to their role in the proceedings.

Over time, however, critics identify a larger pattern of unreliable narration, of actions whose true purposes only become clear via post-hoc justification. A few examples: Early on in Sorrenti's feud with Bonnell, she accused him of going way back with the founder of Kiwi Farms, only for fans to point out that she was incorrect. In response, she replied that she knew all along and was using the accusation as "bait" to draw a reply out of Bonnell. Then there was the swatting story, which also evolved over time—primarily with regards to when and how Sorrenti was deadnamed—to more closely match the police's account. Then there was Sorrenti's decision to publicly blanket-credit the lion's share of harassment against her to Kiwi Farms, even though it later became apparent that the most egregious actions—hacking, physical stalking—seemed to originate from Doxbin. Then there was a big part of the reason she fled to Ireland: not to escape from harassment, which she later declared that she purposefully turned herself into a "lightning rod" for the purposes of *attracting*, but to get away from an ex she deemed abusive.

Sorrenti's desire to keep some of this on the down low is understandable. The public doesn't have a right to somebody's private life just because that person is a streamer.

"I couldn't tell anyone," Sorrenti said during a stream of her decision to obscure the real reason she headed for Ireland after the swatting occurred. "I didn't want it to be a big thing. I didn't want it to be in the papers while all the journalists were circling around and writing their stories. I didn't want that to be known. I didn't want any of this to ever be out in public."

During additional streams and on Twitter, she held up a similarly personal prism to cast her decision-making around Doxbin in a new light. The site had files on her entire family, she explained, and she didn't want to draw attention to it. She figured she could instead use the situation to benefit the greater good by taking down Kiwi Farms, a better-known and more reviled (though perhaps less dangerous) threat.

"I don't think the momentum is there for that," she later said during a stream, in response to the idea that she should have targeted Doxbin instead of Kiwi Farms. "With the #DropKiwiFarms campaign, it was just really opportune timing. I had all this media attention on me, and journalists were following every fucking thing I said and did. I didn't even know about the second website until they went after me."

Sorrenti was in an unprecedented situation. It makes sense that she'd screw up some of the steps to a dance nobody had ever done before. But both before and after the Kiwi Farms campaign, she demonstrated a willingness to plant falsehoods in service of a larger goal—of allowing the ends to justify the means. If you do that for a long enough time, with a live audience hanging on your every word, your house of cards is eventually going to start looking awfully wobbly.

Sorrenti's reputation is not helped by what has become the lynchpin in people's skepticism of her: At the start of all of this, she collected over $100,000 CAD from supporters and sympathizers. Ever since—sometimes fairly, other times unfairly—she's been dogged by questions about where exactly the money went. She has proven unwilling to provide a precise breakdown, saying on Twitter that "because I'm not providing a product to investors, I won't be sharing expense breakdowns" and adding that she's "been advised by lawyers to keep everything close to the vest for legal and safety reasons."

A chunk of the money was earmarked—and presumably used for—moving, including replacing devices taken (and later returned) by the police and paying off a year's worth of rent. The rest was meant to go "directly to my legal fund, which I will be using to seek justice," according to Sorrenti's GoFundMe page. At various points, this has, in Sorrenti's words, meant going after both specific Kiwi Farms users and the police. During this time, she has put together multiple high-quality streaming setups, paid rent on an expensive apartment, struggled with addiction, and done a costly stint in rehab, though she balks at the suggestion that her drug habit claimed whatever remains of her legal account.

"There's this viral clip where they accuse me of spending the entire GoFundMe on cocaine," she says to me after her time in rehab. "One hundred thousand dollars Canadian on cocaine like fucking Pablo Escobar."

Critics, however, take her lack of transparency as a tacit admission of foul play, especially as screenshots begin to circulate purporting to show Sorrenti conversing with collaborators all the way back in November 2022 about having spent an alarming amount of the GoFundMe money.

"Feels really bad watching the GFM deplete," Sorrenti says in one of the screenshots, which comes from an "Editing & Video Production" group chat she used in 2022. "The rest will cover a year rent and my psych fees if I talk to a psychologist once a week for the next 11 months. . . . I keep trying to think of how it depleted so fast, and it's just so many little things. Travel and replacing furniture and helping my friends out and buying new streaming gear and clothes."

In the chat, Sorrenti's collaborators reassure her, saying that it was an emergency fund, and these things happen. It's unreasonable, after all, to expect perfection from somebody under extreme duress. However, over a year later, a former video editor—who requested anonymity out of concern over the many, demonstrated downsides of being part of a controversy in this corner of the streaming world—nonetheless chooses to leak the chat log. After I verify the screenshot's veracity by requesting to view pay stubs that proved Sorrenti had employed the former editor during the aforementioned late-2022 time frame, they explain why they decided to publicize that Sorrenti had spent the money in ways supporters might find objectionable.

"[In 2022] I was worried about the potential negative reactions of other people in that shared social circle towards the breaching of trust of a highly respected community figure, and [I was also worried about] potentially aiding in giving ammunition to opposing political interests," the former editor says. "I also—perhaps delusionally—held out hope that she would eventually use some of her money to pursue legal action against the London Police and make good on the promises laid out in her original GoFundMe statement. However, over a year down the road, I have witnessed a slew of other unethical and unsavory behaviors from Keffals, combined with her general unwillingness to apologize or otherwise reform those negative behaviors."

Speaking to me after the screenshots of her DMs gained traction online, Sorrenti confesses that they are real. She stands by her actions, however.

"I was concerned that people would be upset that my GoFundMe money had already been drained. That's probably true of anyone who has received charity. But that doesn't mean I used the money irresponsibly," she says. "The GoFundMe established several uses for the money, which included moving expenses, equipment expenses, and legal expenses. The GoFundMe also mentioned limitations like my emotional trauma and persistent safety concerns. Those concerns still exist. Just last month someone posted a video of themselves standing outside my apartment to my community's subreddit."

Thus, she says, the need for everything she spent the money on: a move to another country, an expensive apartment with security, the services of a cybersecurity firm, backup equipment even though the police returned the equipment they'd taken from her, multiple lawyers, and so on. At this point, though, it's proven to be far more trouble than it's worth.

"In all honesty, I wish I never got the money to begin with," Sorrenti says. "I wish I was never swatted. My life has only become worse because of it, and I wish I could make people understand how much pain all of this has brought me."

On Sorrenti's end, no legal challenge materializes until the 2023 human rights complaint against the London Police Service. The complaint continues Sorrenti's pattern of not outright changing a story, but brushing up against the limits of what constitutes a more detailed retelling. "At the time of the arrest," a section of the complaint alleges, "one officer pressed her hand against Ms. Sorrenti['s] breast and said, 'Yep, it's a she.'" This is a bombshell, fans and critics alike remark—one it's surprising Sorrenti has never dropped before in her dozens of hours of talking about the swatting.

In response, London Police launch another internal investigation and find "no evidence of misconduct."

Then a year passes, and nothing further comes of Sorrenti's human rights complaint. Critics begin to suspect that it has fallen by the wayside. But after a period of silence on the matter, Sorrenti claims in 2024 that the case is tangled up in bureaucracy.

"Papers have been processed, and we are awaiting dates to appear in the [Human Rights Tribunal of Ontario]," she says on Twitter. "I'm told this could take a minimum of two years at best and six years at worst depending on if this gets escalated to a higher judicial body."

Following further accusations of dishonesty—largely based on a section of the Human Rights Legal Support Centre's website that says the Tribunal's "goal" is to hold a hearing within a year of an application being filed—Sorrenti's lawyer, Justin Anisman, gives a similar account of what's causing the holdup.

"The Tribunal these days is so extremely backed up," he tells me, a claim which is supported by public records of recent Tribunal cases, the original filings for most of which date back to years between 2016 and 2022. "There's, like, five-year delays for any hearings. There's been a lack of appointments for arbitrators. So it's funny to see people quote the mission statement to have things handled as quickly as possible and within one year. . . . I don't anticipate hearing back from them this year."

Not long after, Sorrenti privately tells me the plan has changed, or maybe taken on a form more akin to its original shape, when she hoped the police would decide to settle out of court.

"I talked with my lawyer," she says, "and we are waiting . . . to schedule a mediation with the London Police Service. Basically, it would be a process of coming to a mutual agreement with the police rather than a long, drawn-out legal battle that could last for several years."

Sorrenti, obviously, is not the only one who's begun to feel impatient. At this point, people want justice of a different sort than they put their voices and wallets behind years ago—not so much for Sorrenti, but rather for their own investment in her and her character. Sorrenti insists that they'll have it, but time will tell. Unfortunately, time is not on her side anymore, and it's beginning to look like she's lost the crowd, as well.

- - - - - - -

DESPITE SORRENTI'S APPARENT wishes, 2023 and 2024 see her embroiled in more online drama than ever. She feuds with Hasan "HasanAbi" Piker and other leftist content creators. She feuds with Daniel "Keemstar" Keem on multiple occasions. She feuds with a large portion of the online commentariot when she chooses to publicly defend YouTuber and longtime friend Ian "Vaush" Kochinski in the face of "loli porn" accusations, a saga so lengthy, convoluted, and full of cameos from just about every even slightly politically oriented content creator that it could fill a book of its own. She finds kinship with former foes like Steven "Destiny" Bonnell. Popular YouTuber Mutahar "SomeOrdinaryGamers" Anas repeatedly spars with Sorrenti and ultimately publishes a video that half attempts to hold her accountable for her habit of half-truths and half tries to smear her. The video pulls in over 1 million views. Sorrenti's audience begins to grow tired of all the twists and turns.

"I genuinely have loved watching her, but recently I just can't," said one fan on Sorrenti's subreddit. "The vague [YouTube video] titles with such negative and dramatic names make it hard to want to watch. . . . It feels like she's going down a drama spiral. Obviously she doesn't have to change just because I feel this way. I know it's my personal issue. It's just getting exhausting."

"It always made me laugh how Keffals would say 'I'm done with drama content' every couple months then a week later make some callout video about some random nobody communist," said another fan. "I don't think Keffals is mature enough to handle the position that so many creators would kill for. . . . All that's left is a community of disheartened fans who will slowly leave one by one. It's sad, really, but I think it's for the best. Keffals was not meant for this life."

Arguably, few are. Content creation—and especially leftist political content creation—is a realm in which the snake eats its own tail on a near-daily basis. Even creators who do their best to educate viewers on the issues of the day regularly get caught up in niche drama and inter-factional conflict, making videos and hosting streams about personal grudges nearly as much as they dig into matters of actual import. This is not entirely their fault; algorithms on platforms like YouTube and Twitter thrive on engagement, and nothing gets people more engaged than drama. Twitch is a great place to host lengthier discussions of the drama of the day, which creators and fans can then cut into clips for YouTube. It all filters up. Drama, no matter where you are, often equals views. The same combative impulses that made Sorrenti the ideal person to deal a withering blow to Kiwi Farms also, over time, turned her into an incendiary, exaggeration-prone pundit. The modern platform ecosystem is designed to siphon people's energy away from more productive outlets and transform it into content—to fuel an engine whose only real purpose is to continue consuming fuel. There's more to life than online arguments, but you wouldn't know it from looking at the internet.

I ask Sorrenti why she continues to turn herself into grist for the content mill. Why not, after all this trouble, seek out greener pastures?

"Honestly? I burnt most of my connections from how I acted during the period before I went to rehab," she replies. "Before livestreaming, I was on disability for nearly a decade because of a combination of mental and physical health problems. I managed to luck into a position of getting myself out of poverty with livestreaming, and I don't think I have other options. If I could figure out how to find something to pay my bills without ever having to hit the 'go live' button again, I absolutely would, but I don't know how I'd even go about it. Now I'm in a position where I need [a certain] amount of money in my bank account before the end of the year or I can't renew my visa, then I have to leave Ireland."

Sorrenti tries to turn over yet another new leaf, launching a horror and mystery YouTube channel called Scared Awake. Months after launch, videos with names like *The Paris Catacombs | Scariest Places on Earth* and *The Russian Sleep Experiment | Creepypasta Series* fail to clear ten thousand views. Her most recent video about the Kochinski drama, released within the same time frame, is at nearly one hundred thousand. Sorrenti is a cog in a machine that's difficult to break away from, but following the latest round of drama, she does, at least, seem to see it. She proceeds to take a months-long break from content creation. When she returns, maybe she'll change for real. Or perhaps this is just the same old cycle beginning anew.

"I owe a lot of people apologies for my past actions," Sorrenti says on Twitter in response to accusations that she'd harassed a smaller creator. "I think the drama side of content creation encourages harassment and obsessive behavior that make you a worse person. I fell into the trap of making drama content and engaging in the same behaviors people have used to hurt me. I deeply regret it, and I'm sorry to those I've hurt."

chapter nine

solidarity

Even in a room full of influencers, Hasan "HasanAbi" Piker stands out. The beginning of 2020 would prove pivotal for both Piker and, notably, all of humanity. Los Angeles's biggest content creators have converged on the newly christened compound of 100 Thieves, an esports and lifestyle organization that, even by this point, has already started to lean more latter than former. Its high-ceilinged, white-walled interior teems with YouTubers, streamers, esports players, and industry figures of all shapes and sizes. The crowd spills out onto a back court intended for regular, non-esports, where throngs of drunk influencers sloppily lob basketballs at a hoop.

One towers above all the rest. Soon, he will do so in terms of relevance, ascending into the ranks of Twitch's most-watched streamers and getting singled out by the likes of United States representative Alexandria Ocasio-Cortez (in a good way) and Fox News (in a bad way). But not yet. For now, it's mainly because he's really, really tall. He's also built like a brick house constructed by the Incredible Hulk, with arms as thick as legs and legs as thick as torsos. Even if you don't know quite *who* you're seeing, you'll absolutely see him.

At the end of the night, as streamers stream out of the compound, I work up the nerve to approach Piker. I tell him I'd like shadow him for a book I'm working on about livestreaming. A creator who's managed to quickly amass over two hundred thousand followers talking about politics on a video game website, Piker would seem to be an ideal subject for such a project. Nobody else, I explain, is doing something like this—or at least, nobody else is making it work.

Piker hesitates. Despite already broadcasting to thousands of people per day, he doesn't want the kind of attention mainstream reporting would bring yet. He wants to cultivate a community at his own pace, he says, before flinging open the doors and letting the world see. He wants to build a space that won't immediately be overtaken by far-right trolls, men's rights activists, and endlessly heckling haters. He wants to accomplish all of this while openly advocating for socialism—not exactly an uncontroversial stance in the good old U. S. of A.

Nonetheless, Piker has a plan, and it's clear he wants to do it his way. He *will* do it his way, no matter who tries to force him off course.

But, oh, they will try.

- - - - - - -

DESPITE A CAREER focused on United States politics, Piker spent most of his childhood in Turkey. And despite popular misconceptions about the intent of his political ideology, he feels no need to mythologize himself as the main character of a rags-to-riches tale—or a rags-to-rags tale, as critics regularly posit should be his ultimate goal. Instead, he says during a December 2022 interview from his home, he grew up "relatively affluent" in Turkey after being born in the United States. A switch from private to public school in fourth grade opened his eyes to the cruel realities undergirding modern society.

"I saw the gardener's kid going to the same school as myself, right? And I was like, 'Holy shit, these dudes are not living the same way that I am.' I was taking this for granted," Piker says. "And that is where I started realizing that there was something weird about the way that we existed on this planet."

Other bits and pieces of a childhood in Turkey further informed Piker's nascent political views. After former Turkish Prime Minister and current

President Recep Tayyip Erdoğan came to power, Piker found himself frustrated even by "silly" impacts of a socially conservative regime like Erdoğan's suing his favorite political satire magazine because of imagery he found objectionable.

"I thought that it was unacceptable for someone in a position of power to do such a thing," Piker says.

During his early years, Piker's parents would bring him on summer trips to America, but it wasn't until college that he moved to the United States. This proved to be an eye-opening experience on several levels.

"He was so shocked," says his mother, Sedef Piker. "He said, 'I can't believe these kids, Mom. They're bored.' . . . They had everything that all these people around the world would dream of, and they were bored."

The more Piker observed, however, the more he realized the problem wasn't the people. It was that this supposed land of plenty was not providing for those with less. The American healthcare system, he says, ultimately served as the "final" rung on his ladder to leftism.

"I grew up in a different part of the world where I saw not the immediate impacts of American imperialism, but the secondary shock waves," Piker says. "But then seeing that this service that should be afforded to every single person unconditionally was paywalled—it was really insane. That was definitely the final straw for me to really tilt over in the anti-capitalist direction."

And so, Piker embraced socialism, a political ideology that encompasses a wide range of social and economic beliefs, but which fundamentally argues that workers or a central governing body should control the means of production—aka buildings and tools that create basic necessities, goods, and services—instead of private companies which generally prioritize profit above all else. Socialists like Piker believe more of the benefits of collective labor should be going to individual workers, rather than companies and bosses who rarely, if ever, do the lion's share of the work. Socialists in the United States are often critical of both the Republican and Democratic parties, both of which they argue continually prop up corporate interests even on rare occasions when their rhetoric suggests otherwise. Proponents of socialism often push for socialized systems like universal healthcare and a universal basic income, arguing that a society truly for and by the people should meet everyone's basic needs.

Piker's path to Twitch was a little more circuitous than his one to socialism. He grew up playing pirated video games in Turkey, where legit copies of big hits were hard to come by. For a time, games functioned as his north star; he regularly drew video game characters and aspired to become an illustrator for a video game developer. But Piker went on to abandon that hobby after his first year of college. Even during his self-described "normie" years, however, he maintained a familiarity with the gaming space.

After college, Piker ended up getting a job with *The Young Turks*, a progressive-leaning online news program founded by his uncle, Cenk Uygur. Around this time, in 2014, a right-leaning reactionary movement within video games called Gamergate began to take off on platforms like Twitter, Facebook, and YouTube. Piker, who was producing leftist commentary videos for *The Young Turks*, found himself sharing online real estate with a movement that would go on to pioneer tactics and produce stars for the alt-right.

"I saw the YouTube commentary space infested with these neckbearded weirdos that were super right wing," says Piker. "I mean, they fucking hated me. They were not fond of me at all. They were not fond of *The Young Turks*. They were blowing up. They were gaining a lot of prominence. And a lot of gamers were being radicalized by these commentators that made themselves out to be centrists but clearly weren't."

On the other side of the political spectrum, Piker was finding success with a Facebook show he'd created called *Breakdown*, in which he took a punchy, crunchy approach to analyzing buzzy topics like millennial entitlement and Trump's Muslim ban. But after a while, he began to feel he was hitting a ceiling.

"[Piker] is kind of irrepressible, I think is the right way to describe it," says Uygur, Piker's former boss and current/always uncle. "As soon as he's doing great on Facebook, he's thinking, 'Oh, I gotta expand to a different thing that will give me a different skill set and bring in new eyes.'"

Piker largely concurs with that characterization of events—with the caveat that his uncle's company wasn't paying him enough.

"They basically got other hosts on [*Breakdown*] instead of giving me more money to work with," says Piker. "I had no control over that, and I felt that I was always gonna be in my uncle's shadow no matter what, if I stayed there. . . . And I wanted to get better at speaking off the cuff, because I was horrible at it."

Piker wanted to build a living, breathing community, one united around his principles. He felt that in order to accomplish his goal, he'd need to meet people where they were at—not where po-faced political scholars wanted them to be.

"I wanted to show people authentically that you can be leftist and have fun," says Piker. "It doesn't have to be about constantly woke-scolding people and appearing as the biggest joy killer, as though having fun is actually bourgeois decadence."

Others who've followed in Piker's wake, like a smaller leftist Twitch streamer named Michael "Mike from PA" Beyer, see this as a core element of his appeal.

"[Piker] is, in his person, a refutation of a lot of the stereotypes of the left, right? He is a large, strong, attractive, funny guy who you want to be friends with, but he also has the values of the left," says Beyer, who has previously collaborated with Piker. "He can just refute, in himself, a lot of the stereotypes about soy boy blue-haired cringe—you know, [the idea that] if you vote for the liberals, they won't let you laugh at jokes. He just refutes all of that instantly."

Marcus "DJWheat" Graham, a streamer since the earliest days of the medium and a broadcast journalism major before that, sees in Piker a continuation not just of irreverent political pundits like Jon Stewart but also shock jocks like Howard Stern. Piker is unafraid to communicate complex points using vulgar language. If a viewer comes at him with an idea he finds odious or unsavory, he's just as likely to make a joke about sleeping with their mom as he is to boot them from chat (often he'll do both).

"[Shock jock humor] is always gonna be an entertaining style of content," says Graham. "I think that it transforms and shifts a little bit over time, where you look at the shock jocks of even twenty years ago whether it's on radio or whatever, and there's a lot of misogyny, there's a lot of homophobia, there's a lot of shock for the wrong reasons. I think the shock jocks of today are more creative and clever. It's not just about being a bunch of degenerates. . . . You've got [Piker], who is kind of a shock jock. Definitely in a political world knows how to talk about things in a different way—the way he presents his position and so on."

Piker only really found himself on his current course following the 2018 *Fortnite* boom. Alongside millions of other people, he watched then-Twitch kingpin Tyler "Ninja" Blevins play the sensationally popular battle royale game with rap superstar Drake, and everything clicked into place: He *needed* to be on Twitch. He was already playing *Fortnite* for hours each day, and he was doing so with journalists and podcasters like the hosts of the leftist show *Chapo Trap House*, who similarly endeavored to change people's preconceived notions of leftism by embracing an edgier vibe. Why not broadcast it?

"I could play *Fortnite* and have these conversations that can make for entertaining and interesting commentary," says Piker. "So I strapped a [camera] to my PlayStation 4 and started streaming. I got seventeen people my first stream. Thirty-five people [after that]. . . . And that's how I started in the space."

- - - - - - -

PIKER DID NOT want his Twitch channel to grow explosively—at least, not at first. He'd watched gaming communities, forums, and subreddits get overrun by alt-right elements, and he came to understand the delicate ecosystem that is a new online community. After all, it only takes a handful of loud, determined bad actors to chase away hundreds or thousands of well-meaning individuals. Think of it like going to a bar where somebody's violently drunk or a restaurant with several screaming babies; if you encounter the same unpleasant disruption a few times in a row, you're probably going to give up on coming back.

"I didn't want to be mentioned in mainstream spaces because that opens my community growth," says Piker when I ask him about that interaction. "That changes the speed."

Growing at a deliberate pace allowed Piker to be more hands-on in curating his community. Like other streamers, he relied on moderators to put the riffraff in time-out—or ban them outright—but he also gained a reputation for wading into the muck himself. To this day, Piker pretty regularly calls out chatters who habitually disrupt the flow of conversation or are clearly trying to egg him on. *Consistently* making examples of the worst of the worst, he believes, has allowed him to create an environment in which he's able to actually engage with chat, unlike many other streamers of his size.

"I think that's why I've been able to navigate through the space and maintain a community of thirty to forty thousand—sometimes a hundred and fifty thousand—people [simultaneously]," says Piker, "where I can still have a back-and-forth conversation with anyone and everyone and do that in a productive manner while I'm talking about risky things that most streamers would never even consider talking about."

Members of Piker's community agree with this assessment.

"Even for a Twitch streamer, [Piker]'s intense about keeping up with his chat," says Salem Saberhagen, a fan who runs a popular Piker meme account on Instagram called "Hasanabiposting." "Fifty thousand people can be watching, chat whizzing by, and he'll catch one of us joking, asking questions, or talking shit. And of course the odds of him *actually* going back and forth with chatters makes them even more eager to interact. It tickles this little social need inside all of us, I think, for better or worse."

By many measures, Piker grew quickly despite his best efforts to keep everybody from piling into the pool at once, even in 2019 and early 2020 when he was establishing himself. Regular audiences of hundreds grew to audiences of thousands. In early 2019 he had fewer than thirty thousand Twitch followers. By the same time the next year, he had over two hundred thousand. He couldn't maintain his oasis forever.

Before long, Piker and *The Young Turks* came to what Uygur calls a "mutual decision" to separate due to both Piker's desire for independence and the potential for his unconstrained commentary to be associated with *The Young Turks*. Working outside the bounds of mainstream media but still running a more traditional network than Piker, Uygur now believes his nephew's ascent was inevitable.

"*The Young Turks*, we're not as large as the mainstream media, but we don't get the same leeway [as Piker] because we still have to be cognizant of advertisers generally and other companies," he says. "When you're a one-man shop on Twitch, you can say not only the things that are true like we do, but you can say it in the irreverent way that audiences and especially young audiences connect to. And so a guy like [Piker] was bound to arise. He's just particularly adept at it, so he was the perfect guy for the perfect time."

By the time 2020 rolled around, Twitch audiences began to regard Piker not just as a worthwhile follow, but as indispensable viewing. This is because, in a year of pandemic- and election-borne unpredictability, he did not simply report the news. Instead, he cut through the clutter—curated the chaos— in a distinctly modern fashion. Instead of reading off a teleprompter or argu- ing with talking heads, he pulled information from a variety of sources, web browser bristling with links to breaking news on Twitter and YouTube, as well as networks like CNN and Fox News. He used the same tools any of us might have access to, and viewers saw what he saw: His web browser, a chat panel, and a video feed of Piker himself. There was nothing fancy about it, but that was part of the appeal: Piker effectively showed his work, earning more immediate trust than the distant, suit-clad anchors on mainstream networks. And if somebody doubted him, they could say as much in chat, at which point he'd either throw down with them (verbally, of course) or correct the record.

As *Vice* put it in a piece about Piker's coverage of the 2020 presidential election: "While your parents were most likely watching CNN's John King tap around an electoral map on a giant touchscreen, Piker sorted through exit polls and early reporting the same way I did: clicking frantically between tabs of different news sites, YouTube streams, and various chats. Last night I watched Piker and his guests play for time as he clicked on the wrong tab in his disorganized browser at least three times. I saw myself, and the way that I engage with politics and the news, in not just Piker's political opinions but the way he uses the internet itself. . . . Piker is able to identify and discuss that politician's tweet, the way that reporters analyze the news and comment on it in articles and on social media, and the raw polling data in a way that helps explain our current moment—and he does it in a way that makes politics legible and understandable, even at its most cruel and confusing."

Beyer believes old news media institutions are crumbling away precisely because they failed to take advantage of the sorts of tools to which Piker and himself have access.

"If there's breaking news, I have four thousand people watching [in chat]," says Beyer. "Someone could bring me official stuff right away. I can also [take] that information that people are getting to me and try to teach my audience how to be less susceptible to fake news—to be skeptical and how to interpret information and look at sources and who's saying things. And so I think the generation gap is the biggest reason that old forms of media are dying, because they don't take advantage of the opportunities and they don't provide the interactivity which I think the younger generations want from their content."

Moreover, Piker provided context through a coherent lens: The systems we've relied upon for decades, he posited, are failing us because they're built to turn a quick and dirty profit—not to last. This positioned him as a refreshing alternative to mainstream news in the eyes of fed-up millennials and zoomers; where even liberal networks were, at most, only willing to tickle at the idea that the capitalist status quo might be failing the broader populace, Piker made that case on no uncertain terms every single day. For viewers, it was like having a doctor finally diagnose a sickness after years of being told nothing was wrong. There was a relief in finding someone who could tell them, effectively, that they were not crazy.

This, in part, is why Piker is able to perform the herculean task of functioning as a hybrid political commentator/news network for eight-plus hours per day: The principal characters might change, but the underlying causes of America's biggest problems remain the same.

"I have a worldview and a foundation that I've built on what I believe in and what I want to say about any particular subject. The way things are in America and all around the world, really, is that these systems of oppression don't necessarily change," says Piker. "Sometimes I'll pull up a video from 2016, and I'll be like, 'This is the exact same thing I said in 2016 about abortion.' And unfortunately, it's still the exact same thing I would say about abortion, police brutality, labor rights, wealth inequality—you name it. None of those issues have been solved. So I already have a lot of things that I have said and a lot of things I believe that I find myself repeating."

This is not to say that Piker is infallible, nor does he regard himself that way. He regularly tells viewers that he's just a normal guy and that if he can grasp a concept, anybody can. The rest is a collective effort. In some cases, he leans on his chat—far more media-literate than the average band of Twitch viewers—to pull up and fact-check information. Oftentimes, though, he trusts the expertise of traditional journalists.

"There's a lot legacy media still does that someone like myself will never do," says Piker. "In my opinion, they should never do op-ed stuff. They should keep doing journalism instead—good journalism—because that is the most important part of their job. Whether I agree with them or not, whether I agree with publishers or not, whether I yell about the *New York Times* or the *Washington Post* regularly, it doesn't change the reality that they're still doing something that is necessary and incredibly important."

- - - - - - -

"BIG SHOUT-OUT TO [Piker], because he really helped wrangle all of this together," says United States representative Alexandria Ocasio-Cortez to hundreds of thousands of Twitch viewers.

It's October 2020, and the democratic-socialist superstar is about to start sussing out impostors in a deception-centric multiplayer game called *Among Us*. She's surrounded on all (digital) sides by Twitch and YouTube royalty: Imane "Pokimane" Anys, Charles "Moistcr1tikal" White, Jeremy "Disguised Toast" Wang, Rachell "Valkyrae" Hofstetter, and Seán "Jacksepticeye" McLoughlin, to name a few. A year or two prior, this would have been unthinkable. A day or two before, it *still* would've sounded awfully far-fetched. But it's happening, all because AOC tweeted, "Anyone want to play *Among Us* with me on Twitch to get out the vote?" and Piker took her up on it.

Twenty-four hours later—following a frenzied mobilization on the parts of Twitch, big names like Piker and Anys, AOC's team, and experts in the fields of streaming and content moderation with whom they collaborated—AOC has a custom-made Twitch channel, hundreds of thousands of Twitch followers, and top-of-the-line streaming equipment. Alongside fellow representative Ilhan Omar and the aforementioned stars, she goes live to raucous applause, peaking at 439,000 concurrent viewers. At the time, this means her first stream is Twitch's third most concurrently viewed ever.

Avengers crossover event–level cast aside, it plays out like a pretty standard *Among Us* stream. Players run around a spaceship while a disguised "impostor" tries to quietly kill them off one by one. Galaxy-brained deliberation and deception ensues. Piker, AOC, and the others bicker, yell, and laugh. Nobody makes any impassioned political speeches or debates an ideological rival into submission. There's some light discussion of the importance of voting, but otherwise conversation mostly focuses on the game. Chat, meanwhile, is carefully moderated, with harassing and violent comments quickly zapped out of existence. There are some drive-by political arguments, but this is intentional, according to Frogan (who has not divulged her full name), a public health expert and former moderator for Piker who's since become a popular streamer in her own right.

"[Piker's] mods were asked to mod for AOC when she streamed on Twitch because we are the only moderators that really have the political knowledge to moderate that capacity of a political figure—especially a leftist political figure," she says. "Since [AOC] is a prominent political figure, we weren't allowed to ban people. We were only allowed to time people out. And a lot of people don't like her. And then if there were any threats, we had to escalate them and report them—which there were quite a few. It was insane."

Much of that, however, happens behind the scenes. The resulting sense of normalcy is what viewers love about the broadcast. While other politicians like Bernie Sanders and Donald Trump have by this point established presences on Twitch, they've essentially stranded themselves on tiny, sub-one-thousand-viewer islands—rebroadcasting canned speeches and failing to meaningfully interact with chat or other streamers. Trump's chat, especially, gains a reputation for being a lawless land where racism and sexism flourish. His channel is eventually banned for "hateful conduct," according to Twitch. AOC's team, on the other hand, took a page straight out of Piker's playbook: They engaged with the Twitch community early and often, even before actually streaming.

In many ways, this is *the* reason Piker—not Sanders, a nationally beloved politician—brought socialism to Twitch. As soon as he was able, he linked up with numerous popular streamers regardless of political affiliation: Anys, Félix "xQc" Lengyel, AustinShow, Tyler "Trainwrecks" Niknam, Ludwig Ahgren, and many more. He did not bludgeon them with politics, but he brought up ideas and policies where it made sense. In so doing, he established Twitch's first real, borderline-ubiquitous politics and news empire.

"Consuming his content, [Piker] has helped me understand and reshape my view of politics and have a deeper, more sophisticated understanding," says Show, who brought Piker onto debate broadcasts when he was first getting started on Twitch and with whom he's since become friends. "I think you're kind of naive when you watch CNN and mainstream media. . . . [Piker] has helped me understand how politics are a game and how people play the game."

Piker recalls receiving a less-than-warm welcome from the Twitch community when he first started, however.

"At first everyone was very upset," he says. "[They were like], 'Ugh, all you want to do is talk about politics.' So much pushback. But by the time the election cycle [in 2020] had come around, everyone's talking about politics. You've got [Lengyel] covering shit that's happening. It became, for lack of a better term, the meta."

Big Twitch personalities began to reference Piker and his talking points—and to express more confidence when discussing those ideas even outside of collaborations with Twitch's emerging himbo king of politics.

"I certainly think that him participating in political discourse at this level has encouraged other broadcasters to do the same," says Show, a veteran streamer who used to host edgy broadcasts and employ a mock-Indian accent (despite being white) before a very public change of heart. "I remember a time on Twitch when it just wasn't as progressive in general. I mean, Twitch was very anti-politics for a long time. A lot of [viewers and streamers] didn't like to talk about politics. They considered it taboo, boring, yadda, yadda, yadda. . . . The Wild West of Twitch was not a very inclusive place. Talking about politics, specifically on the left, [Piker's] community has made Twitch a more inclusive place."

While some of this was also a by-product of young streamers maturing and becoming politically activated by the Trump era, Piker absolutely played a role. He made Twitch a more political place, to the point that viewers in *other* streamers' chats now, almost without fail, mention or meme him when political subject matter comes up.

Though Piker did the work of demonstrating all of this on Twitch, it's his mom, Sedef Piker, who puts it best: "I can see there's a really smart new generation that's more aware of what's happening because it's their future that's been stolen from them," she says. "I think they need to be aware of it because political is personal."

The day after AOC's first Twitch stream, there was a flood of tweets and headlines proclaiming Twitch a future political kingmaker. AOC cracked the code, reporters and pundits declared, and imitators were inevitable. But as time passed, shockingly few politicians followed AOC's lead. AOC streamed on Twitch a couple more times in 2020 and 2021, the former time to help out Jagmeet Singh, leader of Canada's New Democratic Party, and the latter time to discuss GameStop's soaring stock price, a gamer-relevant topic of national news interest. She once again attracted hundreds of thousands of viewers. In March 2022, progressive senator Ed Markey introduced a renewable energy bill live on Twitch, but the broadcast peaked at just over five hundred concurrent viewers. In September of the same year, GOP representative Matt Gaetz, at the time under investigation for sex trafficking, also tried his hand at Twitch, with his inaugural broadcast peaking at a disastrous six concurrent viewers. After he ended his stream, trolls deluged his channel's chat with mocking phrases and images.

This is not how political pundits expected things to play out, but Piker and other political streamers are not surprised.

"Twitch is the absolute worst place for a politician, in many ways. You need to be young and have an understanding of online culture to the max, and you have to be a little brain rotted, too. AOC is the perfect person to be able to do that," Piker says. "[Otherwise] it's gonna be fucking failures. . . . And then you have Bernie Sanders. His team tries to make an effort, but they're not doing what is necessary by the platform to have constant engagement. I just knew that wasn't going to be a thing."

"I love AOC, but it's not like she made this a regular thing," says Beyer. "It's not like she's on my show, right? . . . You don't see the same kind of institutional eagerness to support independent media on the left as you do on the right, in my opinion."

Again, the generational gap rears its head, explains Frogan.

"I feel like a lot of politicians don't realize we're in the age of social media," she says. "You see the ones that are active on TikTok and Instagram. They post memes and stuff. Those are the ones that get it. They have zoomer social media teams. Most of them don't. They just tweet."

Twitch is a tougher nut to crack, and Piker doesn't think it really worked as a get-out-the-vote initiative even when AOC—already much more famous than most politicians—gave it a try. But he still thinks it was beneficial in less immediately measurable ways. Then again, he's admittedly a little biased, given what it did for his career.

"It was great for her," says Piker. "She got a lot of tremendously positive coverage out of that. So did I. [It] legitimized my position on the platform and put me in front of millions of people worldwide. Didn't work as a get-out-the-vote initiative, but I don't really care. Get-out-the-vote initiatives, I do that all day every day, talking about what I'm talking about [on stream]. AOC does it as well. . . . I think that probably had an impact on a lot of younger people cherishing AOC. I think [cherish-ability] is this weird thing that is impossible to quantify. And yet, it's so powerful and so important, especially for a political figure."

- - - - - - -

PIKER'S LOS ANGELES home, the site of our December 2022 interview, is the kind of place you could miss if you weren't looking for it. This is largely because it's surrounded by a towering wall, rendering it functionally impossible to see. The wall itself is plain, with only a small camera and a "Beware of Dog" decal differentiating it from the slab of street below. Its gate gives way to a small courtyard, which leads to a two-floor house. The interior is spacious. Piker is splitting it with his mother, who's visiting, but other family members also sporadically occupy the space. This is a major upgrade from the apartment he previously shared with his mother, in which, as Piker puts it, the two were functionally "on top of each other." Highlights include Piker's office, a kitchen with a huge fridge, and a living room practically bifurcated by an enormous couch. Of these first-floor rooms, only the former could be considered anything near cluttered. Most others verge on conspicuously bare. This is the house of someone who is extremely online.

Online, in turn, has at various points fixated on this house. In 2021, it became the latest in a long string of controversies surrounding Piker's personal conduct, which critics argued did not align with his stated views. Thousands across Twitter, other platforms, and websites like Breitbart suggested that Piker, a supposed champion of the people, had no business dropping millions on a house. A true socialist, they insisted, would never do such a thing. Who did he think he was, arguing that the existence of billionaires was evidence of a broken system while also possessing a large (though still vastly smaller) sum of money?

Looking back on the incident at the tail end of 2022, flanked in his office by decorative cardboard cutouts of former president Barack Obama and Vermont senator/fellow socialist Bernie Sanders, Piker furrows his brow in consternation. It's fitting that Flat Sanders sits cross-legged nearby, given that he—the real Sanders, not the flat one—has also faced criticism for owning houses. Piker thinks it all stems from the same source.

"Both on the left and the right—due to Red Scare propaganda, due to a lack of education around what it means to be a socialist or Marxist principles in general—people have this false understanding of what socialism is and what socialism isn't," says Piker. "Socialism has never been and will never be a poverty cult. That's not what it is. As a matter of fact, it's the exact opposite. It's about uplifting others. It's about earning your keep. I say this regularly from [popular video game] *BioShock*: 'Is a man not entitled to the sweat of his brow?' It's delivered by a supposed libertarian [character], but that is actually a socialist principle. . . . It's wage laborers abolishing the profit motive and getting back more of the profits that they generate for their bosses. That's the fucking point."

Whether or not Piker personally owns a house, he doesn't believe it will impact the amount of brow sweat proverbial men will get to take home. Unless underlying systems change, he insists, companies and bosses will continue to come out on top while everybody else squabbles over the scraps. As *Kotaku* put it in a 2021 article about the controversy surrounding Piker's house: "[Sanders] lost the nomination both times and, low-and-behold, years later, nobody actually cares. People probably won't forget so quickly with Piker, in part due to the social media one-upmanship games that spurred them on to care about it in the first place. Meanwhile, the federal minimum wage will still be $7.25 an hour and people will still go bankrupt visiting the hospital." Piker says that until the day change comes, he will continue to advocate for higher taxes on the wealthy (including himself) and decommodification of the housing market, so everyone can have a house.

Frogan concurs with Piker's overall assessment but can also see where some fans are coming from. Piker is visible and, unlike many politicians, responsive. Banging down his door might not actually do anything, but it *feels* empowering in a time when actual agency is hard to come by.

"So many people were talking about how [Piker] should've started a commune-type thing and put funding into that and give people jobs, but he's one person," she says. "I feel like a lot of people don't realize that with these political commentators, they're one person. Sure, they have reach, but they're not political figures in the sense of [being able to] actually make change. They're not in Congress. They can't pass any policies or anything."

Piker considers himself a political entertainer first and foremost—not a political activist. This, somewhat out of necessity, is true for many politics streamers on Twitch.

"I wondered that before: Why doesn't [Piker] do more?" asks Sorrenti. "He could, but he doesn't. The most he does is a charity event every now and then. But now I kind of get it. You have to view yourself as an entertainer first. It's really fucking draining dealing with all of that. And if you start going after other content creators, you will just piss everyone off."

Piker still contributes to causes where it makes sense. Over the years, he's used merchandise drops and on-stream charity drives to contribute hundreds of thousands of dollars to Ukrainian relief funds and strike funds, among others. But he has no intention of trying to become something he's not—of pivoting so hard he breaks a leg.

"I link up with organizers and regularly platform them. I raise money for funds, I donate personally to charities, I engage in mutual aid, I speak at events—that sort of stuff," he says. "[But] I think no matter what I do, it's not going to be enough. People get mad at me, and they'll criticize me like, 'Why don't you start a 501(c)(3) [charitable organization] or something?' I don't know how to do any of that. Why would I stop what I'm good at to do something I'm not good at?"

But while Piker is sometimes frustrated by the extent to which his goals are misunderstood, he's more than used to it by now. Over the years he's been dogged by numerous controversies, most of which stemmed from misinterpreted—or willfully misconstrued—beliefs. In 2019, Twitch suspended his channel for seven days after he said, "America deserved 9/11," igniting a full-on Fox News firestorm fronted by Republican congressman Dan Crenshaw. Granted, Piker made it personal by joking about Crenshaw's eye during a Twitch stream (Crenshaw is a war veteran who's missing an eye), but the bulk of his commentary was in response to Crenshaw's assertion on an episode of the Joe Rogan podcast that prior to 9/11, Bin Laden had no reason to hate America except our "Western ideology" and that "millions" in places like Yemen and Iraq were "begging" for further United States intervention. Piker took issue with that, blaming America's destabilizing foreign policies in the Middle East, which helped arm the groups that eventually became the Taliban and Al Qaeda, for sowing the seeds of 9/11. "We fucking totally brought it on ourselves, dude," Piker said at the time. "We fucking did. Holy shit. Look at the way that this dipshit is running his fucking mouth, justifying genocide right now."

This is not an uncommon set of beliefs among those who oppose American imperialism, but what Piker said—and the way he said it—was red meat to Fox's red state crowd. Crenshaw and Fox News host Laura Ingraham largely used his comments as fodder for a conversation about how leftism is anti-American, ignoring the substance of Piker's criticism and mocking how he spoke. It was a perfect snapshot of how difficult it can be to actually discuss thorny topics on the modern internet, especially from a socialist perspective in a country whose default is militaristic patriotism. In almost no time at all, Piker's words were taken out of context by opportunists on Twitter and YouTube, who in turn escalated them up the opportunism food chain to Fox News. The end result was a game of telephone where everybody was screaming at the same time. Then everybody moved on, because nobody actually cared. It was all dust in the wind, all content in the end.

On another occasion in 2021, Piker and two other streamers were suspended by Twitch for using "cracker" as a derogatory term for white people. This sparked off a platform-wide argument over whether or not "cracker" is a racial slur, something which Piker didn't think was even up for debate when other slurs include the n-word, famously a word that—unlike "cracker"—most people refuse to even say. In Piker's mind, it was a matter of power dynamics: Anybody using "cracker" in earnest, he argued, is likely not white and is therefore "doing it as someone who has been historically oppressed blowing off steam." Still, the debate raged on, even as Piker, temporarily bereft of his Twitch channel, tried to clarify on Twitter.

"White people are oppressed, just on the basis of class—not race," he wrote. "Whiteness is also a concept built around being the dominant in-group. . . . Irish people, Italian people, Polish people, Jews, etc. were all oppressed as non-whites before being accepted into the dominant group."

In other words, whiteness is fake. Whoever is winning is white, and it's nearly impossible to oppress the winners—who are, in unequal societies, to at least some degree, oppressors.

At the time, it was yet another of Piker's pile of stances that were frustratingly misinterpreted. But in hindsight, he's not unhappy with how most controversies surrounding him have played out. In the moment, they got people talking about him, rather than the points he was trying to make, but in the long run, they grew his audience. So in a roundabout way, some of those who first thought him to be a curiosity at best or a pariah at worst eventually absorbed his message.

"What I usually have an issue with is if someone has clipped me completely out of context and is weaponizing something like that against me that goes against a core belief I have," he says. "The cracker thing is funny because I'm white. So I don't give a shit if you think I'm an anti-white racist. I don't think that's a real concept. It's laughable."

"Same with 'Americans deserve 9/11,'" he adds. "That's a foreign policy position I have that is super, super overly simplified. It's supposed to make you angry, right? It's a passionate moment. I don't feel bad about those moments at all, and I would even say that they helped propel my career in some ways."

He views these as teachable moments, and he feels like viewers are learning the right lessons over time.

"The 'America deserved 9/11' take, people understand the sentiment behind it," says Piker. "People might resent the way I said it, but they personally to a certain degree [get it]. Especially in the Afghanistan withdrawal, on the twentieth anniversary of 9/11, so many documentaries came out talking about America's involvement in the lead-up to the [1978–1992] Afghan War. . . . I remember my normie friends coming back to me and being like, 'Oh, I kind of understand what you were saying now.'"

- - - - - - -

PIKER, A SOCIALIST who regularly advocates for unionization, is one of Twitch's most recognizable faces, but he's fully aware that he's hitched his horse to a wagon that is structurally opposed to his values. Twitch streamers are contractors, not employees. They do not receive healthcare or other benefits. When it comes to unionization, this leaves them with the option to either form independent union-like entities or join existing unions like the Screen Actors Guild—American Federation of Television and Radio Artists (SAG-AFTRA), which recently opened its doors to "influencers," but only those who've made money from sponsored deals.

On top of that, Twitch is owned by Amazon, one of the biggest corporations in the world—and one that's demonstrably opposed to unions. That's not to say Piker is afraid to bite the hand that feeds on this front. In 2023, an Amazon Labor Union financial disclosure revealed that more than half of the $850,000 it raised in 2022 was contributed by just three donors: the American Federation of Teachers, the International Commission for Labor Rights, and

Piker. But unionizing Twitch streamers, Piker believes, is a much trickier task than bringing together even thousands of workers at an Amazon warehouse.

"You get the top one percent of Twitch streamers, and you have a union all of the sudden," Piker says. "But scabbing is so easy. And also a lot of the [top] streamers themselves are capital owners and would much rather bargain individually than have any kind of collective bargaining agreement. They want to make sure that their bottom line is protected."

Piker sees the division between big streamers—enterprises in their own right—and smaller streamers as a serious impediment. Recent history suggests he's onto something: Top streamers were nowhere to be found in 2021 when so-called "hate raids"—in which trolls flooded smaller streamers' chats with bot-powered fake accounts that spammed often-racist messages—plagued Twitch, and the company failed to respond in an expedient fashion even after a boycott from smaller streamers.

Piker does believe, however, that he and top creators ultimately have more in common with smaller streamers than they do with the executives running Twitch and Amazon.

"I have more autonomy and less alienation from my labor than the overwhelming majority of workers on this planet. But there's still a big boss up there that dictates how many hours I can be on the platform and how much ad density I have to push and all these other things," he says. "Twitch is a platform owned by Jeff Bezos, ultimately, [that] still wants me to work the most amount of hours for the least amount of money they can pay me. I want to work the least amount of hours for the most amount of pay I can get out of Twitch. That dynamic is the inherent contradiction within capitalism in every wage labor employer-employee relationship: capital owner versus wage labor."

Livestreaming, though seemingly cushier than construction or an office job, is still work, and Piker's belief is that all workers should have each other's back. There's no cutoff point for what, in this case, constitutes work. If somebody's making money off your labor, you're a worker.

"There's this attitude amongst working class Americans that the harder and more backbreaking your labor is, the closer you are to real labor," says Piker. "That's why when Starbucks baristas get together and unionize, people are like, 'Well, you're not really a worker.' The fuck do you mean? They're in the service industry. Not everyone has to get black lung in the coal mines to be designated a worker. There's fifty-five thousand coal miners in this country, total. There's more people that work at Arby's."

But the gig economy, of which Twitch is a part, is moving workers further from reliable structures for collective action, not closer.

"We have a ten percent unionization rate, which is insanely low," says Piker. "Exploitation that workers face under the regular employment structure is not enough, so they want to switch it over to the gig economy so they can further exploit people with no accountability whatsoever, no legal recourse available. People don't recognize it because it's packaged as 'freedom.' It's packaged with American values. Pro-capitalist American values."

Piker holds out hope for a better future, but he's not optimistic that Twitch streamers will lead the way in this particular regard.

"Getting gambling taken off the platform after it dominated its own in-dividual [category on Twitch]—with god knows how many people getting addicted to gambling in the process—it still took a year," Piker says. "I'll take the moral victory. But it wasn't [systemic]. Ultimately we didn't do anything."

- - - - - - -

LISTENING TO PIKER talk, you might begin to get the impression that he rages against the machine simply for the sake of raging. Collaborating with the likes of AOC did not, by his measure, lead to a notably increased youth vote turnout, and organized labor in the United States faces a battle so uphill it verges on Sisyphean. What more can he do? Where's the hope for actual change in any of it? But if Piker aspired only to serve as a hammer for a series of stubborn nails, he would've given up a long time ago. Instead, he's more akin to glue that, given time, can seep into the cracks of a broken system. It's a long play, not a quick fix.

"When people hit certain inflection points in their life, there's a chance they become politically engaged," says Beyer. "One of those is when you're college aged. Another is when you're getting close to getting married or buy-ing a home or launching a career. Another is when you have a kid. These are inflection points that don't necessarily make you political, but if you become political, it tends to be in one of these periods. I think [Piker] is hitting a lot of people in those times."

Piker's entry into this arena has proven a game changer, because many of the alternatives—especially for young men—are not ideal. Whether via Gamergate, the MAGA movement it partially metastasized into, or Joe Rogan's questionable (to put it lightly) taste in podcast guests, there are numerous algorithmic pipelines into far-right extremism that teach young people to bury their grievances in sexism, racism, homophobia, and transphobia. Other content creators on YouTube and TikTok have succeeded in deradicalizing some, but it's a never-ending battle on an internet where engagement is money, and nothing keeps eyeballs glued to screens more reliably than divisiveness, tribalism, and white-hot rage.

At the very least, Piker helps tip the scales away from figures like the controversial yet massively popular Andrew Tate, a misogynistic influencer who managed to position himself as a role model and self-help guru for young men. Tate's unprecedentedly unsubtle shtick—comparing women to property, talking about how he'd assault them if they cheated on him, endorsing adults dating teenagers—allowed him to play influencers on both sides of the divide like fiddles. Whether they endorsed his viewpoints or vociferously opposed them, they felt compelled to make content about him. Just like that, he became a household name.

Piker debated Tate after he'd begun to take off, potentially contributing to his rise despite rhetorically turning him into a pretzel (Piker argues that Tate had already "skyrocketed" by that point and, just to be safe, he went on Tate's broadcast but did not stream the debate on his own channel). Regardless of who benefited more from their verbal showdown, Piker—simply by existing—provides an alternative. He represents a version of masculinity that doesn't root itself in domination of others, and instead of instructing men to blame women for their problems, he points to capitalism, a structural force that is *demonstrably* depriving them of lifestyles they desire.

"The social issues [Piker] talks about are always tangible, because he treats his audience like real people," says Saberhagen. "I know 'himbo' is part of the branding, but he's smart. He just doesn't do what a lot of nerds do: hide behind 'smartness' as a shield. . . . Some leftists Hasan created maybe don't stay leftist long, but he really does stay up their asses about the right path like a good stepdad."

Piker is able to capture younger people's attention because he knows where they're coming from. Unlike news networks and other forms of mainstream media that are, at least to some degree, incentivized to endorse the status quo, he can embody the *feeling* of the moment. He can do this because he's on Twitch, predominantly funded by viewers rather than corporate interests.

"Ultimately young people still don't vote, and why the fuck would they? Why the fuck should they? It's not tangible. It's not immediate. There's no immediate gratification—and maybe no gratification at all," says Piker. "People, I think, ultimately feel powerless in the face of this system that is so crushing and almost autonomous. It's like a robot. It just works on its own. So it's very difficult to make the argument to people that they should vote for one party over the other."

Viewed through the lens of a desire to nurse an ailing system back to health, that's a pretty terminal prognosis. But looked at another way, institutional failure means opportunity—not necessarily for something new to take its place, but for people to advocate for their needs and help each other out beyond the confines of the electoral system. For instances of workplace organization, local-level mutual aid, and other forms of community support to be victories, you don't need to mobilize an entire nation. The results, in Piker's eyes, are immediate.

"If people want to take matters into their own hands, first and foremost, community organizing and organizing your workplace is one of the best ways you can almost immediately achieve a better workplace for yourself and your peers," he says. "The only way to achieve that political power is through organizing. That's something I try to stress whenever I'm doing election coverage."

With the 2024 election on the horizon—and Joe Biden, an incumbent in whom Piker places little faith, waving the flag for the Democrats—Piker plans to keep trying to educate viewers about all the ways in which they're not as powerless as they think.

"I've always stressed the importance of voting down ballot, voting in local elections, voting in the primaries," he says, "because those are areas where you genuinely can make an improvement."

He also plans to get involved on a personal level—at least, to the extent that he is able.

"I don't think the Biden camp would be open to having me on board with them in the same way I could do for the Bernie campaign, if there was one," Piker says.

Otherwise, he's going to enjoy a handsome viewership boost while enjoying much the same experience as those following along at home.

"I'm just gonna strap in for the show," he says. "There's not much more I can do other than that."

- - - - - - -

THESE DAYS, THERE are many political streamers on Twitch. There is only one Hasan Piker.

Nobody else delivers news, day after day, to thirty-five-thousand-plus viewers at any given moment—totaling out to millions over time. Nobody else rubs shoulders with big-name Twitch streamers, politicians, and pop stars alike. Nobody else trends on Twitter all the time. The question is why. The answer is complicated.

Some of it stems from his not-so-humble beginnings: *The Young Turks* was a better launchpad for this kind of thing than most can boast. And while Piker was far from the first political streamer on Twitch, he largely opted to swerve out of the way of the dominant political culture on the platform at the time of his arrival: debates. On both YouTube and Twitch, divisive figures like Steven "Destiny" Bonnell would—and to an extent still do—make a spectacle out of embittered theoretical battles concerning wars, white supremacy, trans rights, and thousands of infinitely more niche topics.

These debates can make for occasionally interesting exchanges of ideas or, more often than not, hypnotic train wrecks, but they're rarely persuasive. Audiences either come in presupposing their guy is gonna come out on top, or they swarm the comments and declare a winner based on who did the best job of forcing their opponent onto the backfoot with bad-faith attacks. The victor is often whoever got the other to show emotion, not the person who made the most coherent or compassionate points. A years-long series of clashes involving a rotating but broadly consistent cast of creators has led to a "debate bro" alternate universe with several *Silmarillions*' worth of lore and regular leaps of logic that require a truly internet-poisoned brain to comprehend. For both creators and viewers within the debate bro bubble, it's a source of infinite content. For everybody else, it's impenetrable.

Piker's had a few dalliances with this bubble over the years, which he largely regrets—especially after one debate saw him share the digital stage with a notorious white supremacist. But for the most part, he's sidestepped the scene entirely.

"When you value debating over your own personal moral code—and what I call empathy-first politics—you create and foster a very toxic environment that isn't necessarily interested in legitimate outcomes or making genuine change," says Piker. "[They're] more so simply interested in winning that conversation, right? . . . I don't think it's a sustainable thing at all, and I don't think it's good in the grand scheme of things. It leads to a lot of bad commentary being out there and bad ideas being spread."

Diehard fans also believe Piker avoided a slow descent into an endless quicksand pit by blazing his own trail instead of joining one of the internet's more established political scenes.

"[Piker] dodged so many bullets by not being a debate bro," says Saberhagen. "There's an acknowledgment when he talks about social issues that they're not fun little hypotheticals. That already put him leagues above other political streamers—mostly other white dudes who had a hard time imagining at all how the system isn't fair, because, after all, they're successful, and their security and success must be because they worked harder and were more talented than most."

While every political streamer walks a line between commentator and personality, Piker is also closer than just about any of his peers to the latter end of that spectrum.

"He'll be hanging out with some of the biggest internet celebrities that exist one day, then squishing watermelons with his thighs for charity or something like that," says Lance (who has not revealed his last name) of a mid-sized leftist Twitch and YouTube channel called The Serfs. "And then the next day, he'll be going on a rant about critical race theory. There isn't really another equivalent in terms of someone who has that kind of leftist philosophy or political stance at that scale."

"I think he's still more connected to the streamer culture of making it about a personal brand, as opposed to a show that talks about politics," says Beyer. "He does gaming, he does that influencer game. He's able to interact with other more straitlaced, corporate-friendly content creators. . . . That is just a pipeline of new people that are interested in him for his nonpolitical content, who he then introduces to that [political] content."

Fans who've discovered Piker via the streamer pipeline view jokes, memes, and Piker's endearing grumpiness as crucial parts of the formula that other political streamers simply can't imitate. He easily gets "stunlocked," meaning that somebody will say something in chat that annoys him to no end, and then he'll go way off track seething about it. The community laughs with and at him, and he does the same to the community. In that sense, Piker is akin to a schoolteacher all the kids like, but also like to mess with.

"It's basically talk-back radio, but for younger people that are terrified of phone calls," says a fan who goes by the handle Vulcan Parrot, who runs a popular Twitter account that catalogs memorable lines from Piker's Twitch chat. "Everyone wants to know what's happening in the world, but as leftists these realities can be very grim. [Piker] being a clown and encouraging jokes within the community makes the streams feel more fun and entertainment-focused than a lecture."

But even when a bad-faith chatter—rather than a well-meaning fan— manages to stunlock Piker, he still believes his response can serve an educational purpose, further adding to his appeal.

"It's giving [fans] talking points to sound smart when they're talking to other people that are less equipped than they are in dealing with those talking points," says Piker. "I'm giving people the opportunity to sound smart. Everybody wants to sound smart."

According to Frogan, general policy among Piker's chat moderators is to time-out and eventually ban repeat offenders, but Piker says there are some purposeful exceptions to the rule.

"I have 'pets' in chat, conservatives we don't ban on purpose," says Piker, "unless they are saying something overtly transphobic, [spouting] Nazi propaganda—that sort of thing. Because oftentimes, you need to have a villain. I need to bounce my ideas off someone."

With other political streamers failing to replicate Piker's unique alchemy, it is, oddly enough, more traditional streamers who've begun to do their best impressions of him when earth-shattering news hits. It's something of a double-edged sword: On one hand, Piker has successfully turned news into a viable genre of Twitch broadcast. On the other, when popular streamers abruptly toss on their press caps, they often don't know what they're talking about. For example, Twitch superstars like Lengyel and Asmongold—both of whom mostly play video games during typical streams—amplified misinformation and sexist narratives during the long-burning tire fire that was the Johnny Depp–Amber Heard trial in 2022.

"[Asmongold] had some takes that were fueling the incel narrative," says Frogan. "You have seventy-five thousand average concurrent viewers and you're an influential character, and you don't even know that what you're saying is wrong. [These streamers] are like, 'Oh well, this is content.' They don't look at it from the perspective of educating people."

Piker's hybrid Twitch streamer–political commentator model puts him in a league of his own on the political left. The right, on the other hand, is a different ballgame—with different players, different rules, and maybe, like, a cube instead of a ball.

"I think people need to recognize that the right, their numbers are monstrous online," says Lance. "Tim Poole pulls in an average of thirty-six to fifty thousand viewers on his daily streams. That's one [Piker]. If I started mentioning other large streamers such as Charlie Kirk, Matt Walsh, [Ben

Shapiro]—even Dave Rubin, who gets a couple thousand, but those are still big numbers. . . . And because of that, maybe part of me gives [Piker] more leeway when a controversy comes up, because there needs to be a figure of that size to be able to push back against other people."

Beyer chalks this dynamic up to institutional support, or a lack thereof. Creators and controversies on the right—as evidenced even by Piker's own experience becoming the Fox News controversy of the day in 2019—often work their way up an online food chain, from Twitter to YouTube to TV, and so on. The American left, on the other hand, tends to favor old media institutions like CNN and the *New York Times* as news sources. But those institutions rarely collaborate with or even acknowledge online creators—at least, not political ones. Moreover, Piker believes his ideological views—which regularly see him trying to heave corporate interests overboard with all his might—further alienate him from the traditional news media ecosystem. In truth, nobody knows quite what to do with him. Networks and publications see him as a threat or don't see him at all. Twitch, though lacking in big right-wing personalities due to ostensibly progressive values like strict rules against hate speech, still views Piker as a potential risk, suspending him on several occasions due to the way he's expressed his views. Brands, meanwhile, often refuse to sponsor him, forcing him to make most of his money directly from viewers.

But even this, Beyer thinks, is in its own way a strength.

"On the right, we don't see a lot of [Piker]-like characters, because they are getting their audiences from institutional support of political content—like advertising, like being on Fox News. They're not organically creating a community. They're being force-fed down other people's throats, through every possible means, whereas [Piker] is organically building up an audience who *want* to see him through blood, sweat, and tears."

At the very least, there's no doubt about the "blood, sweat, and tears" part. Piker typically streams at least two hundred hours per month, sometimes broadcasting for upward of ten hours per day. By comparison, others with similar focuses, like Beyer, Frogan, and Lance, only stream for around half that time per day. This is actually down from Piker's all-time pandemic high of three-hundred-plus hours per month, which to him was still an easier year than 2019, in which he tried to stream full-time and work at *The Young Turks*.

"I was going nonstop. No friends, no girlfriend, no social life. Nothing," says Piker of his 2019. "That was significantly harder than 2020, a year where I spent forty-two percent of my entire year in front of a camera."

That's not to say 2020 was easy. The reason Piker spent an inhuman amount of time on camera that year, he explains, is because it was his way of coping with the pandemic.

"It was lonely," he says. "I had nothing going on. My dog died. It was terrible. It was a fucking one-bedroom apartment in West Hollywood by myself. Hated life. Hadn't seen a human being in a long-ass time. [I was] putting on a VR headset to feel like I'm close to humans. . . . And I needed stability in my life. I still do. I have ADHD. It's very difficult for me to be the person I want to be unless I'm very rigid and following a strict regimen. I have every part of my day mapped out ahead of time in my head exactly how I want to do it. I have it on the calendar."

But Piker's current schedule is still in line with the relentless paces set by other Twitch streamers who dominate their respective categories. As ever, the question is: Can he keep this up indefinitely? Or will he eventually burn out?

Piker's family says they can see the toll working so much takes on him.

"I see [Piker] burning out, right? And here's a guy who should be on top of the world. I think he should be infinitely happier than he is today," says Uygur, Piker's uncle. "And part of the reason for his personal dissatisfaction is because of how hard it is to feed the machine. . . . [Piker] is still going and going healthy and strong, but he's tired, no question. I see him [at] Thanksgiving, Christmas, family get-togethers. He's always tired."

This, in part, is because Piker is not *just* streaming. The job, especially when you're hosting a news show, is a multifaceted menagerie of preparation, community management, business, and hosting—something Uygur knows from experience.

"For gamers, it's still hard because that amount of time wears on anyone, doing anything, especially when your brain has to be alert at all times for incoming stimuli and interaction. And you're under pressure to say something interesting for [twelve hours]," he says. "But at least for gamers, there's nothing you have to prepare ahead of time. [Piker] does politics. There's tons of preparation ahead of time. Especially as you're interacting with the audience, like he does, if you don't know something you're gonna get exposed. That is an enormous amount of stress and pressure to take on any given day, let alone day after day."

Piker admits that maintaining a healthy relationship with chat can be especially taxing. These days, it's his canary in the coal mine for when he needs a break.

"Sometimes I lose my mind after a while of responding to the same dumb shit over and over and over for the millionth fucking time," he says. "And when that happens, sometimes I have a tendency to pop off a little too aggressively, and then I feel bad. And then I realize that maybe I'm burning out, so I shouldn't stream the next day."

Sedef, Piker's mother, has spent long spells living with Piker and has seen how difficult it is for him to turn off.

"When he's off camera, then he's on his phone, going through emails and things," she says. "Sometimes he's like, 'Mom, just give me a minute. I'm trying to talk someone off the ledge.' You have to unplug and de-stress at some point. That's the thing he doesn't realize. I think he needs to do that somehow. I've been trying so hard to get him to do meditation, mindfulness, something, but of course if I say it, he's not gonna do it. So I'm hoping one of his friends will suggest it."

Sedef goes on to open up about additional risks of the trade that Piker prefers to keep to himself. Like other Twitch stars, for example Sorrenti and Kaitlyn "Amouranth Siragusa, he's no stranger to being doxxed and swatted.

"He gets a lot of hate," says Sedef. "That's the thing that's most difficult to deal with, in all honesty. Last year [2021], we went through so much where the cops were showing up at his house. . . . A whole SWAT team showed up in front of his door. We were here at the time. It's very scary to see your son go through this."

She recalls one occasion when Piker got swatted over the holidays. Of course, by that point, the two of them were used to it.

"The day before Christmas Eve I was preparing food, and [Piker] goes, 'Mom, can you talk to the cops? They're here,'" Sedef says. "I go out, I have an apron on. You know, the typical mother preparing food. I looked at them. Seven people walk up. One's got her shotgun, and I was like, 'Oh my god, not again.' They were more surprised than I was. They were like, 'This happened before?'"

When pressed, Piker admits that the hate does sometimes get to him.

"Death threats, doxxing, those sorts of things that come along with the territory—that's not fun," he says. "That does hurt my feelings."

And yet, sitting in his office at the end of a workday in late 2022, surrounded on all sides by streaming equipment and a collection of cardboard politicians, Piker seems at peace. Part of the reason for this is that, like other big streamers, he has a team making sure he's not carrying every ounce of love, hate, and responsibility on his shoulders. His team, however, is smaller and more streamlined than that of, say, Siragusa or Ben "CohhCarnage" Cassell—significantly so. But he'd rather juggle tasks than people.

"All these other streamers, they've got employees. They've got people that are working under them," Piker says. "I have [video] editors that do their own thing. It's so hands-off. I don't tell anybody anything, and it just works. . . . That's the way I wanted to set myself up. I wanted to make sure that I had the most sustainable and best possible way of generating revenue so that I can have full editorial independence and full-blown independence."

It's an approach that, again, fits Piker's worldview. He's spent hundreds of hours ranting about how bosses are functionally dictators that preside over the majority of our time. He has no desire to be one.

"Bosses fucking suck," he says. "And I suck at being a boss. Makes me probably the best boss on the planet, because I will never be like, 'Yo, where are you at? What's going on?'"

- - - - - - -

GET SOME STREAMERS talking, and they'll wax grandiloquent about future goals so lofty that even Icarus wouldn't dare. They're gonna start their own video game company. They're gonna launch a livestreaming platform to put Twitch out of business. They're gonna head up an agency that represents an army of content creators even bigger than they are now.

Piker wants to keep doing what he's doing now, with just a slight tweak: Instead of twenty to thirty thousand concurrent viewers at any given moment, he wants 1 million.

"I want to do exactly what I'm doing, but have two hundred thousand concurrent people tune in, three hundred thousand people, [and so on]," he says. "I don't think it'll happen in the relatively near future, but it can happen, I think."

Fans agree that he'll pull it off, if only because the state of the world is likely to get worse before it gets better.

"Look, it's wild out there," says Saberhagen. "We are always one major disaster or political upheaval from [Piker's] biggest stream. And, for the sake of survival, I *don't* want that. . . . But probably, yes, he will livestream the end of the world."

Moneywise, Piker's got it made. He insists that he no longer needs to do any of this, but passion—and a contract with Twitch—keep him streaming for hundreds of hours per month.

"When I start streaming, when I click that button, everything is just shut off," he says. "I'm in the zone. I'm like a composer or conductor. Everything is silent. . . . I don't think about obligations that I have in the real world. I think about how to entertain thirty to forty thousand people and educate them as best as I can. And that is liberating for me. I love that. It's almost like a coping mechanism."

"I reached the happiness point a long time ago," he adds. "My financial situation now and all the money I make is just a contingency. No matter what happens down the line, I can say whatever the fuck I want. That's the way I see it."

- - - - - - -

IN LATE 2023 and early 2024, Piker's predictions come true, to an extent. While his viewership does not skyrocket into the hundreds of thousands—and even declines as he takes a position most content creators deem too risky for their brand-friendly images—he becomes a news epicenter for many trying to follow Israel's brutal retaliation against Palestinians following an October 2023 attack from Hamas, the political and military movement governing the Gaza Strip, that claimed over one thousand Israeli lives. While mainstream news networks both liberal and conservative broadly adhered to the narrative that Israel's killing of over thirty-five thousand Palestinians is justified, young people look to platforms like Twitch and TikTok for alternatives. During the first few weeks of Israel's bombing campaign, Piker—who has long maintained a pro-Palestinian position in his analyses of Middle Eastern politics—quickly becomes one of the few news sources willing to spend tens of hours per day unpacking decades of propaganda and explaining why opposing Israel's government is not the same thing as opposing an entire ethnic group. He plays a crucial role in changing the discourse around Palestine, in helping explain what experts and residents have known for years: that Gaza was an open-air prison occupied largely by minors, its warden a nuclear power directly supported by the United States, a nuclear *super*power.

Piker also meets more mainstream audiences where they're at, appearing on the BBC and a show hosted by popular British television personality Piers Morgan, among others, to explain his stance. During one broadcast, a BBC host asks him why the Israel-Palestine conflict has been so polarizing.

"I think it's polarizing because people do not see the humanity of those who are under colonial subjugation. Ever since the Nakba, Palestinians have not been able to return back to their homes," Piker replies, referring to a mass displacement of Palestinians during the 1948 Arab-Israeli war. "There has been a brutal occupation that the Human Rights Watch and Amnesty International now correctly consider to be an apartheid state. This is, of course, twenty years after Nelson Mandela had considered Israel to be an apartheid state, and I feel like he knows a thing or two about apartheid states in general."

Piker also takes his show on digital roads much closer to home, primarily

Leftovers, a regular podcast he hosts with Ethan Klein, a popular YouTuber of Jewish descent. While Klein at various points expresses sympathy for Palestinian civilians and even donates to Palestinian relief efforts, the two differ on numerous points, including what their ideal vision for Palestinian liberation would look like and where that would leave the Israeli people. They debate often, and emotions run high. Both end up crying on air in sympathy for Palestinians who've lost children and loved ones.

"The IDF went in and beat the shit out of the Palestinians that were mourning her at her funeral, that were holding her casket, and ripped the Palestinian flag off of her casket," Piker says, through tears, of Shireen Abu Akleh, a Palestinian-American journalist killed by an Israeli soldier in 2022. "This is not Hamas. This is a journalist that was beloved in the Muslim world, and she was assassinated for speaking out and trying to shine a light on the atrocities. It's very hard to hold my composure on this. This is something I've talked about for years and years, but when . . . that kind of brutality is so normal, is so normalized, when that's the everyday existence of Palestinians in the supposed collaborative project with the Israeli government, how can you expect them to do anything but violently retaliate?"

Piker and Klein's repeated debates serve as learning experiences for both content creators, as well as their audiences. However, even as they manage to relieve some tensions, others build, with Klein voicing stances that cause discomfort among members of Piker's community, including Frogan, whom he baselessly accuses of antisemitism. Ultimately, the two decide to put the show on pause.

A handful of other, smaller leftist news streamers on Twitch follow in Piker's footsteps and pivot to prioritizing Palestine, including Caroline Kwan, a rising star who typically focuses on entertainment news. She describes the difficulty she faces not just in preparing and avoiding misinformation, but also in resisting the urge to succumb to hopelessness. "This has been the most challenging thing for me to cover on stream," she says during an interview. "I already feel the fatigue, not just with myself, but with my stream, because it's really hard to spend all day consuming information that includes babies being blown apart [and] thousands of people dying, not having the basic aid and necessities that they need, as bombs are raining down on them. It is very heavy. It's a lot for me to wake up every day and go 'All right, here we go again.' It's also a lot for my community, many of whom are resoundingly pro-Palestine. To consume this, there's just a certain hopelessness when you do this all day or listen to this all day. You go 'How do we stop this? What are we supposed to do?'"

Streamers covering the conflict persist, however, doing their best to roll with months' worth of gut punches. Then, in spring 2024, students at major colleges like New York's Columbia University, Portland State, and UCLA begin to protest en masse, demanding that their places of education divest from companies that support Israel and its war. This leads to thousands of arrests, as well as violent police crackdowns on gatherings and encampments that are largely nonviolent. Twitch streamers, including Piker, Frogan, and Kwan, attend protests. Campus protesters, wary of traditional media, greet the streamers with open arms.

"[The media] loves talking to PR people when it comes to corporations," Piker tells the *Washington Post* at the time. "They have no problem talking to the media liaison when it comes to the NYPD or the LAPD and writing down everything they say without even asking remotely contentious questions. But when it comes to students, they don't treat these students as an organized entity at all."

Piker spends hours at the UCLA encampment, working to show what it's like in a seamless, unedited fashion rather than from the perspective of a news crew or a police report. Hundreds of students chant and raise their voices, but they also chill, laugh and joke, and pass out pamphlets and other resources. It's like a loud, long picnic.

"I think the students are doing a really good job," Piker says to a student during his stream. "The problem is, the media is desperately trying to move the attention away from the main focus. You rarely hear about the demands being made by student organizers. You rarely hear about the fact that the students want to keep the attention on Gaza, on what's going on in Gaza. And unfortunately, you only hear about how the police and the National Guard should come and kill the students."

Piker speaks to and is approached by numerous protesters, including a member of his community who was able to pay part of his college tuition by creating a Twitch channel that broadcasts replays of previous streams when Piker isn't online. Another is wearing a shirt from Piker's merch collection, which Piker is also wearing.

"This is why I do what I do," says Piker. "What I do would be meaningless if people didn't listen and take action."

But what Piker is happiest to see isn't any individual person or group. Rather, it's everybody gathered together, fighting for a cause he's supported his entire career, for which he's been ostracized and smeared since October 7. This, through all the darkness and despondency, is what fuels him.

"I would never have imagined this much of a crowd at a college campus anywhere in solidarity with Palestinians," he says directly into the camera, with his arm around the shoulder of a friend who's been moved to tears by the enormity of the moment. "In my whole fucking life I never would have ever thought I would see this day. I didn't stop advancing. I did not stop advocating for the cause. And now I don't feel lonely; I don't feel as lonely anymore. That's because of you guys. That's because of you in the chat and all of these people out here. They're putting their bodies on the line. They're putting their careers on the line. They're facing possible doxxing. They're facing assault. They're facing being brutally arrested for doing what is right. So I hope that you can continue advocating for the right things."

----

twitch is dead, long live twitch

Twitch as we now know it was in no small part built by many of the creators featured in this book. Marcus "DJWheat" Graham was in the trenches before livestreaming even became a medium, helping forge the bond between creators and chat that undergirds the whole operation to this day. He proceeded to steward Twitch's community forward through multiple eras until doing so from the inside proved a lost cause. Ben "CohhCarnage" Cassell was at the forefront of turning streaming into a legitimate profession with his combination of analysis and dedication. He set the standard and stuck to it, eventually assembling a multifaceted team to support him and becoming a picture of consistency. Every big streamer, in some way large or small, counts Cassell as an influence. Kaitlyn "Amouranth" Siragusa helped pave the way for women on a platform with an unfortunate history of sexism. She also showed everybody that streaming doesn't have to be a one-note job; you can, with sufficient savvy and an appetite for capitalizing on trends that borders on feral, become a full-on business mogul. Tanya "Cypheroftyr" DePass was making inroads for gamers of color long before Twitch began to seriously expand beyond gaming's

269

archetypal, often-white base. Hasan "HasanAbi" Piker turned Twitch into millions of people's hub for news and political commentary. Dream embraced parasociality like few before him and gained a level of celebrity that borders on mainstream among younger generations. Clara "Keffals" Sorrenti carved out space for trans streamers and viewers and fought back against harassers until her past caught up to her and she hit a self-destructive wall. Youna "Code Miko" Kang forced streamers and viewers outside the anime/idol bubble to stand up and take notice of VTubers, now an entire livestreaming genre. Emme "Negaoryx" Montgomery became an internet-wide meme that endures to this day, with all the ups and downs that entails.

These are the messy, complicated, and sometimes ugly sagas that made Twitch what it is. This is why hundreds of millions of people continue to visit the site per month, even during times of discontent. This is why, sometimes try as they might, they cannot look away.

Twitch no longer feels like the same company it was when I began reporting out this book—let alone like the company it was when it was founded. In truth, the Amazon-ification of Twitch was already well underway when I started this project in 2020, but streamers and viewers began to really *feel* it in the following years. High-profile incidents like Twitch's slow response to hate raids—in which trolls overwhelmed marginalized streamers' chats with fake accounts that spammed hateful messages—acted as the canary in the coal mine, and the company's poor communication and pivot toward unpopular, largely ad-based monetization features soured sentiment further. This even as Twitch boasted its two most successful years ever in 2020 and 2021, experiencing record-high watch times while people across the globe were stuck inside as a result of the pandemic.

But it was only once Twitch's internal changes and the rigors of streaming began to take a visible toll on the community that it really felt like we were witnessing the end of an era. Twitch's actual building blocks, the people, slowly crumbled away. Starting in 2021, the company let a startling number of stars, like Ludwig Ahgren, Tim "TimTheTatman" Bejar, Ben "DrLupo" Lupo, and Lily "LilyPichu" Ki walk to YouTube rather than pay them exclusivity money for their services, leaving streamers feeling like Twitch no longer valued them. Other stars burned out and moved on. In June 2023, for example, Turner "Tfue" Tenney, once *Fortnite*'s heir apparent, announced his retirement from livestreaming at the age of twenty-five. In a video explaining his rationale, he choked back tears. "Earlier in my gaming career I used gaming to escape from reality, and I feel like now I use reality to escape from fucking work," he said. "I just need to go live my life." Tenney unretired at the end of 2023, but Imane "Pokimane" Anys—a face of Twitch so prominent that she featured in its marketing materials—headed for the door as Tenney walked back in. Around the same time, nearly a dozen prominent YouTubers announced that they were retiring, going on hiatus, or taking on background roles as a means of freeing themselves from the all-consuming grind. A generation of content creators had reached their limit.

Some streamers depicted in this book ended up walking a similar path. Emme "Negaoryx" Montgomery is now primarily a voice actor, while Tanya "Cypheroftyr" DePass accepted a role as senior writer on the upcoming *Wonder Woman* video game in 2023. Youna "Code Miko" Kang, meanwhile, has her VTuber technology company, MikoVerse, and Marcus "DJWheat" Graham is now VP of community development at a new video game company called Fortis Games, which he believes will "break down the walls between development and community." Burnout took a toll on many of these streamers. They had no choice but to find new, more sustainable careers where they could apply the skills and connections they'd picked up while on Twitch. They've all resumed streaming at least semi-regularly, though some took longer to return than others. Now, however, they're not as dependent on it. They no longer need to break their bodies and sap their spirits to ensure that a few all-important numbers keep going up.

Only two creators in this book, Ben "CohhCarnage" Cassell and Hasan "HasanAbi" Piker, said they plan to keep streaming in a full-time capacity indefinitely. Maybe they are, to borrow an online colloquialism, just built different. The fact that they've made millions and have hired employees to lighten the load probably doesn't hurt. Newer stars like Case "CaseOh" Baker and Kai Cenat (who made national news in 2023 with an in-person giveaway that caused chaos in the streets of Manhattan) have risen up and gained immense popularity—and these stars will doubtless push Twitch in new directions, just as their forebears did. In some ways, this kind of churn is natural in entertainment; just as Hollywood stars and pop musicians rise and fall, so too do content creators. But Twitch has nonetheless started to feel like a patchwork quilt that sports several conspicuously large holes. Content creators burn out hard, and when they do, their viewers lose what has effectively become their watering hole, their midday escape.

Within a similar time span, the final vestiges of Twitch's internal old guard made for the door. One of those long-tenured employees, Marcus "DJWheat" Graham, sent shock waves through the Twitch community when he departed in 2022. Many considered Graham to be the last remaining public-facing Twitch employee who didn't merely function as a company mouthpiece. When he left, so did the spirit of the days when your friendly neighborhood Twitch rep was just a phone call away. Then, at the beginning of 2023, CEO Emmett Shear—who'd helped found Twitch—stepped down as well. Mass layoffs followed shortly thereafter, shaking up Twitch's internal culture even more. Under the stewardship of new CEO Dan Clancy, Twitch spent the first half of 2023 walking back some of its less popular decisions like doing away with the 70/30 revenue split, introducing new features that explored concepts like short-form video, and getting back in touch with the community. Under Clancy, Twitch also introduced a feature that prevents banned chatters from watching streamers' broadcasts, addressing one of the root causes of DePass's stalker situation, albeit years after her specific case had already faded into an unpleasant memory.

Twitch, a communication platform, was finally making a concerted, consistent effort to communicate. Streamers took note, voicing their appreciation. This was not all directly Clancy's doing; Twitch is a big company full of employees with varying priorities, and many spent years doing their best to serve streamers even as public perception suggested that Twitch was growing more and more out of touch. But Clancy facilitated initiatives that might not have gotten as much attention under the previous regime. He made Twitch *feel* a little more like Twitch, at least from the outside looking in. He recognized that, in some ways, streamers are Twitch's main customer—more so than viewers—and sold the idea of Twitch to them. Clancy went on to embrace the role of Twitch emissary far more than Shear ever did, becoming a streamer in his own right. In late 2023 and early 2024, Clancy was practically a fixture on the channels of countless big streamers, engaging in discussions, answering questions, and sometimes just chilling and playing music. Every Twitch streamer is, to an extent, playing a character, and so was Clancy. His just happened to be "Twitch CEO." In most ways that mattered, it worked. For the first time in years, Twitch streamers felt listened to. Criticism—at least, from Twitch's biggest stars—softened.

But Twitch, by Clancy's own admission, remained unprofitable even after the record highs of 2020 and 2021, and Amazon had come to collect. Near the end of 2023, Twitch shuttered operations in Korea—the birthplace of many of the esports that fueled Twitch in its early days—citing costs. In early 2024, the company announced another round of layoffs, bringing the total count of employees let go in a single year to nearly a thousand—or almost half the company. Already running lean after the previous year's cuts, remaining employees wondered how they'd keep the lights on, let alone deliver new features in a timely fashion. In posts and interviews, Clancy insisted that the cuts were all in service of building a more efficient Twitch from the rubble, of ensuring that the platform could sustain itself indefinitely. But creators and viewers continued to eye Twitch warily, especially as Twitch's cost cutting came for partner managers—Twitch employees who aided partnered streamers on an individual basis—and Twitch's Safety Advisory Council, a group of industry experts, streamers, and moderators Twitch had been paying since 2020 to advise on trust and safety matters, work-life balance, and other matters near and dear to streamers. After all, once the unthinkable happens a couple times, nothing is really off the table anymore. Even if Twitch wasn't in danger of suddenly disappearing, it seemed to be on the decline. This perception dovetailed with viewership numbers; after the majority of people began more or less ignoring the pandemic in 2022, Twitch viewership began to trend slowly downward.

Around the same time, Twitch also began to feel heat from a monster of its own making: Kick, a new rival livestreaming platform, arose in late 2022, founded by the owners of a gambling site called Stake after Twitch cracked down on many forms of gambling on its service.

This split the Twitch community in more ways than one. Many streamers lauded the idea of competition for Twitch, which had seemingly grown complacent as a perennial livestreaming king that'd survived Mixer's grand heist and subsequent talent poachings by YouTube. Some of what Kick offered, too, was undeniably appealing: for example, a 95/5 revenue split in streamers' favor where Twitch defaulted to 50/50 (also offering 60/40 and 70/30, but only in conditional circumstances), a salary-like creator incentive program to stabilize streamers' previously boom-and-bust incomes, and more direct company-to-creator communication like in Twitch's old days. But others turned up their noses at Kick's focus on gambling and inconsistent moderation of problematic content like racism and sexualized nudity. They also looked at Kick's promise of an intensely generous pay split and wondered how the site planned on staying afloat.

Kick's seemingly bottomless bank account brings us to the other way Kick divided Twitch streamers: by turning some of them into part-time Kick streamers. After Twitch gambling convert Tyler "Trainwrecks" Niknam threw his hat in with the site at its outset, Lengyel proved to be its first truly high-profile signing in an alleged $100 million deal—a historic sum that, as *Forbes* pointed out at the time, even outstripped LeBron James' $97.1 million Lakers deal. Incredibly, Kick did not even foist exclusivity on Lengyel as Mixer had on Blevins and Grzesiek and YouTube has on others; instead, he simply wraps up his daily Twitch streams and then begins streaming on Kick right after. A streamer featured in this book, Kaitlyn "Amouranth" Siragusa, followed shortly thereafter with a deal that similarly allowed her to split her time between Twitch and Kick, another pillar in her ever-expanding business empire which now also includes a $17 million orchard. After announcing the deal, she tweeted her rationale, expressing a lack of faith in Twitch's future prospects.

"Twitch's 'sin' isn't trying to squeeze their creators," she wrote. "Their sin is making a business model that doesn't succeed except maybe at YouTube scale—but livestreaming is a much smaller [total available market] ... Taking

[an] incremental share of streamer earnings is ham-fisted, and you can't cut your way to profitability that way."

Kick, which evidently hopes to use megastars like Siragusa and Lengyel as funnels to aid in slurping down fed-up Twitch viewers, may or may not succeed in the long run, but it's symptomatic of an increasingly fissured landscape. Streamers no longer view Twitch with anything resembling the reverence they once did, and—as with users on other platforms that have experienced palpable culture shifts, like Twitter—some are looking to jump ship. But for big names, especially, the paydays that come with moves to greener pastures also represent something else: an out. Where once starry-eyed young streamers told themselves they'd keep going live every day forever, many now recognize a sobering truth: This career simply isn't sustainable. Siragusa is far from alone in plotting a course to a future in which she no longer has to appease the unquenchable appetite of the content machine. Ludwig Ahgren, who launched his own creative agency in 2022, has openly framed his self-proclaimed "mogul" moves as a means of setting himself up to retire from streaming in a handful of years.

All of this leaves Twitch in a uniquely volatile position. The platform will not suddenly disappear; Amazon has invested too much in it for that to happen. But it will continue to change. More streamers will leave, whether for opportunities on other platforms or simply because years of acting as one-person shows day in and day out have left them too disillusioned to force a smile and hit the "go live" button. Twitch, at least, has demonstrated a willingness to adapt to this new reality. Toward the end of 2023, the company announced that streamers would be allowed to broadcast across as many platforms as they wanted without violating any agreements. The thinking, more or less, was that the platform ecosystem had shifted. Modern creators no longer restrict themselves to one or two platforms. In order to gain a foothold and make a living, they must be in as many places as possible, contorting their content to fit a variety of resolutions and attention spans. Twitch decided to embrace that, understanding that there's no better ad for Twitch than its own homegrown talent going out and demonstrating how fun a Twitch stream can be. Numbers, so far, seem to support this thinking. For the first time in a year, the end of 2023 saw Twitch's daily hours-watched total trend upward.

For all her doubts about Twitch's business model, Siragusa still sees potential in the platform, especially with Clancy at the helm.

"[I used to think] Twitch was on the down trend. Now I think they are treading water. Maybe they're slightly making progress," she said of the company under Clancy's leadership. "I'm not sure if it'll ever be the peak like it was during Covid and pre-Covid, where Twitch was the ruler of everything, and everyone was on Twitch all the time before these rivals started popping up. . . . Amazon doesn't seem to be really shoveling more money into Twitch. The vibe that I get is that Amazon's kind of letting Twitch figure it out. It's like a parent that's on their phone while the kids are playing on the playground. They're kind of looking up, but they're also kind of not."

Twitch is now an Amazon subsidiary not just in name, but in structure and leadership. There's no going back home because, little by little, all of home's pillars, beams, and tiles have been replaced. This is what happens when corporate overlords see value in a vibrant community like Twitch's: The community becomes a commodity, and commodities are made to be sold—not cherished, curated, and cultivated. Something had to give. This is the common story of today's ruthlessly monetized online world.

There will never be another Twitch. The company and community it created were born of an extremely specific time and place—one that cannot come back. The internet is an almost incomprehensibly different place now than it was then, back before a small group of large companies had carved it up into a series of advertiser-friendly digital continents, landmasses with borders, currencies, and strict systems of governance. That old online world crackled with possibility. This modern one is calcified, save for the odd, disastrous, and entirely preventable slow-motion collapse of a behemoth like Twitter. It's difficult for any new platform to gain traction, unless it has the backing of Meta, Google, or, well, Amazon. TikTok demonstrated that those empires can be destabilized—and, indeed, that the future may lie outside Silicon Valley—but it's a tall order that requires ample funding. It's likely no coincidence, either, that Meta spent a record high $7.6 million lobbying Congress and the White

House on "homeland security" matters during the first quarter of 2024, shortly before the federal government signed into law a bill that could ban TikTok.

Twitch or no Twitch, however, the community will persist. At this point, Twitch culture *is* livestreaming culture. Rivals like YouTube and Kick cannot conceive of alternatives without strains of Twitch DNA, just as Facebook could not have existed without MySpace, and TikTok will forever be indebted to Vine. It's no coincidence that YouTube, Kick, TikTok, Instagram, and other services too numerous to count developed their own variations on many of Twitch's chat features, which in turn were first hacked together by Twitch's community. Other companies understand the value of what Twitch created, even if Twitch came to take its own community for granted. Companies can try to optimize for profit and AI and other whizbang technologies all they want, but if they stop building for the actual human beings who use their services, eventually somebody else will. And if you're not building for people, then who *are* you building for?

Poached Twitch stars function as Trojan horses for what these companies really want: Twitch viewers, Twitch chat emotes, Twitch memes, Twitch lore. Community continuity. Because without that—without the whole family coming along for the ride—the idea of relocating is a nonstarter for streamers and viewers alike. Twitch was born of the unique spark generated by a streamer interacting with chat. Without it, there is no flame, there is no energy. That legacy ensures that even in the face of misguided corporate meddling on an internet that grows colder—more automated and more algorithmic—the core of livestreaming will remain human.

acknowledgments

Thanks first and foremost to everybody who spoke to me for this book. Journalism like this doesn't come together without the perspectives— and therefore lives and careers—of many, many people. Countless streamers, industry folks, community members, and sources repeatedly gave me the time of day for years, at least *seeming* to believe me when I swore up and down that the book was still in the works. More importantly, they trusted me with their stories despite the fact that it's often easier for content creators to just tell their own. I tried my hardest to do right by all of you. I hope I succeeded.

I'm enormously grateful to my agent, William LoTurco, for cold emailing me, at the time a random writer at a gaming blog, and asking if I'd ever thought about writing a book. I had! It was this one. And thanks for walking me through everything from putting together a book proposal to getting a deal with a publisher to requesting a delay due to the ravages of a global pandemic. Writing my first book was a colossal undertaking, but I never felt like I'd bitten off more than I could chew with you in my corner.

All the gratitude in the world to both of my editors over the course of this process, first Amar Deol—who ended up getting a new gig before we could drag this thing across the finish line but whose fingerprints are all over it—and then Sean deLone, who picked up right where Amar left off without missing a beat. A writer is nothing without a good editor. I ended up getting two! I learned a ton from both of you.

279

Thank you to the more seasoned authors who advised me at various points in the pitching, writing, and editing processes: Taylor Lorenz, Jason Schreier, and Lindsay Ellis chief among them. I found a lot of things to freak out about, but you all successfully calmed me down (until I found new things to freak out about).

Respect and admiration to other reporters in this hyperspecific niche, especially Cecilia D'Anastasio and Zach Bussey, both of whom regularly cover Twitch with incredible care and diligence. I'd also be remiss if I didn't thank the numerous other reporters who've shaped the broader video game and digital culture beats over the years, as well as everybody I worked with while this book was in various stages of development: first the Kotaku crew, then the tiny but tenacious Launcher team at the *Washington Post*, and finally all of my cofounders at Aftermath, a worker-owned, reader-supported website about video games, the internet, and everything that comes after (subscribe today!).

My family deserves infinite credit, both for loving me and for putting up with my tendency to go radio silent for months on end. Mom, Dad, Katie, I love you all more than you could ever know, even if I don't say it enough. You shaped me into the person who could write this book.

Endless appreciation to the close friends and significant others who were by my side at various points during this book's four-year gestation: Ari, Garrett, Harry, Silas, Elizabeth, Ali, Kat, Oriana, Nathaniel, and Shoshana. Whether we hang out each weekend or we've drifted apart, you are always in my thoughts.

I will never be able to repay the love and support shown to me by my partner, PJ, who has made me feel happier and more secure than I ever thought possible. But I will spend every day trying.

And thanks most of all to my cat, Biscuit, who can't read this, but who I hope will appreciate it anyway.